D0436058

God Bless America

God Bless America

Tin Pan Alley Goes to War

Kathleen E.R. Smith

THE UNIVERSITY PRESS OF KENTUCKY

Publication of this volume was made possible in part by a grant from the National Endowment for the Humanities.

Scholarly publisher for the Commonwealth,
serving Bellarmine University, Berea College, Centre College of Kentucky, Eastern Kentucky University, The Filson Historical Society, Georgetown College, Kentucky Historical Society, Kentucky State University, Morehead State University, Murray State University, Northern Kentucky University, Transylvania University, University of Kentucky, University of Louisville, and Western Kentucky University.

Editorial and Sales Offices: The University Press of Kentucky
663 South Limestone Street, Lexington, Kentucky 40508-4008

03 04 05 06 07 5 4 3 2 1

Library of Congress Cataloging-in-Publication Data

Smith, Kathleen E. R.
God bless America : Tin Pan Alley goes to war
/ Kathleen E.R. Smith.
p. cm.
Includes bibliographical references (p.),
discography (p.), and index.
ISBN 0-8131-2256-2 (alk. paper)
1. Popular music—United States—1941-1950—History and criticism. 2. World War, 1939-1945—Music and the war.
I. Title.
ML3477 .S65 2002
781.5'99'097309044—dc21
2002152551

This book is printed on acid-free recycled paper meeting the requirements of the American National Standard for Permanence in Paper for Printed Library Materials.

Manufactured in the United States of America.

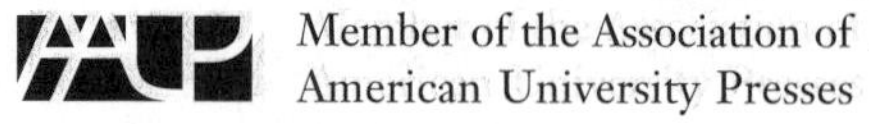

For my husband, Tony; my daughter, Brooke;
and my sisters, Gretchen and Jean.
And to the memory of my parents, Baldwin and Eunice.

Contents

Preface

The quest for the Great American War Song of World War II occupied the American music industry for most of the war years between December 7, 1941, and August 14, 1945. To the amazement of the United States government's Office of War Information and the music industry, the most talented, successful professional songwriters of the era could not create a martial tune that had a lasting impact on the American public. Prior wars always had a song or songs readily identifiable with the conflict. From the Revolutionary War came "Yankee Doodle," while "Hail, Columbia" was a product of the undeclared naval war of 1798–1799 between France and the United States. The War of 1812 gave the country the "Star-Spangled Banner," and the Civil War produced a host of songs: "Battle Cry of Freedom," "Battle Hymn of the Republic," "Dixie," "Maryland, My Maryland," "Marching through Georgia," "Tenting Tonight on the Old Camp Ground," "Tramp, Tramp, Tramp the Boys Are Marching," and "When Johnny Comes Marching Home." The Spanish-American War generated "Strike Up the Band, Here Comes a Sailor," "Break the News to Mother," and "There'll Be a Hot Time in the Old Town Tonight." From World War I Americans sang "It's a Long Way to Tipperary," "There's a Long, Long Trail a Winding," "Mademoiselle from Armentieres," "Till We Meet Again," and especially "Over There."

God Bless America: Tin Pan Alley Goes to War examines the search for a World War II song that would rally Americans in the same way that songs from previous wars had done. My sources include the two foremost music business publications of the years 1941 through 1945—*Variety*, published in New York City, and *The Billboard*, published in Cincinnati, Ohio—and documents from the Office of War Information found in Record Group 208, in the National Archives' Washington National Records Center, Suitland, Maryland. Various sub-groups of Record Group 208 pertain to my topic: Sub-Group 118, "Surveys of Public Attitudes"; Sub-Group 169, "Records of the Deputy Chief, Domestic Radio Bureau, New York, Dec.

1942–Dec. 1945," "Records of the American Theater Wing's Music War Committee"; and Sub-Group 170, "Records of the Deputy Chief of the Domestic Radio Bureau, Dec. 1942–July 1945." Also valuable are the materials in Sub-Group 572, "Records of the Radio Division, 1942–1945."

Unfortunately many of these records are in disarray. Over the years they have been shuffled around within the National Archives' complex of buildings and are now located at the Washington National Record Center in College Park, Maryland. Many record folders are empty or minus some of the cataloged contents; in some cases, entire groups of record boxes are missing. However, a vast collection of popular music of the World War II years is located in the sound recording and sheet music collections of the Performing Arts (Music) Reading Room of the Music and Recorded Sound Division of the Library of Congress. These sources, along with various secondary works, were invaluable in tracing the search conducted by the Office of War Information and Tin Pan Alley writers alike for a best-selling war song during the Second World War.

Tin Pan Alley's quest for a proper war song to help maintain American morale during World War II is a fascinating story. The subject also provided an added bonus: the great music of the war years that kept me dancing all the time I was working on this project. In the process of researching and writing this work, I have incurred a number of personal and professional debts. I would like to express my gratitude to three colleagues at Louisiana State University, Baton Rouge, Louisiana. First, Dr. Burl Noggle, Alumni Emeritus Professor of History, gave freely of his time, expertise, and experience. He encouraged me to persevere and was unfailingly generous with his knowledge and enthusiasm for the subject. I also benefitted enormously from Dr. Robert Becker's careful reading of the manuscript, his perceptive comments, and his support of the project. Dr. Charles Shindo offered excellent advice about interpretation of materials and made suggestions that were most helpful in my approach to the topic.

Numerous librarians and archivists have aided my research. I especially thank Fleming Thomas, head of Interlibrary Loan; Mary Linn Wernet, archivist of the Cammie G. Henry Research Center; the staff of the Eugene P. Watson Memorial Library, Northwestern State University of Louisiana; Iona Boyd of the Houston Public Library; and Deborah Atchison, microfilm and microforms librarian, Troy H. Middleton Library, Louisiana State University. Members of the staff of the Music Division of the Library of Congress and of the Washington National Record Center, a branch of the National Archives, were most helpful.

In addition, I would like to thank my friends and colleagues at Northwestern State University of Louisiana, especially Dr. Frank M. Fuller and Dr. Jane Newcomer Fuller, for their suggestions, patience, and encouragement. Kathy Bills of Our Photo Shop in Natchitoches, Louisiana, provided the excellent photographs of the sheet music. And finally, my most profound thanks belongs to my husband, Tony, my daughter, Brooke, and my sisters, Gretchen and Jean, for their support, their understanding, and their unfailing love.

Permission has been granted to reprint the following song lyrics:

"He's 1-A in the Army and He's A-1 in My Heart"
Words and Music Redd Evans
Copyright © 1941 (Renewed) by Music Sales Corporation (ASCAP).
International Copyright Secured. All Rights Reserved.
Reprinted by Permission.

"The House I Live In"
By Earl Robinson and Lewis Allan
Copyright © 1942 (Renewed) by Music Sales Corporation (ASCAP).
International Copyright Secured. All Rights Reserved. Reprinted by Permission.

"I'm Doin' It For Defense"
Words and Music by Harold Arlen and Johnny Mercer
Copyright © 1943 (Renewed 1971) by Famous Music Corporation.
International Copyright Secured. All Rights Reserved.

"I'm Getting Tired So I Can Sleep" by Irving Berlin
© Copyright 1942 by Irving Berlin, Inc.
© Copyright Renewed by Irving Berlin.
International Copyright Secured. All Rights Reserved. Reprinted by Permission.

"Just A Blue Serge Suit" by Irving Berlin
© Copyright 1945 by Irving Berlin. © Copyright Renewed.
International Copyright Secured. All Rights Reserved. Reprinted by Permission.

"Mairzy Doats"
By Al Hoffman, Milton Drake and Jerry Livingston
Copyright © 1943 (Renewed) by Al Hoffman Songs, Inc. (ASCAP), Hallmark Music Co. & Drake Activities Corporation.
All rights for Al Hoffman Songs, Inc., administered by Music Sales Corporation (ASCAP).
International Copyright Secured. All Rights Reserved. Reprinted by Permission.

"M.P. That's Me"
By Fred Waring and John M. Dolph
Copyright © 1943 (Renewed) by Shawnee Press, Inc. (ASCAP).
International Copyright Secured. All Rights Reserved. Reprinted by Permission.

"On The Swing Shift"
Words and Music by Harold Arlen and Johnny Mercer
Copyright © 1942 (Renewed 1970) by Famous Music Corporation.
International Copyright Secured. All Rights Reserved.

"Remember Pearl Harbor"
By Deon Reid and Sammy Kaye
Copyright © 1941 (Renewed) by Music Sales Corporation and Davadon Music (ASCAP).
International Copyright Secured.All Rights Reserved. Reprinted by Permission.

"Somebody Else Is Taking My Place"
Words and Music by Dick Howard, Bob Ellsworth and Russ Morgan
Copyright © 1937, 1941 Shapiro, Bernstein & Co., Inc., New York
Copyright Renewed.
International Copyright Secured. All Rights Reserved. Used by Permission.

"There Are No Wings On A Foxhole" by Irving Berlin
© Copyright 1944 by Irving Berlin.
© Copyright Renewed by Irving Berlin.
International Copyright Secured. All Rights Reserved. Reprinted by Permission.

"(There'll Be Bluebirds Over) The White Cliffs of Dover"
Words by Nat Burton
Music by Walter Kent
Copyright © 1941 Shapiro, Bernstein & Co., Inc., New York and Walter Kent Music, California.
Copyright Renewed.
All Rights outside the United States Controlled by Shapiro, Bernstein & Co., Inc., New York.
International Copyright Secured. All Rights Reserved.Used by Permission.

"There's a Star Spangled Banner Waving Somewhere"
Words and Music by Paul Roberts, Shelby Darnell
© Copyright 1942 Universal-MCA Music Publishing, A Division of Universal Studios, Inc. (ASCAP).
International Copyright Secured. All Rights Reserved.

"WAVES in Navy Blue"
By Fred Waring and John M. Dolph
Copyright © 1943 (Renewed) by Shawnee Press, Inc. (ASCAP).
International Copyright Secured. All Rights Reserved. Reprinted by Permission.

"White Christmas" by Irving Berlin
© Copyright 1940, 1942 by Irving Berlin.
© Copyright Renewed.
International Copyright Secured. All Rights Reserved. Reprinted by Permission.

Chapter 1

What this Country Needs Is a Good Five-Cent War Song!

World War II had an enormous impact on all aspects of American society: political, economic, and social. The United States was transformed from a nation crippled by economic depression, divided by class, and facing a crisis of confidence, into a prosperous society that was united in purpose and beginning to show limited tolerance for the diversity of its population. The war affected nearly every man, woman, and child in the United States. While young men, and later women, were overseas or stationed at training camps throughout the country, children and adolescents on "the home front" were encouraged to do their part by collecting scrap material and buying war stamps. Older people took civil defense jobs, served on selective service boards, and bought and sold war bonds. Men who stayed on the home front were joined by millions of women and older adolescents working to produce war materials and provide the services needed to run the country. Some argue that World War II was the last time the United States was totally committed to a common goal—the defeat of the Axis powers. Along with this communal effort, the war had a dark side at home: black markets, race prejudice, war profiteers, and organized crime divided Americans along political, economic, and social lines. But most of the time these divisions were overshadowed by the intense patriotism that swept the country following the Japanese attack on Pearl Harbor. A notable exception was the reinforcement of social division by the compulsory interment of Japanese-Americans in relocation camps throughout the country.

The entertainment industry fed a large part of this patriotic fervor. Two of the strongest branches of show business, radio and motion pictures, played a central part in marshaling public sentiment for the war effort: The U.S. Treasury Department sponsored radio shows to stimulate the sale of war bonds. Other programs incorporated public service messages concerning the war effort into their scripts. Motion pictures sought to inspire as well as entertain Americans. Music was the one element common to all these forms of entertainment during World War II—and the music that had the widest audience was popular music. Heated debates arose over popular music's role in maintaining morale, and boosting patriotism sparked as the industry entertained conflicting views about the music's function as a propaganda tool.

Popular music—music that seeks to appeal to the widest possible audience—is initially written, then published, performed, and possibly recorded. David Hatch and Stephen Millward, in *From Blues to Rock: An Analytical History of Pop Music*, maintain that popular music, by virtue of its creation in written form before performance, is akin to the art song of classical music. Popular music is not the same as "pop" music, which is more closely related to jazz in that it is primarily improvised by musicians and learned by others who hear it performed live or from recordings.[1] A "pop" musician does not have to be musically literate, whereas a popular musician, by definition, must be. The audiences of popular and "pop" music take the opposite positions. The "pop" music audience needs to be better educated in the form, style, and substance of jazz-oriented "pop" music in order to more fully appreciate the improvisational character of the music. Popular music audiences, on the other hand, need no prior knowledge or special understanding to enjoy the music; thus, a diverse audience can appreciate popular music.

By the 1940s popular music could also be defined by the number of recordings or sheet music copies a song sold or the number of times a tune was played on the largest broadcasting networks in a specified period of time (usually a week). At the beginning of World War II a "smash" hit song might sell 200 thousand copies of sheet music and 100 thousand records. By the end of the war sheet music sales of 1 million copies or more were not uncommon and record sales of 250–500 thousand marked a song as a best-seller. Any song with large sales was automatically listed on the top ten music charts and would be played an average of forty times per week on the major networks.[2]

Popular music is most often associated with some form of social activity such as dances, parties, or social gatherings where a sense of community and shared emotions is important. Richard Mabry says that popular music "acts as [a] binding force on the group, [in which] the observed responses of the other members are a way of clarifying your own."[3] Another view of the term "popular" comes from Ray Browne of the Center for the

Study of Popular Culture. Browne argues that "popular" is comprised of "all those elements of life which are not narrowly intellectual or creatively elitist and which are generally though not necessarily disseminated through the mass media."[4] It follows that popular music is a composite of musical tastes that consolidate or merge their certain similarities at a given time. There are variables of age, sex, race, class, and education that affect the public's reception of popular music, but the most important variable in defining popular music is the fact that people select what they like to hear. If enough people like the same songs and purchase recordings or sheet music of these tunes in sufficient quantities, then the music is said to be "popular."

In this study "popular music" refers to the specific music associated with the sheet music publishing business, known as Tin Pan Alley, and the recording industry during the years encompassing the United States' involvement in World War II. Although accomplished musicians wrote for a musically informed public, not every person who listened to popular music read and understood printed music; rather, the popular music audience was well-versed (through hours of listening) in the musical form, style, and lyric content of the songs.

During the war years Tin Pan Alley produced an enormous number of popular songs, and, despite the lack of a "proper" war song, the Office of War Information (OWI) did not falter in its attempts to guide popular songwriters in the direction they thought necessary to assure the American public's morale. None of the new songs, however, rallied the American public and the fighting man in the same way that George M. Cohan's "Over There" had sparked the imagination and spirit of the country during World War I. What factors contributed to this lack of a dominant "war song"? What was done to promote the writing of such a song, and how did the United States government attempt to give guidance and direction to composers during the Second World War? Was it even possible for such a song to gain wide popularity in the 1940s? Maybe American society was now so sophisticated that it disdained the use of militant songs to get the public to do the jobs necessary to win the war. Was some other form of popular entertainment available that filled the function of a war song? Or did some other factor explain America's failed search for an inspiring war song?

The federal government debated the relevance of popular music to the daily headlines and life of a nation at war. What *should* be the influence of popular music in a nation at war? Should it become an unofficial arm of the government to be used for propaganda and "education"? The controversy over popular music's role began almost as soon as World War II did.

By December 1941 popular music was a highly profitable, widespread part of American culture, featuring well-known musicians, bandleaders, singers, and songwriters, whose efforts would be heard by millions of radio and jukebox listeners during the war and watched on stage by adoring fans across the nation. The United States government, through the Office of War Information, was quick to realize that here was a reservoir of talent and competence capable of influencing people's feelings and opinions. And popular music might be capable of even greater influence during wartime than before, because for the first time in a generation people had money to spend on entertainment.

The debate about the value of entertainment in a war culture often became hot and bitter. Congress especially seemed subject to polemics and rhetoric during the first year of the war. Recreation is essential, said President Roosevelt. How essential, asked Congress? Should musicians, entertainers, and technical crews be exempt from the draft?[5] Some congressmen were unhappy with what they perceived as preferential treatment for members of the entertainment industry. The head of the Selective Service, Brig. Gen. Lewis B. Hershey, at first sanctioned draft deferments for actors, musicians, writers, directors, producers, sound engineers, cameramen, and other technical jobs related to show business.

His move infuriated members of the House of Representatives who had been attempting to gain deferments for men whose vocations the congressmen considered significantly more essential to the war effort. For example, Rep. August H. Anderson of Minnesota demanded to know why his request for farmers' deferments had been waiting unsigned on General Hershey's desk for six months. Congressman Clevenger of Ohio leveled another criticism at the Selective Service, asking, "May not sugar, milk, canned fruit, and vegetables, meats, and grain be more essential than a lot of this salacious bedroom drama, low comedy, and propaganda so generously interlarded into legitimate entertainment?"[6]

The most galling abuse, according to some in Congress, was the addition of wealthy entertainers to the federal payroll. Rep. John Taber of New York called them parasites, pointing to actor Melvin Douglas's eight-thousand-dollar salary as a member of the Office of Civilian Defense. Rep. Charles Fabbis of Pennsylvania joined Representative Tabor's criticism of extravagant salaries offered show business people. On February 6, 1942, Fabbis summed up the attitudes of many on Capitol Hill when he said that Douglas's salary would be as much "as we are paying that matchless and heroic soldier, General Douglas MacArthur when he is battling in the forests of the Philippines everyday, every hour—yes, even every minute—in danger of his life to preserve the fate of the white race in the Orient."[7]

Ultimately, Congress did not regard entertainers as being essential to the war effort. The Deficiency Appropriations Bill, which passed two-to-one on February 9, 1942, was crucial to the future role of the music industry's war efforts. An amendment to the bill refused to allow the Office of Civilian Defense to use any of its funds to "promote, produce, or carry on instruction in physical fitness by dancers, fan dancing, street shows, theatrical performances, or other public entertainments." In other words, if show business wished to contribute to the war effort, it would have to pay its own way, and there would be no special privileges for actors, musicians, or other professionals in the entertainment industry. Show business would soon invest itself with the "morale factor" to counteract this negative assessment placed on it so early in the war.

Questions about music's role in wartime continued to arise. Among the most pressing were the following: Might popular music be of sustaining value to the war effort?[8] What were the "right types" of war songs and who could be trusted to write them? Should the United States government be a part of the "creative" process of composition?[9] These and many other questions faced the popular music business at the beginning of World War II, and they continued to haunt Tin Pan Alley until August 1945.

Some leading music educators saw a potential in popular music for patriotic excitation and for public instruction, and so they called for the conscious development of patriotic, educational music. Edwin Hughes, president of the National Music Council, addressed the National Music Teachers' Association and the American Musicological Society, meeting in Minneapolis, Minnesota, in December 1941: "Music in America faces difficult and even perilous times. It also faces an extraordinary opportunity to perform a vital function in the nation's hour of need—to sustain public morale and to bear its full share of responsibility in upholding and strengthening the culture of democracy."[10]

Tin Pan Alley composers, publishers, authors, and music-related trade papers quickly took up the debate. *Variety* demanded that American publishers "Sift English War Songs for America Now" and questioned "Show Biz's Role in the War." The *Variety* article "Paeans in Praise of America" compared the strength and morale boosting power of popular Revolutionary War music to the musical output in the first month of World War II and found the latter wanting. Publishers, demanding to know "Where Are the War Songs?," lamented that there were "Too Few Good War Tunes." Tin Pan Alley proposed that the "First Steps [Be] Taken for Fighting Songs." *Billboard's* headlines echoed *Variety's*: "Old Timers Doom New War Songs," "Droopy War Ballads Out—In Theory," "All Out for Uncle Sam: Demand for Patriotic Records Soars," and "Tin Pan Alley Fires Song Salvo at Axis."

Yet publishers stayed away from war songs, claiming the public's interest was in romantic or novelty songs, not battle hymns. Escapism seemed to be a high priority for music listeners, and the composers of Tin Pan

Alley struggled to write a war song that would appeal both to civilians and the armed forces.[11]

Aside from the headlines, three main questions dominated the popular music debate: Did listeners want only escape? Would the public accept war songs? When would the big hit war song appear?

A 1942 straw vote of film reviewers in forty United States cities indicated a desire for fewer serious dramas and war pictures and more comedies in1943.[12] Did the same mood prevail in the field of popular music? There was fierce talk in Congress and the entertainment press, but did Tin Pan Alley and Hollywood truly attempt to turn out war songs that would sell? Did Americans agree with Representative J. Parnell Thomas of New Jersey when he said: "What America needs today is a good five cent war song. The nation is literally crying for a good, peppy marching song, something with plenty of zip, ginger, fire, something like 'Over There,' 'Keep the Home Fires Burning,' 'Pack Up Your Troubles' and some of those good old songs of World War I."[13]

Or was the nation lukewarm to the old-fashioned, rousing, marching song, patterned after "Over There"? Could it be that the search for the Great American War Song was fundamentally flawed from the beginning since it rested on the belief that what had worked in World War I would still work in World War II? Was it also possible the hunt for a war song was merely an illustration of the struggle between private enterprise and the federal government trying to define their roles in the war?

Judging from the amount of time they spent searching for the Great American War Song, both the government and Tin Pan Alley seemed to believe that such a song was vital to the war effort. In the final analysis, music was of little or no consequence in the outcome of the war. One "Higgins boat," an open, ramped landing craft built for the navy by Andrew Jackson Higgins's shipyard in New Orleans, did more to win the war than any song, but the government was convinced a war song was a necessity.

This insistence on a war song reflects the detailed manner in which the government spelled out World War II as a "total" war for the American people. The government needed Americans to recognize the all-encompassing nature of the conflict and the potential threat it posed to every facet of American life: a victorious Axis meant, at best, an uncertain future for the United States and, at worst, the end of a free, independent, democratic country.

The search for the Great American War Song was a distillation of the problems faced by American society during the war: How did society balance public versus private obligation in a democracy? What constituted a war song? To the government and Americans of the World War I generation, a war song was in march tempo and gave voice to America's military might and the righteousness of her cause. During World War II civilians and soldiers put their own blueprints on war songs, which were far different from those Americans sang in previous wars. These questions faced a popular music business that was still reeling, along with the rest of the nation, from the shock of the surprise attack by Japan on Pearl Harbor.

Earlier that fall and winter of 1941, when America's war against Japan had not yet begun, preparations for the holiday season had overshadowed the threat of war. On the first Sunday of December 1941, newspapers carried the usual pre-holiday stories and advertisements. The *New York Times* filled dozens of pages with gift suggestions. W & J Sloan invited shoppers to visit their "Gay Main Floor" for Christmas presents that ranged from crystal seahorse bookends at $3.95 a pair to a $160.00 coffee table made from a drum used in the War of 1812. The Davega Music Company reminded shoppers of the big sale on Emerson "Miracle Tone" table radios at $34.95. Liberty Music Shop extolled the Deluxe Capehart radio-phonograph as "a time-proved record-changer that turns the record for listeners." It played twenty records (forty selections) on both sides, providing three hours of uninterrupted music. Prices started at $595.00.[14]

Front pages all across America on that Sunday reported trouble in the Pacific as well as news of the war already underway in Europe and Asia. The *New York Times* carried the banner headlines "Roosevelt Appeals to Hirohito after New Threat in Indo-China; Germans Trapped at Taganrog." The equally ominous subheading followed: "Direct Appeal to Tokyo Not to Precipitate a Conflict Is Made by President."[15] On the front page, Secretary of the Navy Frank Knox assured Americans that the United States' "Navy Is Superior to Any." The *gravure* section led off with the photo feature "Hawaii—Spearhead of Pacific Defense," emphasizing swimming and surfing at Waikiki in the shadow of U.S. Navy maneuvers.

December 7, 1941, began for most Americans as another early winter Sunday morning. Radio programs on the major networks for Sunday afternoon offered a wide choice for the listener: popular music (Sammy Kaye's *Sunday Serenade*); drama (*Great Play's* version of *Inspector General*); symphonic music (the New York Philharmonic with guest pianist Arthur Rubenstein); pro football (Brooklyn Dodgers vs. New York Giants); and current events (*Wake Up America*'s panel discussion on "Can There Be a Substantial Reduction in Nondefense Expenditures of the Federal Government?"). And in a twist of irony that would not go unnoticed at the time, on their 5:00 P.M. show the Moylan Sisters planned to sing a favorite tune: "The End of a Perfect Day."[16]

Most Americans were going about their usual Sunday routines. At mid-day, radio listeners were jolted by a report over the Mutual Radio Network: "THE JAPANESE HAVE ATTACKED PEARL HARBOR,

HAWAII, BY AIR, President Roosevelt has just announced." WOR's staff announcer, Len Sterling, cut into the network's play-by-play account of the Dodger-Giant contest at New York's Polo Grounds to read the news from a United Press bulletin. He glanced at the studio clock. The hands showed 2:26 P.M. Minutes later CBS and NBC networks sped the news to a stunned America. At CBS newscaster John Daly told of the Pacific air attack. At NBC newswriter Robert Eisenbach seized the teletype sheet, rushed into the studio, and read the bulletin without waiting for a staff announcer.[17]

Within minutes of learning of the attack, radio converted to emergency status, offering airtime and communications assistance to President Roosevelt. To speed news to listeners around the clock, radio networks quickly rearranged schedules to give war-related news bulletins priority over all programming. Appeals were broadcast to military personnel and civilian plane-spotters to report back to their units. Armed forces recruiting messages dominated the air much of the day. Beginning on that Sunday afternoon, newscasters and commentators dealt chiefly with the war effort. Music on the radio, which had provided chiefly entertainment before the attack, also began to march to a different drummer. Now it added a new beat: morale boosting on the battlefield and on the home front.

"Morale" has a wide variety of possible meanings. In the broadest sense, morale may mean that people must be "kept happy" through increased availability of favorite diversions "normally enriching to life." A narrower definition of "morale" implies a "disciplined and unified will: the loyalties of people must be mobilized and directed."[18] According to Herbert Blumer, "Modern war has made morale a consideration of primary importance."[19]

The formation of a huge army of draftees in place of professional or volunteer forces during World War II turned the country's attention to the "so-called spiritual factor." The total warfare aspect of the conflict also led to concerns about the morale of American citizens. Because all citizens were enlisted in the war effort and the smallest details of their lives were subordinated to the mission of winning the war, some thought that the government must cultivate and ensure the people's loyalty.

To do so, the government sought to use music as booster of morale, both in terms of keeping people happy and unifying their will. There was a prevailing view during World War II that people's spirits and thus morale were kept high by entertainment: movies, theatrical performances, concerts, dance bands, and other social events were ranked high as morale boosters. Music, first and foremost a form of entertainment, readily served this purpose. However, using music to mobilize and direct the public was much more difficult. Success depended on joining a memorable melody with lyrics that would convince listeners to follow their leaders loyally.

Between December 7, 1941, and August 14, 1945, thousands of popular songs poured over the airwaves, from bandstands and jukeboxes, from phonographs and pianos in the front parlors, and from loudspeakers in factories and war industry plants. Americans were surrounded by the music of the times. The average radio listener heard music four-and-a-half hours a day.[20] There were talk shows (to elevate the listener), literary shows, newscasts, and broadcasts of classical music. The "Survey of American's Radio Listening Habits," conducted for the Office of War Information on December 8, 1943, asked a cross-section of Americans, "What kinds of programs do you listen to most?" They responded: Straight News Broadcasts—64 percent; News Commentators—62 percent; Comedy and Variety Programs—49 percent; Popular Music—42 percent; and Hillbilly or Country Music—23 percent.[21]

Popular music, as always, was the staple broadcast material. Forty percent of air time on the radio was occupied by music that was popular with all age groups, especially those under age forty who said they wanted a variety of songs without repetition.[22] But now there was a new twist: both the music industry and the U.S. government expected music to be helpful for morale.

Both American society and the United States government embarked on a campaign to maintain high morale. Raising and sustaining morale became all-important, and morale itself (at home and at the front) developed into one of the constant obsessions of the Allies in the Second World War.[23] The Office of War Information's "Survey of Public Attitudes" in May 1943 asked five thousand Americans "What is our biggest problem in winning the war?" They responded: 1. Labor disputes (24 percent) 2. Farm labor shortage/Food production (18 percent) 3. Arousing the public; keeping up the public morale (11 percent). When the OWI asked the question again in April 1944, the public thought: "Arousing the public, keeping up public morale" was the number one problem.

During World War II, the term "morale" came to designate a mystique indispensable to victory. In war time, "high morale" became a substitute for all kinds of lost things—happiness itself "had disappeared along with rubber, silk, and many other staples, to be replaced by the wartime synthetic, high morale, for the duration."[24]

People could not be motivated to fight or support the war effort by filling their minds with lofty principles or political convictions; they were not interested. What did substitute for ideological commitment during World War II was morale.

On the American home front manufacturers of products like beer, chewing gum, and tobacco sold their products by arguing as one advertiser put it, "Morale is a lot of little things." Among them was beer, "best consumed with Wholesome American Food." The advertisement continued, "Yes, morale is a lot of little things like this. Little things that help lift the spirits, keep up the courage. Little things that are . . . our American way of life."[25]

This advertiser was not alone in his use of the war and the premium placed on morale to sell his products. A glance through any magazine from the war years, 1941–1945, will show that almost every product on the American market could, in some way, be tied to the war and to maintaining morale, not to mention keeping the product before the public and hopefully luring post-war consumers who might remember the loyal "service" of a certain brand of soap flakes or breakfast cereal during the war.

There was great concern on the part of the OWI that the home front was not as involved as it could be in winning the war. One OWI survey asked Americans three different times during 1942 and 1943 if they thought people were taking the war seriously enough. In March 1942, fifty-four percent responded "no" and this increased to sixty-two percent in July 1942. When asked if Americans were making enough sacrifices, people responded with a resounding "No." In August 1942 seventy percent thought Americans were not sacrificing enough. This fell to sixty-five percent in December 1942 and fifty-nine percent by June 1943.[26] These surveys convinced the OWI that more had to be done to motivate the public toward a greater involvement in the war effort.

The American music industry lost no time in joining the campaign to boost morale. In a full-page editorial published in *Billboard*, December 13, 1941, J.E. Broyles, president of the Rudolph Wurlitzer Company, said, "The most important qualification for a fighting force is its morale" which must be "supported by the morale of the home forces." Broyles thought the greatest booster of morale was singing, and so he believed, the automatic phonograph industry (jukeboxes) would be vital in maintaining high morale among Americans. Not only must American soldiers keep up their morale, but the morale of those people "back of the line," those left on the home front, must also be supported. Broyles called morale "the personal feelings and efforts of the individuals composing the army," supported by the morale of the home forces. If home front morale failed, he warned, the nation would be in jeopardy. Preserving morale was as vital as manufacturing weapons, and the great booster of morale, according to Broyles' rhetoric, was music. And, as the war news and war-related activities day after day weighed heavily on people's minds, music could give them much-needed relief. Dropping excess change into jukeboxes would relieve stress and keep both army and civilian morale high.[27] It would also keep the manufacturers and owners of jukeboxes in business, which was a concern. There were rumors that the metals used in manufacturing jukeboxes would be rationed or that their production would be halted altogether as were household appliances such as washing machines and refrigerators.

Chapter 2

"Praise the Lord and Pass the Ammunition"

The unprovoked attack on Pearl Harbor sent American songwriters into a flurry of activity, producing combative, war-like songs. According to the lead story in *Billboard* of December 20, 1941, record producers were swamped with anti-Axis songs, and reliable estimates included in the same issue placed the number of tunes peddled in the first weeks of the war at more than one thousand.[1] One publisher claimed to have received over four hundred tunes with Pearl Harbor as the theme following December 7, 1941.[2] "Writers kept rushing into publishers' offices with songs inspired by the event," *Variety* said, though it added, "The effort so far hasn't shown up Tin Pan Alley at its best."[3] *Billboard* agreed, "Most of the ditties penned . . . have topical themes that may not hold water . . . the quality . . . will improve after composers cool off . . . and forget about just trying to be first out with a Jap or Hitler lyric."[4] The record publishers thought that if ten of the songs ever got anywhere, it would be a high number, but they were ready to "come into their own as dispensers of morale builder-uppers."[5]

Some of the titles from this first wave of Tin Pan Alley war song hysteria were "We'll Always Remember Pearl Harbor," "Let's Put the Axe to the Axis," "The Sun Will Soon Be Setting for the Land of the Rising Sun," "We're Going to Find a Fellow Who Is Yellow and Beat Him Red, White and Blue." Others included "You're a Sap, Mr. Jap," "Put the Heat on Hitler, Muss up Mussolini and Tie a Can to Japan," "Oh, You Little Son of an Oriental," "Slap the Jap Right Off the Map," "To Be Specific, It's Our Pacific," "When Those Little Yellow Bellies Meet the Cohens and the Kellys," and "Let's Knock the 'Hit' Out of Hitler."[6] Of these first war songs,

RCA-Victor's music director Leonard Joy said, "Most of them urge us to slap the Japs or axe the Axis. As a rule they're pretty bad, musically, and the rhymes are even worse."[7]

In the first months of the war, songwriters strained to write the Great American War Song, but none of these early songs caught on. Although the Japanese bore the brunt of the songwriters' wrath, the rest of the Axis was not forgotten. The songs were hastily written and rushed to the public in the composers' bid to write the first song to inspire the nation. Songwriter Burt Wheeler won the race to be first when he introduced "We'll Knock the Japs Right into the Laps of the Nazis" before a nightclub audience on the evening of December 7, 1941:

> Oh, we didn't want to do it,
> But they're asking for it now
> So, we'll knock the Japs
> Right into the laps of the Nazis!
> ....
> I'd hate to see Yokohama
> When our brothers make their bow,
> For we'll knock the Japs
> Right into the laps of the Nazis!

One of the first war songs to be written that enjoyed some success was "We Did It Before and We Can Do It Again," by Charles Tobias and Cliff Friend. The men wrote the song on the very day Pearl Harbor was bombed. Two days later, Eddie Cantor (Tobias' brother-in-law) hurriedly inserted it in *Banjo Eyes*, the Broadway musical in which he was then starring, and offered it as a stirring martial number that brought down the house.[8] The lyrics, sung to a rousing, march-like tune faintly reminiscent of George M. Cohan's World War I blockbuster, "Over There," promised to "take the Nip out of the Nipponese and chase 'em back to their cherry trees." "We Did It Before" offered Americans a message that bolstered confidence by reminding them of past military glories and exhorted: "We're one for all and all for one / We've got a job to be done."

By 6 A.M. on December 8, songwriter Max Lerner had finished "The Sun Will Soon Be Setting for the Land of the Rising Sun." Three hours before Congress declared war on Japan, Carl Hoff and Orrin Tucker copyrighted "You're a Sap Mr. Jap." The nation heard "You're a sap, Mr. Jap, to make a Yankee cranky . . . Uncle Sam is gonna spanky" and "The A. B. C. and D.[9] will sink your rising sun . . . You don't know Uncle Sammy—when he fights for his rights you'll take it on the lamee."[10]

Ten days after the attack J. Fred Coots wrote and published the words and music of "Goodbye, Mama, I'm Off to Yokohama." The song had a march-tempo, 4/4 meter with some syncopated rhythm. The tune is cheery and not unlike a Boy Scout hiking song:

Goodbye, Mamma,
I'm off to Yokohama,
For my red, white, and blue,
My country and you.
Goodbye, Mamma,
I'm off to Yokohama,
Just to teach all those Japs,
The Yanks are no saps.
A million fighting sons of Uncle Sam,
If you please,
Will soon have all those Japs right down,
On their Jap-a-knees.
So, Goodbye, Mamma,
I'm off to Yokohama,
For my country, my flag, and you.

The title of the first nationally successful war song was already in the air, waiting for a songwriter to seize it and put it to use. The phrase "Remember Pearl Harbor," supposedly first appearing in spaced capital letters at the top of mimeographed Office of Production Management orders in December 1941, passed into the language and American culture.[11] Several other songs had the words "remember " and "Pearl Harbor" in the title, but "Remember Pearl Harbor," by Don Reid and Sammy Kaye (also written before the smoke above Pearl Harbor cleared), was the Pearl Harbor song to survive and to be identified with that catastrophe. Written in a 6/8 march tempo and recorded by Eddy Howard's band employing a trumpet fanfare introduction and a male chorus, the song had a martial air and called on Americans to remember their past and to be victorious as their forefathers had been:

Let's REMEMBER PEARL HARBOR
As we go to meet the foe.
Let's REMEMBER PEARL HARBOR
As we did the Alamo.
We will always remember
How they died for Liberty.
Let's REMEMBER PEARL HARBOR
And go on to victory.

"Remember Pearl Harbor" was not a big hit (in terms of selling a million copies of sheet music or records) and did not last more than a few weeks on any of the popularity charts the music business had instituted between the years 1935 and 1940, but it filled a void at the beginning of the war.[12] In fact, the song eventually ran afoul of the federal government. Deputy Attorney General Thomas B. Minnick Jr. of the Office of the Coordinator of Inter-American Affairs asked Republic Music to delete the line "As we did the Alamo" from the song. It seemed it was no longer polite to recall that the United States avenged the Alamo in 1848 because Mexico, an enemy then, was now an ally. Minnick declared on April 21, 1942, that the words "Remember the Alamo" were an affront to Mexico "just when we are trying to establish good neighborly relations with the Latin-American Republics. . . . bringing up sore wounds like the Battle of the Alamo . . . is in poor taste to say the least." Republic Music complied with the federal government's request and NBC, CBS, and the Mutual Broadcasting networks agreed not to allow any of their member stations to broadcast the song in its original form. The voluntary prohibition also applied to shortwave radio.[13]

An even greater success, and the first war song to register as a best-seller on the popularity charts, was Frank Loesser's "Praise the Lord and Pass the Ammunition." It was recorded with a trumpet fanfare introduction and sung by a male chorus to a folksong-type tune. The expressionistic sheet music cover vividly portrays battle action: Ten men engage in loading and firing an enormous gun. While the leader shouts orders, an enemy plane looms in the distance, and shells explode around the group. The story of the song, published with the sheet music, says, "The pungent words of the battlefield have found their way into the lyrics of a truly great war song . . . it captures the spirit of a people aroused and an army determined." According to the legend (program note):

> As sailors boiled from below decks of a U.S. Navy warship to fight off low flying Japanese planes, Chaplain William McGuire left his altar where it stood and ran to a gun station where one of the gunners had been killed and another wounded. In the unholy uproar of that torrent of bombs, Chaplain McGuire shouted his now famous words: "I just got one of them!! Praise the Lord and Pass the Ammunition!!"

Frank Loesser borrowed the story and hastily concocted the song which was also his first attempt at writing both the lyric and the tune. Before the war, he had been employed as a successful lyricist for various composers and counted among his successes "Jingle, Jangle, Jingle" and "I

Don't Want to Walk without You." But "Praise the Lord and Pass the Ammunition" was Loesser's entree into the world of full-fledged songwriters. He took the story of the chaplain and, using military slang, put together the first really big hit song to deal directly with the war:

"Praise the Lord and Pass the Ammunition!
Praise the Lord and Pass the Ammunition!
Praise the Lord and Pass the Ammunition
And we'll all stay free!"

The real-life chaplain, Capt. William McGuire, a Roman Catholic priest, later was unable to recall saying the words and wrote to *LIFE*, "If I said it, nobody could have heard me in the din of battle. But I certainly felt what the statement expresses."[14]

Furthermore, Captain McGuire did not fire a gun at all; rather, he helped by carrying ammunition. The account was one of the early myths of the war, and no one wanted to deny it because everyone vaguely believed that American needed incidents of heroism for inspiration. According to an editorial in the *Milwaukee Journal*, reprinted in *Variety*, the song was the contemporary American interpretation of Oliver Cromwell's phrase "Trust in God, but keep your powder dry."[15]

The Office of War Information was solidly behind the song, forbidding its playing on the radio more than once every four hours for fear that this morale booster would be "plugged" (played) to death. The OWI hoped to breathe spirit into and extend interest in the song beyond the usual playing lifetime.[16]

Tin Pan Alley was delighted with "Praise the Lord." In just a few weeks, it sold more than 170,000 copies (with Loesser donating all royalties to Navy Relief). The demand for the tune was so great that Columbia Records was challenged to keep up with the requests for Kay Kyser's version. Columbia also tried unsuccessfully to restrict the number of times the song was played on the networks. Station owners seemed to think that no publishers or network executives could tell them how to run their businesses, and they played "Praise the Lord" as often as they wanted.[17]

By November 18, 1942, "Praise the Lord" had sold 450,000 copies to the chagrin of some members of the clergy. According to *Variety*, "A minority of American religious leaders, mostly Protestant, . . . have condemned the lyrical co-mingling of firearms and theology." Furthermore:

> These vocal ministers soon found themselves the objects of government scrutiny by Washington officials and those who measured morale equations. Washington was "greatly disturbed

> by the anti-patriotic cold-as-ice attitude of numerous members of the clergy many of whom dominated the church publications and/or the church machinery in many denominations. The latter had recently aggravated the situation by refusing to encourage prayers for victory (i.e. shedding our enemies' blood) on Pearl Harbor Sunday."[18]

Variety traced the revulsion of the clergy towards the Second World War to their own excessive emotionalism in World War I and their subsequent vows not to repeat their hysteria. The Virginia Conference of the Methodist Church and its newspaper, the *Virginia Methodist*, refused to help pump up morale for the struggle. The church had long been a "stronghold of pacifism," with leaders like Dr. Ernest Fremont Tittle of Evanston, Illinois; Dr. Henry Hitt Crane of Detroit, Michigan; Dr. Albert Edward Day of Pasadena, California; and Dr. Ralph Washington Sockman of New York. All were uncompromising pacifists who led the Methodist General Conference, meeting in Atlantic City in 1940, to declare: "The Methodist Church . . . will not officially endorse, support, or participate in war. . . . Agencies of the church shall not be used in preparation for war."[19] The Methodists' motto was "The Church, as such, is not at war," and on December 1, 1942, the *Virginia Methodist* asked that "Praise the Lord" be removed from the air: "There's no denying that the tune is a catchy one, but the words are no credit to America's chaplains. . . . whether the song is sacrilegious . . . may be debatable, but the fact that it gives an entirely erroneous concept of a chaplain's activities is not debatable. . . . It certainly is no great credit to sing with great gusto about a 'sky pilot' who becomes a killer . . . we should like to see the song banned from the air."[20]

Not all of the American clergy reacted unfavorably to "Praise the Lord and Pass the Ammunition." The Liberal Church of Denver, Colorado, ended its service with the Lord's Prayer and the congregation singing "Praise the Lord" as a finale every Sunday for the duration of the war. A cantor at a Brooklyn temple, who normally sang "Oh, Jerusalem," a standard song, added "Praise the Lord" as a part of the service.[21]

The song appealed to Americans' view of the war as a holy crusade. The OWI and other government agencies depicted World War II as a struggle of good versus evil, of slavery versus freedom. "Praise the Lord and Pass the Ammunition" allowed all Americans to be a part of this fight by singing along with the recording. To "all stay free" was possible because Americans were "on a mighty mission."

Chapter 3

"There's Nary an 'Over There' in the Lot"

The desire of the public and the Tin Pan Alley songwriters for war songs passed through several stages. The patriotic phase came first. Following the flood of Pearl Harbor songs, *Billboard* counseled smart songwriters and publishers to concentrate their efforts on "tunes of a less specific nature," and no doubt there would be another "Over There" to take the country "by storm." As soon as the war was well under way, *Billboard* added prophetically, the publishers might find the public as receptive to ballads, love songs, and torch songs as they had been in peacetime. American publishers pointed to England where sentimental songs like "Maria Elena," "Daddy," and "I Don't Want to Set the World on Fire" were three of the top songs in 1941, when England had been at war for three years.[1]

Music industry leaders also hinted that record companies wanted to be sure that the tunes they recorded had "all the earmarks of potential hits rather than a reflection of the current newspaper headlines."[2] The anticipated profitability of a song was paramount for companies that published, recorded, and promoted war songs. Music was a business, and the war could be an important factor in their future earnings.

Veteran songwriters watched with amusement as the younger composers tried to write the Great American War Song. Older songwriters expected the percentage of rejections of new songs by publishers to be "terrific." According to a group of veteran songwriters in Philadelphia, most of the new songs were "doomed to oblivion." These experts advised the use of classical composers' tunes (which had been looted for many years—mainly in the service of love songs) as a natural source for war songs. For example, Chopin's "Polonaise Militaire" might be fitted with appropriate words to help a "Polish comeback." Tchaikovsky's "1812 Overture" might be passed off as "Hit Hitler on the Run from Russia."[3] Few of the younger composers took the advice.

In the first few months of World War II, music publishers, songwriters, bandleaders, radio chains, and record companies were dissatisfied, for the most part, with the quality of new patriotic songs. Publishers lacked confidence in publishing and recording these songs. In part they thought that Americans were still in shock, unable to fully comprehend that the nation was at war. Most important, publishers and recording companies hesitated to produce war tunes because they did not want to be laden with unsalable music if the public taste shifted away from war-like, revenge-filled songs.

At the end of January 1942, Leonard Joy said he was still receiving an average of five war tunes per day. He thought that the grim, angry feelings behind these songs would soon be replaced by the more sentimental or "jolly type," such as the nostalgic pieces predominating in England in late 1941 and early 1942. An editorial in *Billboard* by Harold Humphrey pointed out that the best-selling songs in America before the war were almost all sentimental tunes.[4]

On *Billboard*'s "Music Popularity Chart" for the week of April 11, 1942, most of the best-sellers on both the record and sheet music lists were sentimental ballads or novelty tunes: "I Don't Want to Walk without You," "Jersey Bounce," "Deep in the Heart of Texas," and "Miss You." Some pre-war draft songs such as "'Till Reveille" and "Goodbye, Dear, I'll Be Back in a Year" made the "Going Strong" section of *Billboard's* record-buying guide, but these topical songs were the exceptions.[5]

Besides sentiment, Humphrey seemed to think that these songs on the best-seller lists had musical merit and that the American public wanted, first of all, a good tune. The pre-war song "Any Bonds Today?," written by Irving Berlin in early 1941, never reached the top of any chart despite heavy promotion on radio, records, and the stage. For example, Warner Brothers produced a cartoon with Bugs Bunny, Porky Pig, and Daffy Duck singing "Any Bonds Today?"[6] In an effort to sell more defense bonds, jukebox operators campaigned to have "Any Bonds Today?" placed in the number one tray on every jukebox in the nation.[7] The United States Treasury adopted the piece as the official song of the National Defense Savings Program.[8] Although it may have done the job intended for it with a lively tune and syncopated rhythm, "Any Bonds Today?" never sold well, probably because it asked Americans to part with their money before they were in the war:

ANY BONDS TODAY?
Bonds of freedom,

That's what I'm selling—
ANY BONDS TODAY?
Scrape up the most you can;
Here comes the freedom man
Asking you to buy
A share of freedom today.

Following the attack on Pearl Harbor, Irving Berlin added a new verse containing militant lyrics uncharacteristic of his style. Bing Crosby introduced the new version on his radio show, December 16, 1941.[9]

But wait 'till the final text:
We'll wipe Mr. Jap
From the face of the map
And Germany has to be next.

In his *Billboard* column "Wartime Music," Harold Humphrey attributed the failure of "Any Bonds Today?" to the American public's general perception of music as a form of relaxation and entertainment, not a propaganda tool.[10] Even the celebrated composer Irving Berlin was unable to write a hit every time—especially when writing songs meant to rally the troops and the civilians on the home front.

Berlin was by far the most successful of the Tin Pan Alley composers and could rightly be called the greatest war songwriter. Although "God Bless America" appeared in 1938, it soon became synonymous with World War II patriotism. The tunes for his show *This Is the Army*—"This Is the Army, Mister Jones," "I Left My Heart at the Stage Door Canteen," "The Army's Made a Man Out of Me," "I'm Getting Tired So I Can Sleep," "Oh! How I Hate To Get Up In The Morning"—achieved wide notice, and his patriotic numbers written in support of various government drives were certainly superior to the others in the genre, but none made any lasting impression on the popularity charts. The best of these was "Any Bonds Today?" Others included "Arms For The Love Of America (The Army Ordnance Song)" ("Arms for the love of America / And for the love of ev'ry mother's son / Who's depending on the work that must be done / By the man behind the man behind the gun"), "Angel of Mercy," and "I Paid My Income Tax Today." Berlin's "There Are No Wings on a Foxhole (For the Men of the Infantry)" is a prime example of a song written to recognize a component of the military that might not ordinarily receive much attention. As the pedestrian lyrics indicate, the life of a foot soldier is less glamorous than those who fly the planes or drive the tanks:

THERE ARE NO WINGS ON A FOXHOLE,
If it's where you happen to be.
While the shells are flying,
It's doing or dying
For the men of the infantry.

A patriotic theme was not enough to sell a song; it also had to have musical merit and a "strong touch of sentiment."[11] "God Bless America" might be called the foremost example of this rule. The melody originally had been intended for a song titled "I Love My Wife" in Berlin's World War I soldier show *Yip, Yip, Yaphank* but had been put aside. The song lyric was written shortly after Berlin's return home from a 1938 trip abroad, during which he had seen the shadows of fascism lengthening across Europe. The result was "God Bless America," which he thought too excessive and sentimental for a soldier show,[12] especially the lines "God bless America, My home sweet home."

Berlin presented the song, with these new lyrics, to Kate Smith on November 10, 1938, the evening before Armistice Day and a few months before Nazi bombs fell on Poland. In September 1939 she introduced this patriotic song on her weekly radio show, *The Kate Smith Hour*. She closed the show with "God Bless America" three weeks in a row and then omitted it on the fourth week; after the ensuing outcry from listeners, Smith never closed a show during the war without singing the song.[13] As she sang it time and again during the dark years that followed, Berlin's tune became a quasi national anthem; some even mistook it for an official anthem.[14]

There is little doubt that "God Bless America" was sold to the American public by Kate Smith, who sang it countless times over the air and also recorded it.[15] This song, along with "When the Moon Comes over the Mountain," became her signature tune.

"God Bless America" was so popular because it succeeded on several levels: musically, emotionally, and lyrically. Berlin's choice of lyric allows the singer or listener the latitude to imagine the country from the Atlantic to the Pacific or "from the mountains, to the prairies." The ambiguous words, mentioning no actual landmarks or geographical names, allow the singer or listener to interject his own personal understanding of "mountains" or "prairies" or "oceans white with foam." The vague verse in which "storm clouds gather" refers to the clouds of war in Europe, "far across the sea." Berlin urges Americans to "all be grateful" that they live in a "land that's free," and he merely hints at the grandeur of the land and calls on a transcendent deity to watch over the country "from above."

He also uses personification to his advantage when he identifies America as a female: "stand beside her and guide her." The feminine pronoun kindles thoughts of the maternal, an image often invoked by songwriters to capture the essence of their homeland, as in, for example, "Mother Russia." But Berlin's America is also a feminine presence in need of protection.

The song is both personal and impersonal, precise yet vague, marchlike while at the same time being reverent. Berlin's lyrics compel the listener to identify with the song's most personal sentiments by using first person pronouns, "Land that I love." The concluding lines express the same type of personal sentiment: America is "My home, sweet home."

Finally, different musical styles can express the tune. "God Bless America" can be played by a band or orchestra with a march tempo, or it can be interpreted equally as well as a stately hymn. It is a matter of musical arrangement, the type of musical ensemble performing the song, and performance style.[16]

Joining such patriotic war-horses as "Battle Hymn of the Republic," "Anchors Aweigh," "I Am an American," and the World War I number "Say a Prayer for the Boys Over There" were the early World War II flag-waving tunes "We Did It Before," "Let's Put New Glory in Old Glory," "There's a Star Spangled Banner Waving Somewhere," and "We Must Be Vigilant," a call to arms sung to the tune of "American Patrol" and featured by Phil Spitalny and his All Girl Orchestra on the *Hour of Charm* :

We must be vigilant!
We must be vigilant!
American Patrol
With arms for the army, ships for the navy,
Let this be our goal.
We must be diligent!
We must be diligent!
American Patrol.

Other overtly patriotic numbers included "Me and My Uncle Sam," "Ballad for Americans," "This Is Worth Fighting For," and Glenn Miller's bouncy swing arrangement of "American Patrol." Meredith Willson's "America Calling" entreated: "You Sons of America / Take your stand for the Red, White and Blue / North to the boundary / And coast to coast / Your America's calling to you."

Tin Pan Alley's patriotic songs expressing love of country and support for the war effort gave way to more sentimental, romance-driven songs after 1942. These sentimental songs usually had a soldier in them, but now there was a love interest: two of the most popular were "I Left My Heart At The Stage Door Canteen" and "The Shrine of St. Cecilia," by Carroll Loveday and Jo Kern:

I kneel in my solitude
And silently pray
That heaven will protect you dear
And there'll come a day
The storm will be over
And that we'll meet again
AT THE SHRINE OF SAINT CECILIA

"Rose Ann of Charing Cross," "He Wears a Pair of Silver Wings" ("Altho' some people say he's just a crazy guy / To me he means a million other things / For he's the one who taught this happy heart of mine to fly / HE WEARS A PAIR OF SILVER WINGS"), and "A Boy in Khaki, A Girl in Lace" provide further examples of the more romantic war songs.

"When the Lights Go on Again (All Over the World)" (1942) started a trend that alarmed the Office of War Information and other federal government offices charged with maintaining the fighting spirit and morale of the home front. The song looks forward to the end of the war, to a time when soldiers and sailors will return to their homes and the blissful world of peacetime, with no need for blackouts and no more bombs falling from the skies. The Office of War Information actively discouraged such thinking as "overly optimistic," "escapist," and corrupted by wishful thinking that was dangerous to the war effort.[17] Songs like "When the Lights Go on Again" faded, but not before marking a place on the best-seller lists:

When the lights go on again
All over the world
And the boys are home again
All over the world
And rain or snow is all
That may fall from the skies above,
A kiss won't mean "Goodbye,"
But "Hello" to love.[18]

Also in this sentimental mood, but certainly in a category all by itself, was Irving Berlin's "White Christmas." Berlin's greatest war time ballad—and one of the most successful songs ever written—was not intended as a war song. And yet American soldiers fighting in the swamps and jungles of the Pacific islands seized "White Christmas" as a nostalgic remembrance of home and holiday peace and goodwill to savor when the war was at its worst. (Later Allied soldiers in North Africa would rewrite the words to suit their isolated situation: "I'm dreaming of a white mistress.")[19]

Berlin could not have guessed the impact that the song, introduced in plenty of time for the Christmas season by Bing Crosby in the October 1942 movie *Holiday Inn*, would have.[20] Nor could he have gauged the extent of its popularity on the home front, where it became the longest running song on *Your Hit Parade*, with eighteen appearances in 1942 and 1943, ten of these in first place. "White Christmas" was the biggest selling hit of the war, going on to sell more than one million copies in sheet music alone—the first such sale in a decade—and repeating its dominance during the Christmas seasons of 1943 and 1944. In the wartime mood—a bit sad and yearning—the song expressed emotions with which soldiers and civilians could identify.[21]

Author Michael Freedland claims in *Irving Berlin* that the composer never intended "White Christmas" as a wartime theme. Berlin said, "'It came out of a time when we were at war, and it became a peace song in wartime, nothing I ever intended.'"[22] "White Christmas" was linked with the war because of Berlin's genius for expressing the emotions of so many who were far from home for several Christmas seasons. The mood of the song is quiet and dreamy. "White Christmas" evokes a reverie of quiet ease, recalling the past and invoking the future, but cleverly omitting the present. It requires no particular religious faith, since no mention beyond the word "Christmas" is made of the significance of the holiday.

Like other mythic American holiday scenes (for example, the United States Thanksgiving depicted in a New England setting with colorful autumn leaves, a bountiful harvest, and, of course, the Pilgrims—a scene that has little basis in reality for most Americans), Christmas is assumed to be a part of a collective memory that is Christian, rural, and somewhere in the North. But "White Christmas" is all encompassing, and therefore appealing to a nation at war. It asks no commitment of the listeners, but refers to a mythical past and a mist-shrouded future in which listeners can mingle their own dreams and memories. Most important, Berlin paints a glowing picture of something Americans love that can not be destroyed by war: "a White Christmas," which lives in the imagination.

Despite the great success of "White Christmas," the trade papers reported that Berlin considered his tune a fluke. It was written for a stage show that was never produced and finally came out in a movie. Asked by *Variety* if he considered "White Christmas" a war song, Berlin replied: "What is a war song? Some songs are popular during war and others aren't. Goodness knows 'White Christmas' isn't a war song by the farthest stretch of the imagination, but boys in the Solomons and boys in Africa are singing it. So—it's a war song."[23]

The song evoked such strong emotions that Woody Herman reported in January 1943, "We were requested at the Stage Door Canteen not to play 'White Christmas,' so we avoid playing it at camps, too. It makes the boys too nostalgic."[24] Introducing "White Christmas" during his performance on NBC's Sixth War Loan Program, *Let's Talk Turkey to Japan*, Bing Crosby said, "On a holiday like this, . . . is when our men overseas . . . have to swallow the biggest lumps . . . think[ing] of the cozy, quiet warmth of home on a holiday. . . . [T]hey asked to hear, 'White Christmas'. . . . I hesitated . . . it . . . made them sad. Heaven knows making them sad wasn't my job . . . but every time I tried to slack it they'd holler for it. Sometimes we all got a little dewy-eyed. You can't know . . . and yet you must know how . . . [sings] "'They're dreaming of a White Christmas . . .'"[25]

Variety called "White Christmas" the most valuable song copyright in the world. Crosby's recording for Decca sold over 24 million records between 1942–1949[26] and *Billboard* ranked it as the number two song of the 1940s.[27] Berlin must have had some hints as to the potential for success of the song. Michael Freedland claims that upon finishing "White Christmas," Irving Berlin, working in Hollywood, called his agent in New York and told him that not only was it the best song he (Berlin) had ever written, but it was also the best song that anyone had ever written.[28] If continued popularity and sales receipts are any indication, Irving Berlin may truly have written the most popular song of all times.

Contrasting with the sentimental songs, several more vibrant tunes became famous. "Deep in the Heart of Texas" spent twelve weeks on the 1942 *Hit Parade*, and five of these were in the top spot.[29] The song was so popular with munitions plant employees in England that their supervisors suspended playing the song after the workers damaged several machines in tapping out the hand claps of the song with hammers and wrenches.[30]

"I Got Spurs That Jingle, Jangle, Jingle," by Frank Loesser, actually a caricature of the traditional cowboy song, caught the civilian imagination with its theme of packing up belongings and moving on, mirroring the defense workers migrating to the war production centers on the West Coast and soldiers boarding troop trains.

A favorite with the GIs and with the folks on the home front was the cautionary "Don't Sit Under the Apple Tree." A soldier stationed overseas realizes that his buddy's description of a girl back home "who likes to pet" fits his girlfriend "to a T," and he warns her not to "fool around." The melody of the song was first used for a lyric titled "Anywhere the Bluebird Goes," but was then introduced as "Don't Sit Under the Apple Tree" in the Broadway show *Yokel Boy* in 1939. The Andrews Sisters popularized it, first in the movie *Private Buckaroo* (1942) and then in a Decca recording.[31]

Chapter 4

War Songs in Boy-Girl Terms

Although most of the songs discussed, thus far, dealt with civilian life on the home front, Tin Pan Alley had not given up the quest for a solid, military-style war song. The sentimental songs and the songs that looked forward to the end of the war were still considered unsuitable for the purpose of uniting Americans in the war effort. Since the songs about the home front could not do the job, Tin Pan Alley looked to the men and women serving in the military for inspiration in creating the Great American War Song.

The men in the service had been getting their share of attention in popular song since the beginning of the peacetime draft, the first ever in U.S. history, with the passage of the Burke-Wadsworth Selective Service Act in September 1940. The Selective Service Act called for the creation of forty thousand Selective Service boards run by local civilians and the registration of all men between the ages of twenty-one and thirty-six, and the training, for one year, of more than one million soldiers plus another eight hundred thousand reserves.[1]

When the draft extension was passed in 1941, it was duly recorded in song: "I Won't Be Back in a Year, Little Darling," a revision of the original 1940 title, "I'll Be Back in a Year."

Then came the war and an explosion of what Richard Lingeman calls "Soldier Boy" songs, most of which were either sentimental or humorous. Some of the "soldier boy" songs included "Till Reveille," "Last Call for Love," and "After Taps." Others appeared briefly and then faded, such as "I'll Be Marching to a Love Song," "Cleaning My Rifle (and Dreaming of You)," "If He Can Fight Like He Can Love," "He Enlisted in the Navy," "Wait Until the Girls Get in the Army, Boys," and Redd Evans's "He's 1-A in the Army and He's A-1 in My Heart." The last of these was recorded seven weeks before Pearl Harbor was attacked, but within a few weeks of its release the song's lyrics were heightened by the new wave of romantic patriotism accompanying America's entry into the war:

> He's 1-A in the army and he's A-1 in my heart,
> He's gone to help the country that helped him get a start.
> I love him so because I know he wants to do his part,
> For he's 1-A in the army and he's A-1 in my heart.

Irving Berlin's *This Is the Army*, an all-soldier show that he wrote and produced in his single greatest effort of the war, went beyond describing the war in strictly boy-girl terms. Just as he had in World War I, Berlin convinced the army that the soldiers needed entertainment in camp, and the Pentagon assigned him a barracks room at Camp Upton, New Jersey. There he lived and observed daily camp life while he gathered material for his acts, sketches, and songs. *This Is the Army* opened July 2, 1942, on Broadway with a cast of three hundred uniformed soldiers, all amateurs. The show told the story of army life in song and dance with a great deal of comedy.

This Is the Army was entertainment, pure and simple. Berlin included neither war ideology nor fighting or battle scenes. Army camp life was depicted with boyish humor, and songs were either funny or slightly sentimental, with girls, sweethearts, and mothers as the main topics. The impression of army life that passed over the footlights to the audience was that military service was more like a summer camp vacation and not the serious business of preparing for war.

Songs that made their way onto the airwaves from the show included, as mentioned earlier, "This Is the Army, Mister Jones," "The Army's Made a Man Out of Me," "I Left My Heart at the Stage Door Canteen," and "I'm Getting Tired So I Can Sleep." The most popular song from the show was revived from Berlin's World War I soldier show *Yip, Yip, Yaphank* and featured him in his World War I uniform, singing "Oh, How I Hate to Get Up in the Morning."[2]

This Is the Army proved to be so popular that its initial four-week run was extended to twelve weeks; then a national tour was added, followed by a tour of the European, Far East, and Pacific theaters of war. The show grossed $2 million from its U.S. tour, $1.2 million from its British engagement, and $7.5 million from the Warner Brothers film adaptation.

Berlin was quick to insert new songs into the show, depending on the particular audience. For example, for audiences in England he added "My British Buddy," for those in the Pacific he composed "Heaven Watch the Philippines," and for the Women's Army Corps and Red Cross nurses he wrote "Oh, for a Dress Again." Before leaving the Philippines, Berlin introduced another new song just for the soldiers in the Pacific, "Oh, to Be Home Again." When *This Is the Army* finally closed on October 22, 1945, it had earned more than $10 million for the Army Relief Fund.[3]

This Is the Army proved to be an exception to the usual skepticism and occasional outright hostility faced by the entertainment business from some members of Congress who were not convinced that music and theater were essential to winning the war. Speaking in defense of show business, Rep. Emmanuel Celler of New York said, "It [*This Is the Army*] is a sheer pageantry of patriotism. . . . You are lifted out of your seat with enthusiasm. You feel like throwing your loving arms around our army. Do not fail to see it. It is a great gloom antidote." He also suggested that music and the theater were the "greatest vehicle for bolstering up public morale."[4] The fact that Representative Celler's district included New York City might possibly have colored his intense enthusiasm, but the final tabulation of the profits from the stage productions and the motion picture indicate that Celler was not alone in his positive assessment of *This Is the Army*.

Another group of songs celebrated the advent of American women into the armed services in non-combat roles. On May 12, 1942, Congress passed the bill forming the Women's Army Auxiliary Corps (WAAC), and the American public saw an unfamiliar sight: women outfitted in military uniforms that traditionally were a symbol of masculinity. Persuading the American public that the Corps was a hard-working organization, composed of sensible women whose contributions to the war effort were valid, was indeed a difficult task.[5]

Numerous songs commemorated the entrance of women into the military: "Tillie the Toiler (The WAAC)," "The Girl of the Year Is a SPAR,"[6] and other "service" songs. Several songs induced women to enlist in the military by assuring them that they would still be feminine and still be doing what had traditionally been "women's work":

> Men must fight
> But women needn't stand aside and weep.
> ....
> A Woman's Place is where she's needed,
> And she's needed in the Cadet Nurse Corps.
> So step up Mary, Jane and Sue!
> Here's a uniform for you.
> Here's the chance for all of you to roam
> A Woman's Place is no longer in the home.[7]

The most popular of the Soldier Boy songs were "jumpin'" numbers like "GI Jive" and "The Boogie-Woogie Bugle Boy of Company B." While

"Boogie-Woogie Bugle Boy" was a standard Hollywood production number, made famous by the Andrews Sisters; Johnny Mercer's "GI Jive" had a fast-driving syncopation and clever lyrics, laced with GI slang that informed the listener, "This is the G.I. Jive / Man, alive." The song described army drills as "make with the feet" and army protocol for privates as "Your duty / Is to salute the L-I-E-U-T." The tune jumped all over the scale and had enough jazz and "jive" in it to make weary GIs smile.

By 1943 time and experience made the Soldier Boy songs give way to the "Fighting Man" songs, like the "Ballad of Roger Young," "Comin' in on a Wing and a Prayer," "A Guy 24 in a B-29," "Johnny Got a Zero" (in which schoolboys' jeers at a poor student are thrown back into their faces when he enlists in the Air Corps and shoots down a Japanese Zero), and "The U.S.A. by Day and the R.A.F. at Night," the first song ever written about a bombing pattern.

"Comin' in on a Wing and a Prayer," by Harold Adamson and Jimmy McHugh, has much in common with "Remember Pearl Harbor." In one recording by the male voices of the Golden Gate Quartet, the song is performed in African American spiritual style. This hymn-like quality accents a simple melody and a standard 4/4 rhythm pattern. The chorus of the song is repeated several times, and the lyrics tell a story, making it easy for a listener to remember after one or two hearings:

> Comin' in on a wing and a prayer,
> We're comin' in on a wing and a prayer.
> Oh, there's one motor gone,
> But we still can carry on,
> Comin' in on a wing and a prayer.

In the wake of the success of "Don't Sit Under the Apple Tree" came "Three Little Sisters," in which three sisters vow to be true to their boyfriends in three branches of service. Another tune that reassured the absent GI of his sweetheart's faithfulness was "My Yankee Doodle Boy Can Count on Me." Conversely, "I Came Here to Talk for Joe" recreated the old Miles Standish scenario: an absent GI sends his buddy to plead his case and tell his girl how much he loves her. Out of step with the other songs of this period were "Johnny Doughboy Found a Rose in Ireland" and "Somebody Else Is Taking My Place," with implications that the American GI could be drawn to foreign girls or, even worse, might find somebody else taking his place back home:

> Somebody else is taking my place;
> Somebody else now shares your embrace.

While I am trying to keep from crying,
You go around with a smile on your face.[8]

These songs of faithlessness were aberrations. The trend was songs of dialogue between the Soldier Boy and the Girl Back Home. Following Pearl Harbor, the Soldier Boy would tell his girl not to sit under the apple tree or would vow "I'm in Love with the Girl I Left behind Me," and he would tell her to "Stick to Your Knittin', Kitten," or "Be Brave, My Beloved." Then he was awarded his aviator wings, while the girl looked on adoringly, and went overseas to "He Wears a Pair of Silver Wings," a song by Eric Maschwitz and Michael Carr:

Altho' some people say he's just a crazy guy
To me he means a million other things.
For me he's the one who taught
This happy heart of mine to fly,
HE WEARS A PAIR OF SILVER WINGS.

Strangely, except for an occasional Japanese Zero he shot down, the soldier was rarely heard from again, at least in song. In any case, he seldom wrote, leaving the poor girl at home to suffer the pangs of loneliness, as expressed in "I'll Pray for You," "I'll Be a Good Soldier, Too," "I'll Keep the Love-Light Burning," and "My Devotion." The most popular of this particular type were "Always in My Heart," "I'll Wait for You," "Miss You," and "I'll Never Smile Again," a revival of a 1941 Frank Sinatra hit written by Ruth Lowe and originally published in 1939.

In the 1943 song by Frank Loesser and Arthur Schwartz, "They're Either Too Young or Too Old," the girl reassures her soldier that no matter where his duty takes him, whether to India, Egypt, Australia, or Russia, she won't sit under the apple tree with another man. She says, "There is no secret lover / That the draft board didn't discover." The song also served as a reminder to men not to shirk their military duty, assuring them that "What's good is in the army / What's left will never harm me."

In late 1942 and in 1943 the songs of loneliness began to take on a tone of frustration (yet the girl remained loyal to the soldier), as in Bob Russell's lyric for the Duke Ellington tune "Don't Get around Much Anymore." The girl in this song shuns all social activities and says (as if in a letter to her service man),

Been invited on dates
Could have gone, but what for?

Awfully diff'rent without you
Don't get around much anymore."

Such hit songs as "You'll Never Know," "No Love, No Nuthin'," "Saturday Night Is the Loneliest Night of the Week," "A Little on the Lonely Side," "I Don't Want to Walk Without You," and "I'll Walk Alone" express similar sentiments. The last song, probably the most popular of the group, led the *Hit Parade* eight times in 1944.[9] Dinah Shore introduced "I'll Walk Alone" in the 1944 film *Follow the Boys*. Written by Jule Styne and Sammy Cahn, it was nominated for an Academy Award in 1944 but lost to "Swingin' on a Star."[10] One of the definitive love songs of World War II, Styne and Cahn's words expressed the mood of the nation as well as any other piece of the era:

I'll walk alone
Because to tell you the truth,
I'll be lonely.
I don't mind being lonely
When my heart tells me you
Are lonely too.
....
Please walk alone
And send your love
And your kisses to guide me.
Till you're walking beside me,
I'll walk alone.

Some risqué songs—"You Can't Say No to a Soldier," "He Loved Me Till the All-Clear Came," "Love Isn't Born, It's Made," and "I'm Doin' It for Defense"—were written during this period, but most of them were parodies by soldiers or originated in the movies, since any song that even whispered of impropriety or alcohol would not be given air time on the radio networks. Johnny Mercer and Harold Arlen's "I'm Doin' It for Defense" was sung by Betty Hutton to a carload of sailors in the movie *Star Spangled Rhythm*, and its lyric is typical of the slightly suggestive wartime songs generated by Tin Pan Alley songwriters when they were not constrained by radio's censorship:

This ain't love this is war,
I'm doing it for defense.
Once I start, I can't quit,
I said I'd do my bit

So it's sad, but you're it
I'm doin' it for defense.

In a category defined not only by its provocative lyric but also by the performance of its author was Sophie Tucker's "The Bigger the Army and Navy (Is the Better the Lovin' Will Be)." Sung in the movie *Follow the Boys* by the "Last of the Red Hot Mamas" to a packed grandstand of sailors at the Naval Training Center in San Diego, California, the song suggests that once a man puts on a military uniform he becomes a fighter and a lover:

The bigger the Army and Navy is,
The better the lovin' will be.
The women who went through the last war
Know what I mean.
We're getting thrills we haven't had,
Since 1918.
....
They get into a uniform,
And it's Bang! Bang! Right away!
The bigger the Army and the Navy,
The better the lovin' will be
And it's gonna' be perfect for me.

Such songs provided a different interpretation of the faithfulness vows; it was all right for a girl to bestow her favors as long as she did so out of patriotism. None of these songs had wide popularity, and even though their lyrics were pure on the surface, people were certainly aware of their concealed meaning—for example, "If he's physically 1-A / Don't you be socially 4-F" ("The Bigger the Army and Navy").

Because radio's standards were even stricter than Hollywood's, anything even remotely suggestive would not be broadcast. The words "hell" and "damn" were beyond the boundaries of radio. The hillbilly tune "Pistol Packin' Mama" became a national hit but not before it was laundered considerably to be sung on *Your Hit Parade*. It would not do, the radio censors said, for the man in the song to be "drinkin' beer in a cabaret"; he had to be "singing songs" (the ban on mentioning alcoholic beverages on the air applied to song lyrics as well). Even the cause of "Mama's" wielding her pistol had to be changed to avoid any hint of adultery. The fact that "Papa" was dancing with a blonde was unacceptable.

Written by former honky-tonk proprietor Al Dexter and released on Okeh Records in March 1943, the song tells of a gun-toting woman who chases her husband's girlfriend out of a bar. The lively, rollicking tune was even recorded by Bing Crosby and the Andrews Sisters in September 1943. According to Bill C. Malone in *Country Music U.S.A.*, many songs of the forties had popular appeal, but few were as "commercially successful" as "Pistol Packin' Mama."[11] Its sales of over a million copies in six months made it one of the two or three most popular songs of the war period.[12] When a New York City kindergarten teacher leading her class in song on the first day of school with numbers such as "God Bless America" and "Onward Christian Soldiers" asked for requests from the class, the children cried out, "Pistol Packin' Mama"! And they sang it.[13]

Despite the song's popularity, it did not appear on the *Lucky Strike Hit Parade* until October 1943. *LIFE* speculated that the sponsor disliked the song or that Frank Sinatra, the show's star vocalist, could not sing the hillbilly song. The magazine called "'Pistol Packin' Mama' . . . a national scourge," saying the song was "naive, folksy and almost completely devoid of meaning," and a "national earache."[14]

It was the first song recorded by Decca Records after the company reached an agreement to end Decca's portion of the strike by the American Federation of Musicians. An editorial in the *Charlotte (NC) Observer* wondered if this song was the most popular one born out of the crisis of war: "[Do] we have a country worth saving or a culture that is worth defending with the blood . . . of the best . . . of the land?"[15]

The words of "Pistol Packin' Mama" are rather simplistic to have caused such a division in the music world, but the opinions of the critics did not much matter. The American people bought the records and the sheet music and made a huge success of the song.

> Drinkin' beer in a cabaret,
> And was I havin' fun!
> Until one night she caught me right,
> And now I'm on the run.
> Lay that pistol down, Babe.
> Lay that pistol down,
> Pistol Packin' Mama,
> Lay that pistol down!

The war experience, for both soldier and civilian alike, was instrumental in exposing a new generation of potential fans to country music. When men left their homes in the South for military bases elsewhere in the United States or in other parts of the world, they took their music, what would come to be known as "country and western," with them. Civilians looking for jobs and better lives for their families poured out of the South into industrial centers in the Midwest and on the West Coast. Also bringing their love of hillbilly music with them, the transplanted Southerners requested their music on jukeboxes and in dance halls.

Through this shifting of the population, a regional music form, country music, became a national phenomenon. It introduced Americans to Roy Acuff, Ernest Tubb, Al Dexter, and other musicians of the new country and western style. By the final months of the war, country music was so widespread and recognized as American music that the Japanese included country music in their list of American institutions to insult over the loudspeaker systems they maintained around the Pacific. Nightly, American servicemen would hear anti-American broadcasts with such invectives as "To hell with Franklin D. Roosevelt! To hell with Babe Ruth! To hell with Roy Acuff!"[16]

Songs from country artists were not the only ones that had to be modified in order to pass the radio network censors' standards. Like "Pistol Packin' Mama," the Andrews Sisters' "Rum and Coca-Cola" had to be rewritten because of radio's ban on mentioning alcohol. The song was imported from Trinidad and banned on many radio networks, which argued that it gave free advertising for both of the products mentioned in the title.[17]

Morey Amsterdam supposedly discovered the calypso tune, which was then recorded in the United States, eventually making *Your Hit Parade*. Trinidad native Rupert Grant objected, arguing he had copyrighted the original words, which were set to the tune of a Creole lullaby. Grant claimed that his lyric satirized the American soldiers' occupation of the island; for example, "Both the mothers and the daughters / Working for the Yankee dollar" is a thinly veiled reference to local women selling themselves to American servicemen.[18] Whatever the case, the immensely popular song finally was heard over the airwaves as "Lime and Coca-Cola" before the networks eventually banned the playing of any arrangement of the song that included words. Occasionally instrumental versions were allowed, but the majority of Americans put their nickels in jukeboxes or purchased the records or sheet music and enjoyed the uncensored version.[19] Almost any song about sailors had ribald connotations; "As Mabel Goes—So Goes the Navy," which suggested women bestow sexual favors on sailors, was forbidden by the Office of War Information. But "Bell Bottom Trousers" was sufficiently cleaned up and went on to make *Your Hit Parade* in 1945.

Making up for lost time was the theme of songs as the war wound down: "It's Been a Long, Long Time," and "I'm Going to Love That Gal (Like She's Never Been Loved Before)." Perry Como's interpretation of the latter made *Variety* comment, "None of his squealing admirers was under any apprehension as to what those lyrics suggested."[20] Sex had not been entirely removed from love songs; it had just gone underground.

When the lonely girls of 1944 had had enough of being brave at home and exchanging Victory Mail,[21] a new song cycle emerged: dream songs. Songs with an emphasis on dreams were not new, but a fresh wave of them crested at the end of 1944 and into 1945. They had a simple plot: the love, happiness, or contentment denied by the real or waking world was possible in a dream. Beginning in 1942 with Irving Berlin's "I'm Getting Tired So I Can Sleep" (about a soldier dreaming of his girl), the dream became the popular meeting place:

I'm getting tired so I can sleep;
I want to sleep so I can dream;
I want to dream so I can be with you.

The following year brought Mack Gordon and Harry Warrens's "I Had the Craziest Dream" ("There you were in love with me / When I'm awake such a break never happens") and "Thanks for the Dream" ("Thanks for the dream, it was sweet / There were your arms wrapped around me. . . . Then I awoke, calling your name / Crying for you, wondering who put out the flame"); 1944 saw the popularity of "Long Ago and Far Away" and "I'm Making Believe." Dream songs of 1945 included "I Dream of You," "I'll Buy That Dream," "Sweet Dreams Sweetheart," "My Dreams Are Getting Better All the Time," "What's Your Favorite Dream?" and "Linda":

When I go to sleep
I never count sheep
I count all the charms about Linda.[22]

Joining "Linda" was "Laura" (1945): "That was Laura, but she's only a dream." And perhaps the most popular one of all (five times on *Your Hit Parade*) was "Dream," published in 1944 but not on the best-seller lists until 1945. The song was blatant fantasy; no longer did the dream provide comfort by supplying an absent or languid loved one. Johnny Mercer's lyrics, which told listeners dreaming was "the thing to do" because when one did dream "things never are" as "bad as they seem," were essentially narcotic. The song also relied on dreams to help people find their "share of memories."

Expressing the kindred emotions of war-weariness and happiness at the prospect of returning to a normal life were a group of homecoming and victory songs that began to appear in early 1945. Some of the titles that did not make it to *Your Hit Parade* were "Victory Day," "From the Arms of War to the Arms of Love," "Put Your Guns at Rest Soldier Boy,"

"The Lights Are on Again," "They're Home Again," "Veterans on Parade," and "We've Won the War."

The trend of nostalgic longing for a rosy peacetime actually began in 1941, before the United States entered the war, with Nat Burton and Walter Kent's ballad "(There'll Be Bluebirds Over) The White Cliffs of Dover":

There'll be bluebirds over
The white cliffs of Dover
Tomorrow, just you wait and see
There'll be love and laughter
And peace ever after
Tomorrow when the world is free.

The trend continued in 1942 with "When the Lights Go on Again (All Over the World)." But, as previously stated, the officials at the Office of War Information discouraged such songs as dangerous to the war effort, and composers and publishers let these songs fade from the popular music charts.[23]

The songwriters were soon back with more rousing, if less sentimental, numbers such as "Vict'ry Polka" (1944) and "Hot Time in the Town of Berlin" (1943), a swing tune given peppy performances by various artists such as Glenn Miller, Bing Crosby, Frank Sinatra, and the Andrews Sisters. The latter song, written by John De Vries and Joe Bushkin, reminded listeners of two previous American wars. The title is a variation of the song most closely identified with the Spanish-American War—"Hot Time in the Old Time Tonight"—and the lyrics allude to the World War I tune "How You Gonna' Keep Them Down on the Farm, After They've Seen Paree?" "Hot Time in the Town of Berlin" is full of American bravado and good humor, with an ending in homage of "Der Fuehrer's Face":

There'll be a hot time in the town of Berlin
When the Yanks go marching in.
I want to be there, boy,
To spread some joy,
When they take old Berlin.
....
We'll go "Heil! Heil!"
Right in Der Fuehrer's Face!

"Vict'ry Polka" was a war song in name only but still considered a rousing attempt to cheer Americans and remind them that victory was at hand as the war neared its conclusion. One of the most successful of the

1945 homecoming songs was by Sammy Cahn and Jule Styne. As recorded by Harry James, the most popular trumpet player of the day, "It's Been a Long, Long Time" spoke to parted lovers of the hope that the war would end soon and they would be reunited:

Kiss me once and kiss me twice
And kiss me once again
It's been a long, long time.

Written by Irving Kahal and Sammy Fain and originally recorded in 1938, the haunting and more tentative homecoming song "I'll Be Seeing You" was the most popular tune of 1944. It, too, seemed apropos for the soldier and his girlfriend:

I'll be seeing you
In all the old familiar places
That this heart of mine embraces
All day through.
....
I'll be seeing you in every lovely summer's day
In everything that's light and gay
....
And when the day is through
I'll be looking at the moon
But I'll be seeing you.

Although its lyrics do not stress wartime separation, "I'll Be Seeing You," like so many of the sentimental love songs of the period, holds a tantalizing promise of future reunification. Men and women listeners could read their own situations into the words of love ballads, and even though the songs' lyrics do not mention the war, the song's popularity during wartime made it a war song. The images of small-town life and of simple everyday places and things ("the park, the wishing well") come together in this song to present a nostalgic look at the recent past and a hopeful view to a future day when the lovers will once again share these ordinary things.

Furlough songs also reunited lovers temporarily: "He's Home for a Little While," "Back to My Country and You," and "Ten Bucks and Twenty-four Hours Leave." In "A Fellow on Furlough" the dream song idea was merged with reality, as the song exhorted the girl to be nice to the lonely GI who had been dreaming of a girl just like her: "He's just a fellow on furlough, out looking for a dream," so she should do as the words of another song suggest and "Send Me Away with a Smile" and be sure to "Autograph Your Photograph" when a girl sits down to "Write to the Boys Over There." More songs of optimism and homecoming followed: "My Guy's Come Back," "If I Ever Get Back to America," "When I Get Back to My Home Town," "I'm Gonna' See My Baby," and "I'll Be Walking with My Honey Soon, Soon, Soon."

In an unusual departure into political and social commentary, two 1945 songs addressed a cautionary message to the new United Nations Organization meeting in San Francisco—"The World Must Have Peace" and Henry Prichard's "Don't Let It Happen Again":

> When we round the final bend
> At the end of the scrappin'
> DON'T LET IT HAPPEN AGAIN!
> Keep a light that never fails
> On the trails we'll be mappin'
> DON'T LET IT HAPPEN AGAIN!

But the general view of the postwar world was painted in glowing terms of prosperity and, most importantly for the rationed and restricted American home front—material comforts: "There'll be strawberries floatin' in cream," as one song had it. In Phil Moore's "Shoo Shoo Baby," another hit for the Andrews Sisters and Bing Crosby, a mother sings a swing lullaby to her baby, whose "papa's off to the seven seas," cajoling, "don't cry, baby," and promising that "when he gets back we'll lead a life of ease." The speaker is sorry that "papa's gotta be rough now," in leaving, but it is only "so he can be sweet to you," when he returns some day.

Chapter 5

War Is Good for the Music Business

The songwriters' view of a radiant future might have been shaped by their own wartime prosperity. The music business claimed a huge share of the increasing amount of money Americans spent on amusements during the war. With material goods rationed or completely unavailable, Americans spent their money on entertainment: movies, sheet music, records, and the theater. Sheet music sales were never better, often topping the six hundred thousand mark for a single tune—one rarely reached before this time.

The American Society of Composers, Authors, and Publishers (ASCAP) reported a 25 percent increase in sales royalties in 1944 over the same period in 1943.[1] This prosperity occurred despite three key restrictions: 1) a rationing of shellac, used to make records (the government considered it a strategic material); 2) a ban on the use of records for public performance (such as in jukeboxes or on the radio) by ASCAP; and 3) the American Federation of Musicians (AFM)'s ban on any new recordings using instruments.

Shellac was a primary ingredient in the materials used to press records before 1945. The main supply of shellac came from India, and shipments had been in jeopardy since the beginning of the war in Europe in 1939. Fortunately, American recording companies had large reserve supplies of shellac, and when the War Production Board cut allotments by 40 percent, record production continued. Chemical engineers for Columbia Records experimented with substitute materials and other methods of diluting shellac. Shellac rationing affected smaller recording companies more than the large ones, but none of them went out of business for lack of materials with which to press records.[2]

The ASCAP strike, as it was known, lasted for ten months, from January 1941 until October 1941. Despite these obstacles, the record business soared.[3] The American Society of Composers, Authors, and Publishers held conflicting views with the national broadcasters over music licensing rights. When a five-year contract between ASCAP and the networks expired on December 30, 1940, ASCAP demanded $9 million a year in royalty payments, twice the amount of the old contract.[4]

The national broadcasters refused to pay, having already anticipated such a move from ASCAP by forming their own organization, Broadcast Music, Incorporated (BMI), on October 14, 1939. The new group was a great deal weaker than ASCAP, which owned the rights to most music written and published in the United States after 1884. Exceptions were songs in the public domain and a small catalog of music owned by Selected Editions of Standard American Catalogues.

On January 1, 1941, the broadcasters banned the use of all ASCAP material in favor of other licensing organizations. BMI had few songs in its holdings until Edward B. Marks, publisher of popular and Latin American music, joined the organization. Two other publishers with extensive hillbilly and country and western catalogs enlisted with BMI: Ralph Peer's Southern Music and M.M. Cole of Chicago. BMI gradually expanded its holdings until it had over thirty-six thousand works from fifty-two publishers. ASCAP and the radio networks resolved their differences in October 1941, but BMI had grown strong enough to be a real competitor to ASCAP and would eventually be instrumental in breaking ASCAP's monopoly on Tin Pan Alley.

In less than a year, the music business was once again interrupted by a strike. This time James Caesar Petrillo and the American Federation of Musicians were in conflict with the publishers and record companies. Petrillo argued that jukeboxes, estimated to be around four hundred thousand in number, were driving musicians out of work, and as a result, a fund should be set up to aid unemployed musicians. Petrillo decided to coerce the recording industry into paying higher fees to counteract the effect of records being played on the radio and jukeboxes. The recording companies refused and the musicians went on strike August 1,1942. There would be no more recordings made by instrumentalists. Players of ukuleles and harmonicas were exempt—Petrillo did not consider these real instruments.[5]

The record companies had tried to fill their vaults with around-the-clock recording sessions, but by mid-1943, the selection of new music was falling short of listeners' expectations. Singers, who were not members of the AFM, could still make records but without orchestral backing. Consequently, Americans heard the a cappella gospel harmonies of the Golden Gate Quartet and some artfully arranged choral performances accompanying Bing Crosby and Dick Haymes. Even an appeal from President Roosevelt did not sway Petrillo from his stand.

Live radio broadcasts, not intended for public sale or permanent preservation, were not affected, and many more performances were preserved on unbreakable transcription discs by Armed Forces Radio Service. The American public heard new songs in movie and Broadway musicals and in live performances by the dance bands and orchestras, but these tunes were not available on record.[6]

The musicians' union did make one exception to the recording ban. James Petrillo lifted all sanctions against recording for servicemen. Under Col. Howard C. Bronson and Maj. Harry Salter of the Special Services Division, the Army was given carte blanche to use AFM musicians without paying the usual fees to the union. The musicians also donated their time and talent. The first pressing of 50,000 records proved to be so popular with the servicemen that within a year's time 250,000 recordings were sent abroad each month. In isolated areas the records, made from the new material Vinylite, were dropped by parachute in specially packaged boxes also containing portable hand-wound record players. These unique phonograph records produced between the years 1943 and 1949 were known as V-Disks. Over eight million recordings of popular, jazz, country and western, and classical music were distributed to the troops overseas.

The music was divided according to category, with about 80 percent of the pressings in the popular bracket and the remaining 20 percent apportioned between folk, hillbilly, "race," and semi-classical music. V-Disk recording artists included Roy Acuff, Marian Anderson, the Andrews Sisters, Gene Autry, Pearl Bailey, Louis Armstrong, Count Basie, and the Boston Pops Orchestra. Other favorites were Les Brown, Cab Calloway, Rosemary Clooney, Nat King Cole, Bing Crosby, Jimmy and Tommy Dorsey, Duke Ellington, Ella Fitzgerald, and Eileen Ferrell. Further artists offering their services included Benny Goodman, Woody Herman, Lena Horne, Harry James, Andre Kostelanetz, Kay Kyser, Johnny Mercer, Glenn Miller, the NBC Symphony, the Philadelphia Orchestra, Tex Ritter, Artie Shaw, Dinah Shore, Frank Sinatra, the Voice of Firestone, Fats Waller, and Fred Waring.[7]

Although V-Disks were the brainchild of the army, it was not long before the navy, marines, and the Coast Guard saw how popular the Disks were. The other services negotiated with the army to "borrow" the master recordings so that they could contract with regular commercial firms for pressing copies to send to their men. Eventually the Office of War Information and the Coordinator of Intra-American Affairs also would gain access to the master recordings in order to press disks for use in entertaining servicemen. The one stipulation that the AFM placed on the V-Disk recordings was that all pressings, many containing unique, non-commercial recordings, were to be destroyed after the war or when the AFM strike was settled—whichever came first. Fortunately, for posterity, these stipulations were ignored and some never-to-be replicated V-Disk recordings survived.

Decca Records was the first company to capitulate to the American Federation of Musicians' strike. Decca's entire revenue came from popular music, and it felt the money crunch first. Faced with bankruptcy, Decca signed a new contract with the AFM in September 1943.[8] Its first new release after settling with the musicians' union was "Pistol Packin' Mama," recorded by the Andrews Sisters and Bing Crosby. A year later in November 1944, Columbia and Victor Records settled with the musicians' union.[9]

The strike was a gift to many small recording companies who were able to sign with Petrillo and gain a place in the recording business when the giant firms were out of the picture. The newly formed Capitol Records, headed by Johnny Mercer, profited from the strike and gained a strong position in the Hollywood movie industry and also with country and western artists who had discovered the West Coast.[10]

As a direct result of the ASCAP strike, and perhaps from a longing for a simpler time, revivals of older, previously recorded songs became the mainstay of radio broadcasts (aside from live performances) and some older songs gained great popularity. "As Time Goes By" was resurrected for the movie *Casablanca*, and "I'll Get By," written in 1928 by Roy Turk and Fred Ahlert, became the immortal rhapsody for American's wartime lovers as well as for Irene Dunn and Spencer Tracy in *A Guy Named Joe*:

> I'll get by
> As long as I have you.
> Though there be rain
> And darkness too,
>
> ....
> Dear, I'll get by
> As long as I have you.

The genre of purely nonsense or fantasy songs, which had been popular in the Great Depression of the 1930s, regained a certain appeal during the Second World War. "The Hut Sut Song" was supposedly in Swedish lovers' talk; "Mairzy Doats" in baby talk; and "Chickery Chick" in gibberish. Each had its turn on *Your Hit Parade*. Cole Porter's "Don't Fence Me In," the big hit of 1945 from the film *Hollywood Canteen*, was an imitation cowboy song in which Porter attempted to cash in on the craze for the American West and the freedom it implied for the future when the soldier would return and fulfill his destiny in America-the-boundless. To men and women who had lived regimented lives in the armed forces or in war work on the home front, the appeal of unlimited freedom in this song is understandable. They wanted "land, lots of land . . . under starry skies above," and they wanted to be "turn[ed] loose" to "ride through the wide open country." Americans were looking for freedom to resume their lives and to be with their families, without the specter of war and the shadow it cast on all aspects of American life.

The popularity of Latin American rhythms, sparked by bandleader Xavier Cugat in the 1930s, continued through the World War II years. Much of this popularity resulted from the ASCAP strike. Latin American composers were not members of ASCAP, so their music was outside the boundaries of the strike and could be recorded and played on the air.[11] Latin titles that sauntered through listeners' ears during the war included "Tico Tico," "Amor," "Brazil," "Besame Mucho," "Frenesi," "Poinciana," and "Magic in the Moonlight." Late in the war, a dash of calypso added spice to the Latin rhythms in songs like "Sing a Tropical Song," "Rum and Coca-Cola," and "Come with Me My Honey."

The ASCAP strike also was a blessing to country music; artists and composers who had been shunned by major publishers were now given opportunities, most notably by members of BMI, to be recorded and heard nationally. Consistent nationwide commercial success eluded country music, but the stage was set for the future. With the exception of "There's a Star Spangled Banner Waving Somewhere" and "Pistol Packin' Mama," both of which made it to *Your Hit Parade*,[12] this multimillion-dollar country music business remained the sovereign territory of its twenty-five million fans.

The war was a popular theme for country performers and songwriters. Patriotic songs and those with war-related themes made the first hillbilly music (sometimes labeled as country and western, folk, or cowboy) popularity charts established by *Billboard.* Country music was lumped in with cowboy tunes and "race" music—as African American music (blues and jazz) was called—because the statistics compilers at *Billboard* and *Variety* were unsure of both the exact category in which to place this music and its potential popularity.

In February 1942 *Billboard* placed hillbilly and country and western music in the "American Folk Music" category, where it remained throughout the war.[13] Unlike other composers and lyricists of music for popular consumption, country songwriters did not hesitate to write of the sufferings and death of soldiers or of the traumatic experiences of those left behind. By far the most popular song was Elton Britt's recording of the Paul Roberts and Shelby Darnell composition "There's a Star Spangled Banner Waving Somewhere." It tells the story of a crippled mountain boy who longs to "take the Axis down a peg":

There's a Star Spangled Banner Waving Somewhere
In a distant land so many miles away,
Only Uncle Sam's great heroes get to go there,
Where I wish that I could also live someday.
I'd see Lincoln, Custer, Washington and Perry
And Nathan Hale and Colin Kelley[14] too!
There's a Star Spangled Banner Waving Somewhere
Waving o'er the land of heroes brave and true.

Popular with both hillbilly music fans and popular music followers, the record told a sentimental story and linked past American heroes with a World War II hero, Captain Kelley. It sold over 1.5 million copies and was recorded by Elton Britt.[15]

Other hillbilly songs expressed the outrage Americans felt at the treachery of the Japanese: Roy Acuff 's "Cowards Over Pearl Harbor" and Zeke Clements's "Smoke on the Water" were two of the most successful of this type. Eddy Arnold sang "I Don't Want to Be Buried at the Bottom of the Sea." There were also the usual love songs and those dealing with the anxieties of unfaithful love: "We'll Meet Again, Sweetheart," "At Mail Call Today," and "Have I Stayed Away Too Long?"

Many hillbilly songs were poignant ones that dealt with the tragedies of war. For example, "Gold Star Window," sung by Tex Ritter, tells of the sacrifice of a mother—the loss of a soldier son signified by a small banner with a gold star that was hung in the front windows of homes of men who had died "to keep us free." "Stars and Stripes on Iwo Jima," "White Cross on Okinawa," and "The Soldier's Last Letter" also detailed the sacrifices of American servicemen. Another set of songs featured the tragedies of those at home who lost loved ones: "Teardrops in the Snow" tells of a mother's trip to the railroad depot to claim the coffin, "wrapped in red and white and blue," of her fallen soldier son. Another song, "Searching for a Soldier's Grave," follows an American abroad to locate the final resting place of a loved one. These songs never made it to *Your Hit Parade* because country and western artists rarely made the transition to the popular music charts and also because popular music consumers were not interested in the realities of war.

Tin Pan Alley composers continued to turn out war-related songs. All the armed service branches were glorified in song several times over. The new Army Air Corps flew "Off . . . in the wild, blue yonder," while old standards like "The Marines' Hymn," "Anchors Aweigh," and "The Caissons Go Rolling Along" enjoyed renewed popularity.

The songs about the home front were not nearly as popular. "Cooperate with Your Air Raid Warden" and "He Loved Me Till the All Clear

Came" were not as glamorous as songs about the men in uniform. Love was no longer as cheerful. Instead civilians were faced with songs about rationing, bureaucracy, shortages, and the black market: "Don't Put Me on a Ration of Love," "Who Needs Sugar, When I've Got Honey?" "I've Got Four Brand New Tires," and "Ration Blues."[16] Thomas "Fats" Waller and George Marion wrote "I'll Be Happy When the Nylons Bloom Again," a naughty ditty about rationing and shortages:

> I'll be happy when the nylons bloom again,
> Cotton is monotonous to mend,
> Only way to keep affection fresh,
> Get some mesh for your flesh.
> ....
> And the WACs come back to join their men,
> In a world that Mr. Wallace[17] planned,
> Strolling hand-in-hand.

Other writers channeled their energies into patriotic and propaganda songs at the request of the newly formed Songwriters War Committee, one of many organizations formed during the war with the intent of encouraging American songwriters to aid the war effort through their compositions. Americans were invited to give their all to the war effort with songs such as "We Can, We Must, We Will" by Harold Gardner and Leland Brown's "The Way to Victory."

Most of these morale boosting, propaganda songs were dashed off in a hurry and most were highly forgettable. Bond drives were the most popular subject and brought forth such sales pitches as "Swing the Quota," "Get Aboard the Bond Wagon," and "Unconditional Surrender."

One song in particular, "Ev'rybody Ev'ry Payday," by Dick Uhl and Tom Adair, was singled out by the United States Treasury for a "super-dooper song plug drive." The Treasury's radio division made arrangements with 872 radio stations, 370,000 jukeboxes, public schools, and phonograph companies to popularize "Ev'rybody Ev'ry Payday." The song encouraged Americans to enroll in a 10 percent payroll deduction plan for the purchase of war bonds. Organizers planned to distribute the song through music counters and stores; write special arrangements for dance orchestras; provide scores to school brass bands and singing classes; distribute free records to radio stations; and make special recordings of the song by Barry Wood for Victor, Guy Lombardo for Decca, and Tommy Tucker for Columbia.[18]

The song did not become popular, despite the advertising, the fact that it was free to anyone, and the message:

Ev'rybody Ev'ry Payday,
Buy a Bond the U.S.A. way!
That's the job, it's up to you and me.
Butcher, baker, banker, scholar,
. . . .
Ten percent! That's the rent!
Ev'ryone can pay
For a home in the U.S.A.

Scrap drives to collect used items made of metal, rubber, nylon, and paper netted such songs as "While Melting All Our Memories," "Junk Ain't Junk No More (Cause Junk Could Win the War)," and another jaunty Fats Waller tune, "Cash for Your Trash":

Save up all your pots and pans,
Save up every little thing you can,
Don't give it away, no, no, no,
Get some cash for your trash.
Save up all your old newspapers,
Save and pile them like a high skyscraper,
Don't give them away, no, no, no,
Get some cash for your trash.

Songs also encouraged the planting of victory gardens: "Get Out and Dig, Dig, Dig" and "Harvey the Victory Garden Man." Another category included a role for dogs in the war: "The K-9 Corps" and "I'd Like to Give My Dog to Uncle Sam." Propaganda songs aimed at preventing gossip, panic, and the unknowing betrayal of American secrets were "Rumor Man," "A Slip of the Lip Can Sink a Ship," and "Shhh! It's a Military Secret."

Songs were composed to remind the home front that theirs was an important job, too. "Knit One, Purl Two," "The Woman Behind the Man Behind the Gun," and "Fighting on the Home Front Wins (The Official War Song of the American Housewife)" were aimed at making those left at home feel important and vital to the war effort. Air raid drills, the subject of "When the Air Raid Siren Sounds" and "Cooperate with Your Air Raid Warden," were part of the effort.

A song sponsored by the U.S. Treasury Department, Tom Adair and Dick Uhl's "It's the Little Things That Count," was typical of the tunes emphasizing the importance of the home front to the war effort:

Don't forget, put out the light;
Last year's dress will look all right;

You can save while others fight—
It's the little things that count.
Wear the hat you bought last spring,
Save your paper, wind up string,
Pick up pins,
Don't waste a thing—
It's the little things that count.
....
Mend your stockings, sole your shoes;
Scraps of meat make tasty stews;
Do your part and you can't lose!
It's the little things that count!

American popular music composers became a part of the diplomatic mission of the United States with such songs for our British allies as "Who Are the British?" and "My British Buddy." To cement Pan-American relationships there were "Hands Across the Border" and "Good Night Neighbor." The Soviet Union, now an ally of the United States, was praised with "And Russia Is Her Name," "You Can't Brush Off a Russian," "And Still the Volga Flows," and, finally, "That Russian Winter." None of these morale-builders or propaganda songs made it to *Your Hit Parade* or even made a showing on *Billboard* or *Variety* popularity charts.

Civilian war workers were the target of musical persuasion. They heard "Arms for the Love of America," "We Build 'Em, You Sail 'Em," "Give Us the Tools," "On the Old Production Line," "I Like a Man Who Comes to Work on Time," and "On the Swing Shift," a song by Johnny Mercer and Harold Arlen that intimated romance could be found while working in a defense plant:

Life is fine with my baby on the swing shift,
On the line with my baby on the swing shift.
....
What care I if they put me on the wing shift,
When he's near by in the fuselage?
Overtime, here's why I'm doing it free,
Baby's with me on the swing shift jamboree.

Songs aimed at women war workers flattered the feminine ego: "The Lady at Lockheed," "We're the Janes Who Make the Planes," "The Lady's on the Job," and "Rosie the Riveter." The temptations, upheaval, and stresses in war workers' lives found a voice in song: "Don't Steal the Sweetheart of a Soldier," "Annie Doesn't Live Here Anymore," and "Milkman, Keep

Those Bottles Quiet" ("Been workin' on the swing shift all night / Turning out my quota all right"), by Don Raye and Gene de Paul.[19]

"The House I Live In" urged calmer thinking about home-front racial tensions that had erupted in race riots. Appealing for racial harmony, the song issued a call to a type of patriotism that would put the good of the nation above personal concerns:

The house I live, a plot of earth, a street,
The grocer and the butcher,
And the people that I meet,
The children in the playground,
The faces that I see,
All races and religions,
That's America to me.
. . . .
The church, the school, the clubhouse,
The million lights I see,
But especially the people,
That's America to me.[20]

Richard Lingeman sums up the songs of World War II, saying, "The enduring songs that came out of the war were basically standard peacetime songs." People wanted their popular music "for humming, for mental chewing gum, for a backdrop to their work"; it was also used as "low-level poetry to articulate the chaotic emotions of adolescent love, to dance to, to cheer them up, and to color their romantic reveries."[21] But within the context of their everyday lives, Americans transported their situations into the popular song lyrics and managed to relate popular songs to a wartime message.

Of the thousands of songs written in patriotic fervor, most were destined to be forgotten almost immediately. Don Reid and Sammy Kaye's "Remember Pearl Harbor" had a restless tune that is memorable even today, but who can hum "We'll Remember Pearl Harbor," a hastily written song that came out too soon? "Remember Hawaii," in the same mode, did not make it, nor did "Cheer Up, Blue Hawaii." In general the public dismissed provincial nonsense such as "Go Back to Where You Belong, If You Can't Be True to the Red, White, and Blue," "All You Japs Look Alike to Me," "Hitler's Got the White House Blues," and "At the Setting of the Rising Sun." Also shunned were overtly sentimental songs like "That Boy Is Not Coming Back," "Missing in Action," "The Boy Who Didn't Come Back," and "From Baby Shoes to Silver Wings." Banal, virtuous songs such as "Let Your Mother Be Your Sweetheart," "She Is Every Serviceman's Girl and Everybody's Sweetheart," and falsely religious songs like "Look,

God, I Have Never Spoken to You," and "A Tiny Little Voice (In a Tiny Little Prayer)" did not make much of an impact on the profits of Tin Pan Alley publishers.

The American public also rejected war-mother songs such as "Don't Worry Mother," "Show Us Your Medals, Mother Malone," "The Star in Our Window," "Here's My Boy, Dear Uncle Sammy," and "There's a Blue Star Shinin' in the Window Tonight"—though all were presumably written with honesty of feeling. While a mother's love had been liberally written about in World War I, it seems not to have been a choice topic for *Your Hit Parade.* Happy soldier songs did not fare much better. There were few titles in this category that made more than a dent in the public's music taste. One of the happy soldier songs combined a soldier's love of his mother and his fondness for home-cooked meals. The Jesters were successful in recording and performing on live radio programs "Ma, I Miss Your Apple Pie," by Carmen Lombardo and John Jacob Loeb:

Ma, I Miss Your Apple Pie.
Ma, I miss your stew.
Ma, they're treating me all right,
But they can't cook like you.
Oh, Ma, nobody's spoiling me,
Like you used to do.
They won't let me stay in bed until noon.
At five-forty-five, they play me a tune.
Oh, Ma, I Miss Your Apple Pie.
And by the way I miss you, too.

The heroes and heroic battles celebrated in songs also had short lives. There were such forgettable celebratory tunes as "The Man of the Hour Is General Eisenhower," "A Prayer for General Eisenhower and His Men," "Hats Off to MacArthur! and Our Boys Down There," "God Bless MacArthur," "Here's to You, MacArthur," "MacArthur's Men Are Holding," (all of which celebrated MacArthur's stand on Bataan Peninsula), "There's a White Cross in Normandy Tonight," "Stars and Stripes on Iwo Jima," "There's a New Flag on Iwo Jima," and "Yanks in Tokio." It seemed as if the fighting might end before Tin Pan Alley produced the Great American War Song of World War II.

Chapter 6

"Yearnful Bellowings"

Despite the enormous outpouring of songs from every part of the nation, no single war song emerged from World War II that rallied the American public and the fighting man as George M. Cohan's "Over There" had during World War I. Those responsible for boosting morale during the war worried about this and wondered what contributed to the lack of a "war song." The United States government attempted to guide and encourage composers to provide this war's "Over There." But was it even possible for such a song to gain wide popularity in the 1940s?

Had the mental and social makeup of American society achieved such a new level of sophistication that the public disdained the use of props such as militant songs as a means of uniting the public and increasing war production? Or did the American people view World War II as more than a military endeavor? Perhaps the technology of the music industry in the 1940s made a new "Over There" not only less likely, but impossible.

An unlikely central institution became involved in the quest for the song that would unite all Americans behind the war. The Office of War Information (OWI) did not originally plan to interact with the music industry, but as the war progressed, the OWI became more and more involved in what had once been a strictly private business.

The OWI developed from a previous program, the Office of Facts and Figures (OFF), whose responsibility was to bolster American morale and to explain the importance of defense measures enacted prior to World War II.[1] Although avoiding actual military intervention in the war in Europe before 1942, the Roosevelt administration in 1941 and 1942 gradually increased military spending and began to assist the Allies in their war against Germany.

Two men, Archibald MacLeish and Robert Sherwood, both noted

forces in American literature and both dedicated antifascists, piloted the American propaganda programs in the last days before the United States entered the war. MacLeish was especially passionate about American democracy and wary of the uses of propaganda. He believed that in a democracy propaganda had to be based on the "strategy of truth."[2] This meant giving the American people the facts and then trusting them to make correct decisions. Both men agreed that the purpose of propaganda was to convince the American people that the outcome of the war was crucial to themselves, and not just to Europeans. Formed in October 1941, the Office of Facts and Figures was charged with deciding which issues the American people needed more information about and then setting up plans for various government agencies to make that information public.[3]

From the beginning, the Office of Facts and Figures was controversial. It had to balance information dispersal with discretion to avoid revealing too much about the United States' military preparedness or lack thereof. Personality conflicts among administrators, the precise definition of the OFF's mission, and the sprawling growth of the agency after Pearl Harbor created a chaotic situation. After Pearl Harbor, the OFF's inability to do the job intended was painfully evident, and it was decided that the agency would be scrapped rather than reorganized. Out of this disorder came the Office of War Information, with the responsibility for all propaganda, both foreign and domestic, vested in one agency. Elmer Davis, journalist, author, and radio commentator, agreed to head the new agency when it was created by executive order on June 13, 1942.[4]

The OWI faced problems from the outset. Americans' mistrust of propaganda had been growing since the end of World War I. Worldwide communications made propaganda on a large scale possible for the first time during World War I, and the United States joined the British, French, and Germans in campaigns to gain support from their own citizens and the rest of the world. American propaganda in the First World War was directed by the Committee on Public Information, headed by journalist George Creel. The committee consisted of the heads of the Department of War, Department of the Navy, and the Department of State, but it met only once. After that initial meeting, George Creel made all the committee's decisions.[5]

Because there had been significant opposition to the United States' entry into the war, the Committee on Public Information's first mission was to unite Americans behind the war effort. Using posters, pamphlets, bands, mass rallies, and rousing speakers, Creel embarked on what he referred to as "the world's greatest adventure in advertising."[6]

The Committee on Public Information aroused Americans, but it also sparked unrealistic hopes for the future. Woodrow Wilson's Fourteen

Points, according to the Committee on Public Information, would bring about a new world order. When the Versailles peace conference turned away from reconciliation and degenerated into an assembly bent on revenge and the exacting of punitive damages from the Germans, the gap between overly optimistic propaganda and the reality of world politics left many Americans wary of propaganda. The Committee on Public Information's version of America and the future had been "too boisterous, too exuberant" in a world that had not been made safe for democracy.

Following World War I, the country became fixated upon the idea that good propaganda was difficult to detect and could easily dupe normally rational people. The rise of Adolph Hitler and the Nazi Party in Germany was proof of the power of propaganda to manipulate ideas and minds. Propaganda also was criticized for its association with advertising, a newly powerful tool of American business that induced people to buy products they did not want or need. Allen Winkler says that the public continued to "shy away from the very term" and that President Roosevelt "shared their suspicions." Aware of the legacy of doubt and mistrust left over from Creel's Committee on Public Information, Roosevelt did not allocate the widespread powers of the committee to the OWI. His lack of support would eventually doom the OWI to a feeble network of poorly funded offices with no real authority on the home front.[7]

Initially, the OWI comprised fourteen branches and bureaus. Among these were the Overseas Branch, the Domestic Branch, the Policy Development Branch, the Bureau of Publications and Graphics, the Bureau of Motion Pictures, the Domestic Radio Bureau, and the Bureau of Campaigns.[8] From the beginning, the OWI was hampered by internal conflicts arising from differing perceptions of its mission. Robert Sherwood and Archibald MacLeish thought it should educate the American public and eventually the world about the benefits of American democracy in the postwar future. Other administrators like Milton Eisenhower of the War Relocation Agency and Gardner Cowles Jr., Midwestern newspaper publisher and co-founder of *Look*, saw the OWI as an organization to be used in conveying the nation's war goals to the American people.

Furthermore, there was little cooperation from the military and other branches of government. Congress was suspicious of a government agency (with presidentially appointed administrators) that aimed propaganda not only overseas but also at the American public. Republicans saw the OWI as yet another platform from which President Roosevelt could broadcast what they perceived as his liberal internationalism and New Deal philosophy into Americans' ears. And different agencies and politicians disagreed over the question of what and how much to tell the American public about the kind of war the country was fighting.

The OWI's mission was to oversee propaganda output in all parts of the media—radio, motion pictures, and the press. It attempted to assist in the free dissemination of war news but was blocked at almost every attempt by another government agency or department. The navy, under Adm. Ernest J. King, chief of naval operations and commander-in-chief of the United States Fleet, steadfastly refused to allow information concerning the U.S. Navy and its battles in the Pacific into the public press. Americans' indignation grew at this scarcity of news, especially when the navy released its dead, wounded, and missing totals from the Battle of the Coral Sea months after the May 1942 fight. The figures were far worse than the public had been led to believe, and the resulting outcry convinced the OWI and finally the navy to be more forthcoming with its military news.[9]

The OWI tried to clear up misunderstandings that occurred when other departments issued conflicting or confusing statements. For example, faced with a serious shortage of rubber following Japan's takeover of the major sources of this raw material, the government diverted petroleum to use in manufacturing artificial rubber and decided to ration gasoline to prevent Americans from wearing out automobile and truck tires. The problem was the government refused to tell the American people the real reason behind the rationing program, and as a result many Americans became outraged when it became common knowledge that good supplies of gasoline were available all across the country except on the East Coast. The OWI tried to explain the apparent deception behind gas rationing in terms of the overall war effort, but got absolutely no cooperation from the other agencies involved.[10]

The Bureau of Publications and Graphics attempted to explain the war to the public. In pamphlets like *The Unconquered People*, which gave details of Europeans resisting fascism, and *The Thousand Million*, which consisted of stories about the United Nations, the OWI sought to educate Americans about the global importance of the war and its aftermath. On the home front, the OWI concerned itself with publications such as *How to Raise $16 Billion*, which detailed the need for tax money to fight the war; *Battle Stations All*, which explained how to fight inflation; and *Negroes and the War*, which showed that African Americans, in all kinds of jobs and on all social levels, also had a stake in winning the war.[11]

The OWI's Bureau of Motion Pictures attempted to clarify war aims and problems and unite support for the war effort, especially among those who were not inclined to read newspapers. The OWI produced a number of films with self-explanatory titles: *Food for Fighters*, *Manpower*, *Salvage*, and *Troop Train*. Hollywood also came under the scrutiny of the propaganda agency. The OWI criticized motion pictures for presenting an incomplete view of the war. The United Nations (the OWI's term for the

Allies, adopted from the Atlantic Charter) fought and won in Hollywood films, but there was little mention of what they were fighting for. Law, justice, and human dignity failed to surface often enough in these films, the OWI complained. Instead, Americans were shown films like *Tarzan Triumphs*, in which Tarzan battles and defeats Nazis, or they watched light musicals such as *Star Spangled Rhythm*, *Follow the Boys*, *4 Jills in a Jeep*, and *The Fleet's In*, which used the war as background for love stories and song and dance routines. The OWI criticized movies that portrayed the home front in comical terms, claiming these films were detrimental both to the war effort and civilian volunteerism. In the OWI's opinion, Hollywood's serious battle pictures were not much better: the enemy was stereotyped and ideological differences were almost always settled by brute strength instead of through force of character or negotiation.[12]

The Domestic Radio Division of the OWI was the most successful of its home front divisions. Cooperation from the major networks enabled the OWI to superimpose wartime priorities on an already established medium. Networks donated time for government-sponsored messages, and the OWI saw that these messages were coordinated with the proper programs. It also helped popular shows incorporate war-related themes into their scripts.[13]

The OWI saw itself as coming to the rescue of the nationwide radio networks' "surrealist nightmare" in which there was little coordination of war information either from the government or from the broadcasters. There was no coordination of radio facilities, and "everyone was grabbing whatever part of the station schedule he could get." It was apparent to the OWI that radio executives and their managers had "seized the nearest available pitchfork . . . and [were] marching off to war . . . without plans or strategy." Many commercials and news programs were capitalizing on the war in ways that exceeded, in the OWI's estimation, "all bounds of reason or good taste." Some stations overemphasized simple subjects and neglected the more difficult ones. The OWI feared this would lead to Americans being overwhelmed with "things to do" but without a clear understanding of the reasons behind the government's requests.

Stations scheduled too many war-related broadcasts in a small amount of time. One station broadcast information on forty-four different war topics in one week. The handling of money matters was another crucial problem. There were too many announcements over a brief span of time asking Americans to save money for their taxes, buy war bonds, or give to numerous war charities. Most of these were short, only seconds long, and this was not enough time to present a clear message. Often announcements were clustered at odd times or in rapid succession or the same message was repeated numerous times. Not all of the confusion was caused by the radio stations; government agencies flooded stations with material to be broadcast, with little or no explanation about which material was the most important.[14]

Clarifying war information for American radio listeners was the first course of action for the OWI. The "best brains" in the radio and advertising businesses were called into service and charged with setting in motion plans that would "weld Government and industry together into one efficient team to do the job." The OWI's three objectives were: 1) to give the largest possible audience an effective, well-balanced fare of war information through the medium of radio; 2) to superimpose OWI's plans on the established radio structure in a way that would preserve its enormous listening audience; and 3) to allow the radio industry to do the job with as little interference from the OWI as possible.

The biggest concern of the OWI, other than getting war information to Americans in an "understandable" form, was that radio audiences would simply stop listening—a potential economic catastrophe for the stations and a serious problem for the government, which had grown dependent on radio to convey announcements and, in some cases, propaganda. The Hooper Rating Corporation, which monitored radio listening audiences for statistics regarding numbers of listeners and their preferences, showed in their "sets-in-use" surveys for 1941 and 1942 a steep decline in radio listening in late 1941 that "tobogganed" in early 1942. In April 1942 the downward trend halted and the number of listeners rose steadily. OWI thought it was "more than coincidence" that the Domestic Radio Bureau's plans to coordinate radio were first inaugurated April 27, 1942.[15]

The Office of War Information constantly reminded those it worked with (other government agencies, radio networks, and show business) that the plans it laid out were always forged with cooperation and input from the radio industry and its associates. OWI claimed to have plans for only two types of war information: The first was background information to give Americans a better understanding of the "issues of the war, the enemy, the allies, the war plan, the post-war plans, the need for all-out production, sacrifice, and fighting spirit." The second type of information detailed specific things Americans could do to "help speed the victory." In order to carry out these plans, OWI devised eight different types of radio programs; three would provide "background" information, and five would give "action" information.[16]

The first of three "feature series" presented background information needed for "understanding" the war, covering such topics as the nature of the enemy and of the United Nations (Allies); war aims and post-war plans; the fighting forces, including the training, jobs, morale, leadership, and objectives of the U.S. Army, Navy, Marines, Coast Guard, and Merchant

Marine; the working forces and the need for high production from management and labor, including manpower mobilization; and the need for "home force" participation through rationing, conservation, taxation, the purchase of war bonds, health maintenance and nutrition, and relocation.

The second grouping of the "feature series" comprised five types of programs: The first program type treated a single subject for an extended length of time (for example, *The Army Hour*, which provided information about all branches of the army, and the *U. S. Navy Band*, a concert hour that used music as a recruiting aid); the second type consisted of programs continuing in their particular pre-war format but devoting a show from time to time to various subjects of war information (*People's Platform* and *America's Town Meeting* normally discussed a wide range of topics that did not center on the war). The third type, shows devoted to covering several war information subjects, included such programs as *Confidentially Yours* with Arthur Hale and *Story Behind the Headlines* with Cesar Saerchinger. The fourth, covering all phases of war information, targeted specific audiences: women, youth (at various age levels), and minorities (for example, *Victory Hour*). The fifth type consisted of programs dividing listeners in terms of intellect: *Voice of Firestone* and *University of Chicago Roundtable* sought "high intelligence ratings," as opposed to the "medium intelligence ratings" of *Chicago Theatre of the Air* and *National History Mystery Quiz* and the "low intelligence ratings" of *Lum and Abner* and *Young Dr. Malone*.[17]

The OWI's insistence on complete control of these radio series was controversial. In the beginning, the radio networks' fear of a government takeover of broadcasting, in the name of national defense, led them to cooperate voluntarily. Overt coercion was not necessary; the radio networks gave free airtime to the war effort. However, the office wanted balanced coverage of the many war information subjects and required that all scripts for these programs be cleared by the agency. As a result, writers resigned en masse, feeling their work had been devalued and their ideas pushed aside in favor of advertising methods imported along with "ad men" from Madison Avenue. The OWI writers saw themselves as artists first and propaganda manufacturers second. Many were offended that their talents and expertise were ignored.[18]

Understanding the United States' war aims, as outlined by the OWI, was thought to be crucial to morale, which in turn was thought to be essential to winning the war. In order to achieve high morale, the OWI mandated fewer programs but higher quality. If a program was to be informative, it had to meet OWI guidelines, and most importantly, contribute to a better understanding of the war. OWI decided to apply what it termed its "quality yardstick" to shows. It would analyze the time of the broadcast (for optimum number of listeners), the writing's directness in explaining the subject), the production and talent, and, most importantly, the show's adherence to the war information policy as set out by the OWI.

Shows receiving poor marks were rejected. In order to prevent some stations from broadcasting entertainment and calling it war information, the OWI warned that the appearance of military bands on broadcasts could not be classified as war information. In fact, entertainment programs of any type, whether emanating from stations or training camps, were not endorsed as war information programs, even though they might carry recruiting messages.[19] (Eventually, the OWI's firm stance changed when it was discovered that the listening public wanted entertainment and had no second thoughts about turning the radio dial from officially sponsored OWI programs to less pedantic programs.)

The OWI had valid reasons for its policies. If stations had continued to offer the blizzard of programs they considered to be war information, it is conceivable that radio might have continued to lose more listeners and the government would have lost a valuable communication tool. Many of the so-called war information programs were vague in purpose, or they were merely a cover for advertising. (One hair-removal product's advertisement warned listeners: "For a nation under arms, watch your under arms."[20])

OWI guidelines reduced the number of shows and increased the quality of war information programs by giving the stations definite, planned topics (for example, "Get a railway job," "OPA food tokens," and "'Cookies for rookies' campaign"), some of which had not been addressed previously. But the most important service the OWI performed was coordinating the broadcasting networks to make it possible for stations to return a large portion of their schedules to sheer entertainment. This allowed radio audiences to relax and prevented them from being "burdened with too much war."[21]

Recognizing the need for entertainment that would also deliver messages, the OWI organized its "Special Assignment Plan," which allowed for programs that were primarily entertainment or public-service oriented. These shows already had established audiences, and OWI wisely decided to not interfere with them. Although the OWI said it was neither telling broadcasters how to write nor censoring their shows, the plan's goal of "quality not quantity" carried an implied threat: programs that did not seem to be "handling their assigned messages with the anticipated effectiveness" might be replaced in the OWI's Special Assignments Plan. By this OWI meant it would select a replacement from among already existing radio shows—not that it would remove a network's show from the air. With this "understanding," certain shows volunteered to take part in the plan.

Some shows were to broadcast information on a single subject. For example, the Metropolitan Opera broadcasts for the 1942–1943 season dealt each week with some aspect of the United Nations. Another program, *Information Please*, presented basic information about the "food problem." Other shows had rotating topics, and some presented a variety of war information subjects.[22]

The Special Assignment Plan was to be operated by the OWI's Special Assignment Section, with a chief and a small staff of "writer-expediters" assigning subjects to radio program producers and providing "background material and ideas" for the shows. The "writer-expediters" also provided their "aid and counsel" to a program's staff of writers. The OWI insisted it was only attempting to "help" writers and producers integrate war information into their programs.[23] The chief and his writer-expediters traveled to New York, Chicago, and Hollywood to ensure that the "stars" of selected programs understood their function in disseminating war information. There are no records indicating that any OWI personnel turned down these assignments.

Prior to February 1, 1943, the OWI sent complete pre-recorded programs to radio stations for broadcast once or twice a week; shows included *Treasury Star Parade*, by the Treasury Department; *Victory Front*, *Victory Volunteers*, and *This Is Our Enemy*, by the OWI; and *Voice of the Army*, by the U.S. Army. Other distributed programs, based on "timely and topical" war information, appeared only once. With the exception of *Treasury Star Parade*, the OWI discontinued after February 1 all of its pre-recorded shows, the majority of which had small audiences. Thereafter, radio networks would use their own programs and rely on OWI for information, not programming.[24]

Treasury Star Parade, produced by the Radio Section of the Treasury Department Defense Savings Staff with the approval of the OWI, was on the air during 1942 and 1943.[25] An overtly propagandistic program whose mission was to sell war bonds and World War II to the American public, *Treasury Star Parade* presented the war as a just war being fought by a democratic nation with a citizen-soldier army composed of free and equal citizens. It emphasized American values—fair play and rooting for the "little guy." *Treasury Star Parade* used sports metaphors to explain war aims and emphasized the Judeo-Christian religious foundation of the nation.

In a break with OWI's officially stated policy, *Treasury Star Parade* treated the two enemy nations quite differently. The Germans were portrayed as the victims of the Nazi Party and its leaders, captives in their own land, whereas all the Japanese were described as barbaric "Nips," "Japs," "yellow bellies," "flat eyes," "rats," and "monkeys."[26] The Nazis, as opposed to the German people, were madmen, but all the Japanese people were subhuman butchers.

To maintain its listening audience, *Treasury Star Parade* relied on famous entertainers. Some of the most popular musicians of the time appeared on the show. The bands of Harry James, Bob Crosby, Kay Kyser, and Vaughn Monroe all performed in the name of Treasury Bonds. Fred Waring and his Pennsylvanians, Xavier Cugat, and Ted Lewis provided an alternative to swing. Singers ranged from Rudy Vallee to Bing Crosby.[27] *Treasury Star Parade's* guest musicians sold the war and war bonds to the sounds of hit tunes and newly composed war songs. The latter usually were performed only once.

Beginning February 1, 1943, the OWI tried a different tactic. It sent complete scripts to the networks to produce and broadcast. The first of these was a new war information program titled *Uncle Sam*. The program treated subjects such as the home front, the United Nations, manpower, working forces, the enemy, minorities, and fighting forces. Topics ranged from food hoarding, getting a war job, and joining the WAAC, to Brotherhood Week and systematic starvation of conquered peoples by the enemy. The programs were only fifteen minutes once a week. Of course, OWI had great hopes for *Uncle Sam*, and the office advised stations that the success of the show might induce local advertisers to sponsor the programs, making them profitable for the stations to air.[28]

Financial loss was a great concern of radio stations during the opening months of World War II. The OWI warned that as the war progressed many stations might have to shut down because a potential lack of consumer goods would lead to diminished advertising revenues. In addition, stations in sparsely populated areas would lose listeners as people moved in search of employment and better opportunities. The OWI was convinced it had to step in and get war information to Americans while the commercial communications network was still intact. The OWI regarded "sponsoring," or simply approving, "official" war programs as the most expedient way to get its message to the public.[29]

As it turned out, radio stations did not close as the Office of War Information had feared. Instead they prospered. There had been serious doubt in the 1930s that radio could survive the Depression, but enough stations held on to reap great rewards during the war. The real threat to radio's future would be television, not the loss of the listening audience or advertisers during the war. Stations expanded during the war, increased the number of listeners, began offering live broadcasts from military training camps and other war-related sites, and converted to twenty-four hour broadcasts to accommodate the new audience working the swing (4 P.M. to midnight) and night shifts.[30]

Radio was a vital force in the everyday life of Americans, and the OWI was not above using scare tactics and subtle coercion to gain access to the networks. Predicting the failure of radio stations was one ploy. The OWI policy led to something never before experienced in the United States: privately owned radio stations broadcasting government produced programs. The OWI insisted, of course, it was stepping in as a rescuer to bring order to chaos and would gladly drop its "sponsorship" (a euphemism for air time that stations gave to OWI programs) as soon as circumstances permitted. Thus, the OWI encouraged stations to seek private sponsors who would subsidize time for *Treasury Star Parade* and *Uncle Sam*.

Since it was the patriotic thing to do, advertisers jumped at the opportunity to have their names connected with war shows. The OWI set two restrictions: no wine or beer advertising accounts could be accepted, and the first series of commercials from advertisers had to be approved by the OWI in Washington, D.C., after passing the Domestic Radio Bureau.[31]

In addition to providing background information, OWI's Domestic Radio Bureau endeavored to provide "action messages," which told Americans to buy bonds, save scrap, enlist in the armed forces, and conserve energy. Before the OWI's Network Allocation Plans were instituted, stations barraged listeners with as many as eighty or ninety different messages a day. To prevent listener boredom the OWI assigned "action messages" to particular advertisers at specific times.[32]

Another OWI plan for getting war information to American radio audiences was the "Spot Plan," which employed short announcements that were sponsored by one of the seventy-four approved OWI advertisers. When local station writers were given the opportunity to create their own announcements, the OWI found that the writers were quite capable of taking the fact sheets and writing excellent messages. All that was necessary was guidance in the form of suggested topics.

Local "live" programs proved less amenable to OWI control. Although live shows often incorporated the content of the prerecorded OWI programs, the scripts were composed by local radio writers, and the scripts, as OWI described them, ranged "from poor to good." The failure of these local shows, which were broadcast by understaffed and underfunded radio stations to small towns and rural areas, concerned the OWI.

OWI proposed eliminating war information programs that could not be improved, as well as local programs that duplicated "good" national network programs. The OWI used its authority as a government agency to intimidate local radio stations and national networks alike. The mention of removing programs from the air was often enough to send shockwaves through the industry. The war was a new experience for the OWI and broadcasters, and they were both unsure of the methods that would bring about the desired results: getting vital war information to the public without losing the broadcasters' audience.[33]

The OWI sought to control the content and flow of war information from the smallest radio station in rural areas to the enormously powerful nationally syndicated networks. Knowing that its methods and motives would be questioned, the OWI tried to reassure stations of its good intentions. Radio in a democracy, it told the station owners, "is a complex, diffuse business that cannot be turned overnight into a single-minded, smooth-functioning instrument of war information." Because the government was not interested in taking over privately owned and managed stations, the OWI insisted that all it offered was "coordination" services, not "co-opting" services.[34]

As the casualty lists grew, the OWI also worried that the amount of "war" on the radio would still be too much. If people who had lost brothers, fathers, sweethearts, and sons could not turn to radio programs for some relief and escape from the war through a "needed balance of entertainment," then they might seek out other forms of relief or distraction—forms not controlled by the OWI. The OWI continued to streamline and coordinate war information in order to improve its effectiveness. The agency tried to get the most information to the American public in the least objectionable way; the quantity of war information on the air was lessened and replaced with direct, single-minded information in amounts that the public could absorb without becoming weary of the subject.

To make sure that OWI-approved war information reached the American public, the OWI formulated a series of guidelines for writers. These directives came, so the OWI claimed, at the request of radio writers for the best way to present war information. The OWI sent its "handbook of practical suggestions for use in the preparation of wartime radio scripts" to every radio station in the country; the recommendations included no duplication of national news, no nonessential war news, and no reworking of good nationally broadcast shows at the local level. After comment from broadcasters, these directions were reworked and refined by the OWI and offered as suggestions to American songwriters, publishers, and recording companies.

Having planned for the worst, the OWI got more cooperation that it had anticipated. The broadcasting industry joined the war effort so wholeheartedly that containing the networks' enthusiasm became the OWI's focus.[35]

Chapter 7

Recipes for War Songs

In its continuing search for the Great American War Song, the OWI offered songwriters the following guidelines: Songs should focus on enemies of the "United Nations [Allies]" and not minimize their abilities. Consequently, the enemy should not be the object of humorous songs; ridiculing him might lead the American public to underestimate his strength, which in turn would lead to complacency and a lessening of the intensity of the war effort. Songs that called the enemy by derogatory names, such as "yellow rats" or "dirty Huns" would not help win the war. OWI's reasoning was that the real enemy was not the German or Japanese people, who had been misled by their "despotic rulers, by lies, [and] by false promises based on false premises." (Most Americans, believing that the German citizens had been duped, made no distinction between the Japanese people and Japan's government: all were warmongers and equally guilty.) When the war was over, the people of Germany and Japan would be "re-educated" and "permitted to know the fuller, better life that is our aim for all the world."

The OWI cautioned songwriters that the enemy existed within the United States, too. Any songs that fostered disunity among Americans, by dealing with racial prejudice, labor unrest, or discontent with rationing, or by fostering isolationism, appeasement, or compromise with the enemy, were taboo.[1]

The OWI explicitly encouraged songs that were complimentary to members of the United Nations, especially those with themes of unity: "common action, common love of freedom, common consideration and esteem of one group of people for another." Writers and composers were encouraged to look on the United Nations as people with many different languages, religions, customs, histories, and governments who were "bonded" by a fundamental respect for freedom (Stalin's totalitarian government in the U.S.S.R. was conveniently ignored by the OWI). Complimentary songs included "And Still the Volga Flows," "Brave Britain," "British Children's Prayer," "Everything Will Be Like Home in Ireland," "Hello, Broadway, London Calling," "The King Is Still in London," "March of the Volunteers (A Fighting Song of China)," "My British Buddy," "Paris Will Be Paris Once Again," "Ring out Big Ben," "Spirit of Aberdeen," "Stalin Wasn't Stallin'," "That Russian Winter," "There'll Always Be an England," and "United Nations."[2]

The OWI wanted the United Nations represented, not merely as allies, but as the best hope for a "successful post-war period." Thus, songs should not present a "superior viewpoint" that the Yanks were coming and the world's troubles would soon be over. Furthermore, songs should not take the view that the rest of the world was following America or that America was the future center of world culture. American war efforts should not downplay the work of the United Nations: other countries made tanks and planes. And there should be caution about writing songs that contained statements about Americans being the "best fighters" in the world.

A quick perusal of war song titles from American songwriters reveals that the OWI's directives about the enemy and the United Nations were not followed too closely, especially in the case of songs dealing with the fighting abilities of the U.S. military. Tin Pan Alley created the following boastful songs: "All Out for America," "America United Is Rolling Along," "The American Way," "Because We Are Americans," "Defend Your Country," "Fighting Men of Uncle Sam," "Let's Bring New Glory to Old Glory," "Long Live America, the Savior of Democracy." Other proud, combative pieces included "They Started Something," "This Is Our Side of the Ocean," "Song of the Bombardiers," "The Song of the Fighting Marines," "Song of the Tank Destroyer Men," "When the Yanks Go Marching In," and "Uncle Sam Gets Around."[3]

The OWI's suggestions for writing about the world after the war were inspired by the example of the Atlantic Charter, a joint statement of war aims mixed with the idealistic goals of the New Deal and Woodrow Wilson's Fourteen Points. The Charter, formulated by Roosevelt and Churchill during a secret shipboard meeting in Placentia Bay, Newfoundland, in the summer of 1941, laid out the plans for the postwar world and included "common principles" upon which the parties based "their hopes for a better future for the world." Songwriters were encouraged to incorporate the terms of the Charter into their work, including the end of territorial ambitions by any nation against another, equal participation in world trade, improved labor and economic standards for all countries, freedom of the seas, and universal abandonment of force by all the world. The OWI said that radio and entertainment could get people to think about and discuss the kind of world they wanted to live in after the war.

Very few of the songs written between 1943 and 1945 incorporated OWI's suggestions, though the following might have observed the guidelines, at least in part: "After It's Over," "Bill of Rights," "For the Flag, for the Country, for the Future of All Mankind," "Freedom for the World," and "Fun to Be Free." Other titles included "Let Us All Sing Auld Lang Syne," "The Song of Liberation," and "We Fight for Peace."

Songwriters were cautioned to avoid overstatement and superlatives such as "This is the *only* way" or "The *best* way" to help win the war. Additionally, fearing that "unhealthy competition" among groups for "recognition" would detract from the cooperative effort needed to win the war, OWI asked songwriters to stress the total strength of the country, not one separate asset.

A further concern of Office of War Information was that songwriters would use their skills to influence Americans in the wrong way. Songs aimed at military recruiting might, for example, glorify the armed services too much. Writers were reminded that "war is not pretty," and that people should not join the service to "wear flashy uniforms" or "see the world." The OWI labeled as misleading any "sales talk" that stressed ideas such as "Join the WAACs (or WAVES) and wear good-looking uniforms"; "Nurses have a high percentage of marriage in their ranks"; or "Join the merchant marine . . . see Waikiki Beach." These directions apparently reached Tin Pan Alley too late, or they were ignored, judging from the number of songs treating these subjects in the very manner OWI cautioned against: "The Army's Made a Man Out of Me," "The Blond Sailor," "Cleanin' My Rifle and Dreamin' of You," "Corns for My Country," "He Wears a Pair of Silver Wings," "I Wanna Dance with a Sailor," "Jumpin' with a G.I. Gal," "My Beloved is Rugged," "My Heart Belongs to a Sailor," and "That Star-Spangled Baby of Mine.""The Blond Sailor," first appearing in 1937 (by Parish, Leib, and Pfeil) and returning in 1945, was typical of the type of song presenting an overly romantic view of military service that the OWI wished to discourage:

> Farewell, your Blond Sailor must leave for a while dear.
> Farewell, send me off with a kiss and a smile, dear.
> All my love and devotion I will leave in your care;
> As deep as the ocean and as true as a pray'r.

The horrific side of war was to be avoided in song as well. Sad tales of "blood baths" or "seaman fried in oil" were detrimental to all Americans, to recruitment, and especially to the "womenfolk . . . [who] can picture all too vividly the horrors that may befall their men." Songs of death or loss should be curtailed, too. Only cheerful, brave soldiers and their loyal families should populate the stories told in song. There could be an occasional dead hero, such as "The Ballad of Rodger Young," a folk ballad about a twenty-five-year-old soldier killed in the Solomon Islands, and "The Dying Soldier," but his actions should be told with as little detail as possible while the songwriter emphasized the hero's sacrifice for all Americans.

Overzealous patriotic songs filled with unconscious jingoism posed a threat to postwar harmony among the nations of the world, and the OWI cautioned against them. For example, the word "yellow" as applied to the Japanese could just as easily refer to America's Chinese allies and other cooperative Asian nationalities. Warnings were issued against calling the British "limeys," the Japanese "Japs," the Germans "Huns," the Chinese "Chinamen," and against giving African American song characters names such as "Eight-ball," "Ironhead," or "Razor." Stereotypes were to be avoided: songs should not minimize the Japanese as enemies by characterizing them as "funny little men whose teeth protrude, who always wear thick-lenses spectacles, and say 'so solly.'" Once again, the OWI message fell on deaf ears in Tin Pan Alley, which cranked out songs like "Bye, Bye, Benito," "Der Fuehrer's Face," "Hitler's Funeral March," "Let's Put the Axe to the Axis," "Mow the Japs Down!," "Put Another Nail in Hitler's Coffin," "Son of a Gun Who Picks on Uncle Sam," "We're Gonna Have to Slap the Dirty Little Jap (and Uncle Sam's the Guy Who Can Do It)," and "We've Got a Job to Do on the Japs, Baby."

Boasting about the United States' past glories in song would not help win this war, according to the OWI. After all, some of the countries we were fighting alongside in World War II had been our enemies in past wars. If songwriters had to boast of past glories, it would be better to extol our defense of liberty and freedom instead of past military exploits. Yet boastful songs abounded: "The American Way," "America's on the March," "Be Glad You're an American," "Because We Are Americans," "God Must Have Loved America," "I'm a Son of a Yankee Doodle Dandy," "Long Live America," "Remember Pearl Harbor," "There's a Star Spangled Banner Waving Somewhere," and "We Did It Before and We Can Do It Again."

Songwriters were not expected to lose their sense of humor when writing songs for wartime, but some humorous peacetime situations were no longer funny during WWII. Losing girlfriends to best friends or men with more money or good looks was no longer acceptable material for humorous songs. Funny songs about wartime restrictions or sacrifices— rationing, shortages, curfews, higher taxes, or the shortage of consumer goods— were not a good idea either because the OWI thought the message (if there was one) could get lost in the humor. Songs in this vein included "Duration Blues," "G.I. Blues," "G.I. Jive," "Good-for Nothing Is Good-for Something Now," "I Feel a Draft Coming On," "I've Been Drafted (Now I'm Drafting You)," "Make with the Bullets, Benny" "'Oh, My Achin' Back,'" "(Bomb) Shelter Lullaby," "There'll Never Be a Black-Out in My Heart for You," "There Won't Be a Shortage of Love," and "There's No Ceiling on Love."

The OWI cautioned songwriters to choose the right words for their songs carefully. "War effort" was too apologetic; the OWI preferred "war job, war drive, fighting the war." "Sabotage," an overused word, was said to be in danger of losing its effectiveness. For example, it was sabotage to arrive late for work, to drive on Sunday, or to fail to vote. Songs warned Americans, "Shhh!!! It's a Military Secret," and "A Slip of the Lip (Can Sink a Ship)." Other words and phrases to avoid were "game" in connection with war, "exterminate the enemy" (that was "Hitler's policy—not ours"), and "conquer" when referring to the enemy. Americans "liberated" Axis countries in order to "restore" countries to their "rightful owners." However, only a few songs mentioned "liberation" (e.g., "The Song of Liberation"), while numerous songs told of "victory": "Fight to Victory," "Let's Keep a V in Every Heart," "On, On to Victory," "'V' Calls for Victory," "V for Victory," "The 'V' Song," "Victory Cavalcade," and "Vic'try Polka."

These guidelines were not enforced by the OWI in the case of commercial publishing or private recording, but if a song was to be used on a program in cooperation with government agencies, clearance by the Domestic Radio Bureau of the OWI was mandatory. Songs used in radio scripts broadcast overseas also had to be cleared by the Office of Censorship.

The OWI and its controversial mission did not survive the congressional elections of 1942. Near the end of 1942 a coalition of conservative Republicans and Southern Democrats began to dismantle the New Deal and the OWI along with it. Between 1942 and 1943, Congress eliminated the Civilian Conservation Corps, the Works Progress Administration, and the National Youth Administration. The attack on OWI was led by Senator Rufus C. Holoman of Oregon and Representative John Taber of New York, both Republicans, and by a Democrat, Senator Harry F. Byrd of West Virginia. Their objection to OWI was the publication of a magazine called *Victory*, which was intended for distribution overseas to explain American democracy and culture. The cover of the first issue was a full color photograph of President Franklin D. Roosevelt, against the background of an American flag. Senator Holoman and members of Congress opposed to Roosevelt attacked OWI and *Victory* as "mere window dressing for a personal political campaign for a fourth term."[4] The head of the OWI, Elmer Davis, found his budget slashed by Congress, forcing the closure of regional offices. Congress put a stop to the OWI's propaganda publications for use on the home front; subsequently, commercial news channels distributed all domestic war information emanating from government agencies.

Liberal propagandists in the OWI's Overseas Bureau, headed by Sherwood Anderson, continued to foster their interpretation of the war in terms of the Atlantic Charter and belief in the Four Freedoms, as outlined by President Roosevelt in his pre-Pearl Harbor message to Congress on January 6, 1941: freedom of speech and expression, freedom of worship, freedom from want, and freedom from fear. The OWI used the pledges of the Atlantic Charter, published in pamphlet form, and the declarations of the Four Freedoms to give a sense of purpose and meaning to America's entry into the war.[5]

The OWI also made great efforts to present Americans as they wanted to be seen: sympathetic, sentimental, shrewd, aggressive, tough, and endowed with "horse sense." American ingenuity and industry were praised. Ordinary life was celebrated in films and stories about picnics, baseball games, town meetings, and church services. The message of the OWI, said Executive Director Elmer Davis, was "We are coming, we are going to win, and in the long run everybody will be better off because we won."[6]

Chapter 8

Just Love Songs with a Once-Over-Lightly War Background

From the commencement of the war, the OWI recognized the power of radio. Here was a tool for propaganda already in place that could reach millions of listeners. Ninety percent of American homes had a radio.[1] After coordinating the "correct" music and organizing propaganda "spot" announcements with already existing radio shows, seeing that popular shows included war-related themes and if applicable, music, into their plots, and convincing the radio networks to donate free air time to government-sponsored war messages and entertainment shows,[2] the OWI's Elmer Davis turned his attention to the music industry and stepped into the search for the Great American War Song. The OWI took its cue from President Franklin D. Roosevelt and cited a letter he wrote to Mrs. Vincent Ober, president of the National Federation of Music Clubs, about the strength of music: "The inspiration of great music can help to instill a fervor for the spiritual values in our way of life; and thus to strengthen democracy against those forces which would subjugate and enthrall mankind."[3]

The OWI wanted to assist musicians in finding the Great American War Song, but these same government administrators harshly criticized early examples of wartime music. Lyman Bryson, head of the Music Committee of the OWI, complained of pop tunes that the ballads were too saccharine and that the war songs were "just love songs with a once-over-lightly-war background."[4] Lyricists had merely slipped a soldier into their songs: "It was still boy-meets-girl stuff." For example, "We'll Meet Again," "The White Cliffs of Dover," and "Blue Skies Are Just Around the Corner" contained lyrics that could be relevant to many situations; the connotations of the songs depended on the listeners and their circumstances.

The personalization of popular music lyrics by the American public was not new to the music industry, but the advent of the war made it seem more important than ever to produce songs that would bolster morale and support the war effort.

Some feared that these simple, sweet, love songs would lull audiences into a false sense of security. The ultimate goal of the OWI was the manufacture of "freedom songs" that would "wave the flag and shout Hallelujah for all conquered and oppressed peoples."[5] The OWI thought that after a strong start in 1942, popular music "fizzled out" in its effort to rally the American people behind the war. During America's first full year of fighting, 17 percent of all popular songs reaching the top ten were war songs, but the number of patriotic and martial tunes being produced by Tin Pan Alley fell steadily during 1942. The same types of songs that had been popular prior to the war, ballads and swing tunes, continued at the top of the popularity charts in 1942.[6]

The problem was not antiwar songs. The only artists to question the conflict, once the United States was formally in the war, were a few blues singers who noted at the end of the war, in tunes such as Big Bill Broonzy's "When Will I Get to Be Called a Man?"[7] and "Fighting for Dear Old Uncle Sam" by J.D. Short, that African American contributions to the war effort did not weaken racial segregation.

Desperate for good war songs and contradicting its own advice to songwriters not to trivialize the enemy, the OWI singled out for praise Spike Jones's 1942 recording of "Der Fuehrer's Face," a very successful novelty tune about an admittedly unfunny man. Although a great deal was already known about Hitler's character, methods, and beliefs, the prewar tendency in the popular media to depict Hitler in comic caricatures persisted throughout most of the war. The cut of his hair and mustache, his mannerisms of speech and gesture, and his exaggerated boastfulness made the German leader a favorite model for humorists and impressionists for years. The enormity of Nazi inhumanity was hidden from full view until the Allied troops overran the interior of Europe and discovered the camps in which millions had been starved, tortured, and killed. "Der Fuehrer's Face," written by Disney studio composer Oliver Wallace for the animated propaganda short film *Donald Duck in Nutziland*, sold over two hundred thousand records in its first month of release and was number five on the sheet music best-seller chart.[8]

The song's melody was a parody of the "Horst Wessell Lied," a Nazi anthem. The tune was immediately picked up by many entertainers, but the most successful recording and live performances were by the group that introduced the number, Spike Jones and His City Slickers. One can only speculate on how this zany novelty song, notable for the Donald-

Duck-type voicings, the employment of a rubber razzer following every mock "Heil" in the song to simulate a Bronx cheer, and the hint at homosexuality among the Fuehrer's followers (crafted by the singers' vocal inflections at the lyrics "Super-dooper-super Men") improved on the romantic tunes the OWI disdained:

> Ven der Fuehrer says, "Ve iss der Master Race!"
> Ve heil! heil! right in der Fuehrer's face.
> Not to love der Fuehrer iss a great disgrace,
> So ve heil! heil! right in der Fuehrer's face.
> ....
> Ve bring der vorldt New Order—
> Heil Hilter's vorldt New Order!
> Ef-ry one off foreign race,
> Ve love der Fuehrer's face,
> Ven ve bring to der vorldt dis(-)order.

Spike Jones's recording of "Der Feuhrer's Face" evidently found favor with the men in America's armed forces. A soldier on Ascension Island took three currently popular songs—"Long Ago and Far Away," "The Music Goes Round and Round," and "As Time Goes By"—to task when he wrote about Jones:

> To us, Mr. Jones's orchestrations furnish a refreshing departure from Frank Sinatra's groaning and Andre Kostelanetz's symphonic sirup [sic]. . . . We need more of Mr. Jones's syncopated arrangements to keep us from believing in a sugar-plum world where everyone has a tingling spine [a lyric in "Long Ago and Far Away"] and goes round and round. All is not as simple as "woman needs man and man must have his mate" [a lyric in "As Time Goes By"]. Our ability to laugh at ourselves is an American tradition to be cherished. The world needs fewer Goerings and Himmlers and more guys like Jones.[9]

The OWI's anxiety concerning the failure of war songs was grounded in the nation's past. Americans had been singers, especially during World War I when group or community singing was considered as much a part of the nation's war effort as "rolling bandages, serving out coffee and cigarettes at canteens and knitting socks for soldiers."[10] Group singing accustomed people to doing things in unison; therefore, mass singing became an ally of military drill. In America's previous wars there were songs that seemed to be on the lips of every citizen. Now there seemed to be very little material published that captured the fancy of the public for longer than a few weeks, and the OWI complained that Tin Pan Alley did not seem to be doing its best for the war effort.

During World War II the music industry never quite caught fire as it had in 1917–1918. Only in World War I did the number of songs about war approximate those about love. Americans rallied behind the government and the war, and Tin Pan Alley helped lead the way with hundreds of songs supporting the war. Between April 1917 and November 1918, when the war ended, Tin Pan Alley produced more songs than during any other comparable period in history.[11] No American war, with the possible exception of the Civil War, yielded as many martial tunes as did the Great War, nor has any war added such numbers of sentimental songs to the permanent repertory of American popular song.

In the course of World War I, popular music reflected and capitalized on the new national mood. Tin Pan Alley had developed into an efficient machine. If the country demanded a particular type of song, the Alley could produce it. And the demand for war songs was phenomenal.

Tin Pan Alley also responded to the government's encouragement. The official propaganda agency, the Committee on Public Information (CPI), headed by George Creel, believed that singing was vital to the war effort, and agitated for composition of martial tunes. Creel did not go so far as to outline song topics or suggest how Tin Pan Alley writers should go about their business, but he made his presence and desires for war songs known.

The Committee on Public Education also distributed songbooks and dispatched song leaders to theaters around the country to lead people in group singing of war songs. The military distributed songbooks in camps and commissioned special officers to lead singing. Another indication of how important the government thought music was to the war effort was that despite paper rationing, music publishers continued to receive their full quota of paper for printing sheet music, although the traditional large format gave way to the standard page size used today with some smaller and miniature sizes also produced as conservation efforts.[12]

Sheet music sales soared. Sales of one and two million copies of a song were not uncommon. One explanation for this sales boom is that there was a shortage of entertainment outside the home. Many theaters, both vaudeville and legitimate, closed for want of fuel, power, and entertainers (many of whom were drafted).[13] Americans were compelled to entertain themselves, often around a family piano. People sang at community gatherings, in theaters, and at war bond rallies. Tin Pan Alley sponsored war song contests in movie theaters—before the advent of sound motion pictures—and several of World War I's best songs came from these venues.

Without radio or television to bring the horrors of battle into the home, Americans in the months between April 1917 and November 1918 still held to an old-fashioned, romantic view of war. A majority of World War I songs were martial and at the same time romantic in spirit. In these songs, the soldiers were handsome, brave, and noble, while the fragile women at home waited patiently and lovingly for them.

Representative of the militant-style song was the war's biggest hit, George M. Cohan's exhilarating "Over There." Written the day after Wilson signed the Declaration of War, the catchy ditty was introduced at a Red Cross benefit at the Hippodrome in New York City in the fall of 1917. Warning that America was on its way to straighten out the trouble in Europe, the tune sold more than one million records and two million copies of sheet music and was recorded by many singers, including the great opera star Enrico Caruso. Among the different sheet music cover illustrations for the successive printings of the song, Norman Rockwell's depiction of young soldiers gathered around a campfire, singing heartily while one of the boys plays a banjo, is striking for its depiction of innocence. These young men could be at summer camp instead of an army-training site. The caption above the song's name on the title page salutes "Over There" as "Your Song—My Song—Our Boys' Song." The words were simple, and the catchy tune was easy to remember:

> Johnnie get your gun, get your gun, get your gun,
> Take it on the run, on the run, on the run;
> Hear them calling you and me;
> Ev'ry son of liberty.
> Hurry right away, no delay, go today,
> Make your daddy glad, to have had such a lad,
> Tell your sweetheart not to pine,
> To be proud her boy's in line.
> CHORUS:
> Over there, over there,
> Send the word, send the word over there,
> That the Yanks are coming,
> The Yanks are coming,
> The drums rum-tumming everywhere
> So prepare, say a pray'r
> Send the word, send the word, to beware,
> We'll be over, We're coming over,
> And we won't come back till it's over Over There.

Cohan, long known as an ardent patriot, donated all of his royalties from the song to war charities. His generosity did not go unnoticed in high places, for it eventually earned him a congressional medal by a special act of Congress.[14]

During World War I the government could not have asked for a better presentation from popular music. Tin Pan Alley wholeheartedly responded to the government's call. War songs comprised part of a government-wide crusade that by mid-1918 nearly eradicated most organized opposition to the war.[15] The end of the war found most of Tin Pan Alley and other Americans anxious to return to life as it had been before the war. Shortly after the armistice ending the First World War, November 11, 1918, the deluge of war song manuscripts declined to a trickle. The public seemed so anxious to erase the war from memory that vaudeville house managers in 1919, sensing the shift in the public's mood, tacked up signs prohibiting war songs.[16]

The disillusionment many Americans experienced following the postwar failure of President Wilson's new world order at the Versailles Peace Conference, returned in 1939 when Nazi aggression thrust Europe into war. Americans were divided between isolationists, who wanted to keep the United States from becoming involved in Europe's troubles, and interventionists, who tried to aid the French and British and prepare the country for eventual entry into the war.[17]

American musicians also were divided before Pearl Harbor. A group of folk-style, urban musicians—with ties to the Communist party—created a small following in New York and Detroit. These musicians hoped to use songs as ideological weapons to persuade Americans to stay out of the war in Europe. The best known of these folksingers was a group called The Almanac Singers. The Almanacs shifted personnel frequently, but included, at one time or another, Woody Guthrie, Pete Seeger, Lee Hays, Ronnie Gilbert, Millard Lampell, Allen Sloane, Beth Lomax, Arthur Stern, Butch Hawes, Brownie McGee, Charley Polachek, and Sis Cunningham. Other singers, such as Burl Ives and Will Geer, came and went repeatedly. In spring 1941 the Almanacs released their strongly worded album *Songs for John Doe*.[18] The songs left little room for compromise or loose interpretation. They were openly hostile to the capitalist system, insulting to the United States government and public figures, and purposefully inflammatory. The song "Washington Breakdown" illustrates the point:

Wendell Willkie and Franklin D.,
Seems to me they both agree,
They both agree on killing me.

Another song from the album received wide coverage in the press, and excerpts from it were published later when the Almanacs came under fire from the New York dailies. The Selective Service Training Act, which registered 16.5 million American men between the ages of twenty-one and thirty-five, was the subject of "The Ballad of October 16"—the date in 1940 when this first-ever peacetime military conscription went into effect:

> Oh Franklin Roosevelt told the people how he felt,
> We damned near believed what he said.
> He said "I hate war and so does Eleanor but
> We won't be safe till everybody's dead."

One of the most devastating of the *Songs for John Doe* was "Plow Under," by Allen Sloane. It was decidedly opposed to intervention in Europe and also cautioned Americans against using militarism as a way out of economic depression: "Plow under, plow under, / Plow under every fourth American boy."

Following the attack on Pearl Harbor, the Almanacs reversed their antiwar position and began to write militant patriotic songs. One of the first songs, written in February 1942 by Pete Seeger, was "Dear Mister President." It apologized to Roosevelt for *Songs for John Doe*:

> Now Mister President, we haven't always agreed in
> the past I know,
> ....
> We got to lick Mr. Hitler, and until we do,
> Other things can wait,
> In other words, first we got a skunk to skin.

In 1942, the Almanacs released the song on an album by the same name, advertising the record as "war songs for Americans." Five other new compositions joined the title song: "Round and Round Hitler's Grave," "Deliver the Goods," "Belt Line Girl," "Side by Side," and "Reuben James." The songs also were published in sheet music form by Bob Miller, and it seemed for a time that they might answer the question posed by Samuel Sillen in *New Masses*, "Why don't we have a good war song?" The Almanacs' latest music seemed to fit Sillen's criteria: "We need songs not corn. Songs that make us burn and hate against the Fascist enemy. Songs that make us cheer the heroism of our armed forces. Songs of dignity and hope and courage. Fighting songs that rouse and rally. . . . The people are sick and tired of jerks and jeeps and oceanic caresses. Tin Pan Alley: business as usual with a few war angles thrown in."[19]

After the Almanacs began to urge all-out efforts to win the war, a larger audience was willing to accept their songs. Norwin Corbin, of the

Columbia Broadcasting System (CBS), hired the Almanacs to sing on several radio programs that emphasized the war effort. They also sang to the Allied Armies overseas on shortwave broadcasts produced by the Office of War Information. This wide exposure allowed the Almanacs to reach audiences beyond their usual devotees of union members, intellectuals, and leftists, and it helped them gain an agent from the prestigious William Morris Agency, a contract with Decca Records, and an audition at New York's Rainbow Room in Rockefeller Center. The latter opportunity was ironic since John D. Rockefeller, the founder of the Center, often had been attacked as an immoral capitalist in the Almanacs' songs. Avoiding the label of "Show Biz" and declining to wear "Lil Abner" outfits when they performed, the Almanacs drew the conclusion that the Rainbow Room was not the best showcase for their material.[20]

Although the Almanacs continued to assist the war effort in song, their support was eroded by a series of articles published in New York newspapers beginning February 1942. The group's antiwar past was exposed, including a songbook they had produced for the American Peace Mobilization (a communist "front" organization), along with details of the many rallies they had attended to perform peace and anti-intervention songs. The Almanacs were accused of being disloyal to the United States. As the *New York Times Herald* said, "These [are] lads and lassies who, before Russia went to war against Germany, had nothing but the ugliest things to say about FDR, the Congress and other things American."[21] Following these newspaper attacks, William Morris quit representing the group, their recording contract was nullified, and the Rainbow Room job offer was rescinded. The Almanacs' personnel continued to fluctuate, but the group still performed.

The New York newspapers renewed their attack on the Almanacs on January 4, 1943, again citing pre-Pearl Harbor antiwar activities. The *New York Times Herald* said the group had gone from "peace singers" to "war minstrels." But the most serious issue in this article was the question of why the OWI had employed and still continued to employ these "subversives."[22] The next day, a *New York Times* article raised similar points about the Almanacs, but reported that the group was "no longer thumping out their alleged folk songs for the short wave propaganda service."[23]

The Almanacs were especially criticized for their pro-labor songs performed on OWI programs. Songs that favored unions in conflict with management were seen as counterproductive to the drive for national unity. Retreating from an earlier position praising the Almanacs for writing and singing their militant war songs, the OWI now declared that it had been a mistake to hire the "hillbilly group." Leonard Carlton, in charge of the International Radio Bureau of OWI, said, "We pulled a blunder. These boys are no longer doing broadcasts for us. We put on [oversee the content of] 2,500 programs [U.S. domestic and foreign broadcasts] a day. . . . It was natural that somebody should pull a blunder sometime." The Almanacs did not perform any of their anti-war or anti-government songs for OWI broadcasts, but they sang one tune about "everybody [having] joined the union" on a program saluting the state of Michigan. They had previously recorded songs that attacked Henry Ford and praised the C.I.O. (Congress of Industrial Organization) victory over Ford Motors. Neither of these recordings was broadcast by the OWI.[24]

Shortly after the group was fired by the OWI, most of its members entered the military or joined in other war-related work. The Almanacs' firing might be considered an act of political expediency and not an act of thoughtful reasoning. For almost a year the singers had shown their ability to communicate with some groups of people that possibly had not been reached by media before—former union laborers who were now workers and soldiers for Uncle Sam. Despite the Almanacs' proven effectiveness, an OWI spokesman said, "They'll jolly well stay canned."[25]

The OWI treatment of the Almanacs was just a hint of what lay in the future for folk entertainers: "blacklisting" in the late 1940s and 1950s as a result of the House Committee on Un-American Activities investigation of "Communism in motion pictures," under its chairman, Congressman J. Parnell Thomas (of "five-cent-war-song" fame).[26]

The government was just as anxious for spirited, rousing war songs in World War II (if not more so), as it was in 1918. Despite the OWI's efforts the number and popularity of such songs produced for World War II pale in comparison to those generated by Tin Pan Alley during World War I. The American public no longer seemed interested in militant war songs, and after 1943, their numbers on the charts dropped sharply. The enthusiasm that pervaded World War I songs was missing; World War II had no "Over There." A few energetic tunes like the lively "Don't Sit Under the Apple Tree (With Anyone Else but Me)" appeared, but more songs were wistful. "I Left My Heart at the Stage Door Canteen," "When the Lights Go on Again (All Over the World)," and "Rodger Young" focused on wartime tragedy and disrupted relationships. "Comin' in on a Wing and a Prayer," which reached number one on the general popularity charts in 1943, was the last of the songs with a real war background to make a significant showing.

Casting about for a scapegoat on which to blame the failure of stirring war songs, an OWI spokesman faulted the popular foxtrot and swing rhythms for the lack of high-quality war songs and argued that the new rhythms were less conducive to stirring martial tunes than the one-and-two-steps of the 1910s.[27] The criteria OWI used to determine a war song were out of line with popular musical tastes, especially the new dance rhythms that the public as well as the soldiers preferred. Soldiers were even known to execute their drills while whistling Glenn Miller tunes.[28]

What were these different dances and rhythms that caused so much anguish for war song composers? The foxtrot, a slow, simple, ballroom dance in 2/4 time, originated before World War I. Vernon and Irene Castle are credited with its invention, but a more likely source is the African American bandleader James Reese Europe, who brought the dance to the Castles' attention.[29] The leisurely, graceful tempo was ill-suited to the type of songs the OWI desired. People had a difficult time identifying lovely foxtrot dance music with parades, marching soldiers, tanks, planes, and jeeps. But Americans had no trouble transferring their feelings about the war and its effect on their lives to these same popular songs.

Swing, the other rhythm found culpable in the matter of war song failure, developed during the 1920s. Jelly Roll Morton is credited with the first use of the term in his 1928 "Georgia Swing," and Duke Ellington wrote "It Don't Mean a Thing if It Ain't Got That Swing" in 1932. But it was not until 1935, when Benny Goodman played swing style at the Palomar Ballroom in Los Angeles and the Congress Hotel in Chicago, that swing emerged as a nationwide form of popular music. Luckily for Goodman and his band, the Palomar was one of the first West Coast ballrooms to have a national network radio connection, and night after night the music and the dancers' enthusiasm for it were broadcast nationwide.[30]

Swing music had been the property of African American dance bands and some white bands, such as the Dorsey brothers, but remained on the fringes of popular music until Goodman, in the words of Duke Ellington, had "done the right thing at the right time in front of the right people." Goodman's popularity increased, and following a nationwide tour, he returned to New York to play a regular "live" show at the Paramount Theater between movie screenings from ten-thirty in the morning through the day and evening. At seven in the morning, teenagers were already lining up for the show, and when the band played between movies, the adolescents became so caught up in the music that they left their seats and began jitterbugging in the aisles.[31]

This action sensationalized Goodman's appearances and caused worried adults to fear for the future of the nation. The spontaneity and reckless abandon with which teenagers joined swing music with dance was truly alarming. Here was the youth of America refusing to stay in their seats in a motion picture theater and ignoring the pleas of the management to stop dancing in the aisles. In some eyes this type of behavior was tantamount to anarchy.

Swing bands numbered about fifteen players with rhythm, brass, and reed sections. Some bands also included string sections, vocalists, or a singing group. Swing music was sensual, often producing a physical reaction on the part of the listener and always connected to dancing. Sitting still was difficult when swing music was playing. Swing consists of a four-beat measure with a chugging-type of rhythm; the different instrument sections play call and response passages, and individual soloists improvise against set patterns from the band.

Swing was a hybrid of an African American musical style, namely jazz, with a more harmonious, less-threatening musical style that middle-class, white Americans would accept and purchase. Many adults considered the musical form to be "garbage," a sentiment their children often did not share. The deviant aspects of the music stemmed not necessarily from the lyrics but from the structure and the loudness of the instrumental solos and the dance steps enacted by teenagers to "swing." Swing also was capable of what is termed "covering," the rewording, changing, or rewriting of messages, themes, tonal structure, or rhythms of songs; thus, numerous songs by "unacceptable," relatively unknown musicians were covered by major artists and boosted into the mainstream of American culture.[32]

William Allen White of the America First Committee attacked swing as "blood raw emotion, without harmony, without consistent rhythm, and with no more tune than the yearnful bellowings of a lonely, yearning and romantic cow in the pastures or the raucous staccatic meditation of a bulldog barking in a barrel." A Barnard College professor termed the dance music "musical Hitlerism."[33]

By the Second World War swing came to dominate American popular music, and most of the arguments against it disappeared. American youth was not, as some feared, led to rebellion by swing music. Instead, they marched or rode away to war humming swing tunes. Swing became synonymous with Americans. One young Dutch woman recalled the GIs entering her liberated town playing Glenn Miller's version of "St. Louis Blues": "I cried. I thought it was the most beautiful music I had ever heard. It was so bold, so brash, so American. It meant we were free."[34]

The OWI quickly realized that criticizing swing was not going to produce war songs, so it looked for other areas of the entertainment business to chide for the insufficient supply of war songs. Although radio had offered its services to the nation, it did not escape criticism. The OWI noted that radio had become the primary transmitter of music, overshadowing dances, theaters, and concerts; love songs prevailed on the airwaves.[35] Radio was aware of this but did little to change its music broadcasting patterns.

Other developments might be added to the list of reasons for a lack of a "proper" war song. Graphic radio, newsreel, and magazine reports from the battlefield made the naive exuberance of 1917–1918 impossible. A strike by the musicians' union in 1943 hindered instrumental recording. And Tin Pan Alley, though still huge, was no longer the sole source of white, mainstream popular music as it had been in World War I. Weakened by a fight between ASCAP and BMI over song licensing, and competing with swing, folk, and country, Tin Pan Alley could not flood the market with war songs.

The music business also witnessed a critical development. David Ewen states that Tin Pan Alley underwent "a major revolution" between World War I and II. Tin Pan Alley was no longer the "nursery in which composers could be developed," or a place where "songs were manufactured by the carload to meet every mood" or interest of the American public.[36] It was no longer possible to promote a song to success by songplugging,[37] and, most important, the music publishers had lost complete control of the product.

The single most important factor of the "revolution" in Tin Pan Alley was that after 1930 most of the major publishing houses were acquired by motion-picture studios for their "all-talking, all-singing" productions. The publishing houses became branches of movie studios, and the music publishers answered to the movie studio executives. Songs were written for specific films, not for independent release. Composers and lyricists had little incentive to attempt to circumvent the studio system. Songs written to stand on their own were a "luxury" few could enjoy; most were composed on commission by musicians who were contracted to film studios. Without the assembly-line method of song production that fueled Tin Pan Alley before 1930, it is easy to see why World War II yielded drastically fewer songs than World War I.

The OWI had so much difficulty in finding popular militant war songs that appealed to the American public that it began to seek solutions on its own. The OWI said that the audience, who formerly participated actively by going to dances to hear the latest music, was made passive by radio. The OWI even talked of getting Arthur Murray and Fred Astaire to invent a new style of dance so the United States would become "more oompah and militaristic."[38]

The idea of inventing and popularizing a new dance explicitly to influence the American public to think and behave in a more militaristic manner illustrates the extent to which the OWI was willing to go in order to wage a war that was "total" from both a social and cultural standpoint. During World War I, the government had been interested in the public's support of a military endeavor, but in World War II it wanted a commitment from the American people that extended to all levels of society and touched every aspect of American culture.

Despite gas rationing and curfews in some areas of the country, Americans went out to dances where they wanted to hear tunes they already knew from radio. New songs were introduced on the radio for maximum audience exposure. One record or live performance on radio reached a larger audience than a band could in a year's worth of concert and dance dates. The OWI recognized the power of radio to reach a large audience and formulated plans to aid songwriters in producing "proper" war songs and then having them broadcast.

Chapter 9

THE NATIONAL WARTIME MUSIC COMMITTEE

From its inception the OWI framed directives that offered guidelines for songwriters to aid them in the composition of "proper" war songs, and, in the public press, the OWI rebuked Tin Pan Alley for its uninterrupted production of "nostalgic" hit songs. Finally, the OWI decided to become directly involved with the music business and established the National Wartime Music Committee in November 1942, with representatives from each area of the federal government that had a need for music in any form. The National Wartime Music Committee was organized to seek out and pass judgment on the suitability of "morale" tunes for civilian and military use.[1]

The National Wartime Music Committee's function, according to a memorandum from OWI Domestic Radio Bureau chief William B. Lewis to Merritt W. Barnum at the New York City bureau, was purely advisory. It would: (1) Answer inquiries from private interests in the United States that might assist the government with wartime popular music for radio and films for both military and civilian use; American music for foreign language groups; community sing-a-longs; contributions by individual musicians, orchestras, opera companies, and choral societies; compositions by classical music composers (both in and out of the service); folk music; music in schools and colleges; and United Nations music. (2) Coordinate all of the music programs used by government agencies in the war effort (war bond rallies, Victory Garden programs, and scrap collection drives), so that these separate programs would be of mutual benefit to the different agencies. (3) Channel all requests for use of commercially produced music by government agencies through the National Wartime Music Committee to prevent duplication of effort and confusion—for example in the area of music copyrights. (4) Survey government operations, both domestic and abroad, to discern what agreements, contracts, policies, and procedures were already in effect with civilian musicians or composers and publishers.[2] Especially crucial were agreements between the government and the Music Publishers' Protective Association, the Songwriters' Protective Association, the American Federation of Musicians, the American Guild of Musical Artists, the American Federation of Radio Artists, the Screen Actors' Guild, the Radio Writers' Guild, and the various Victory Committees—such as the Songwriters' Victory Committee, the Publishers' Victory Committee, and the Writers' Victory Committee—established throughout areas of specialization in the music business by private citizens to work for the war effort.

Eventually, after the initial organization period, it was hoped that the National Wartime Music Committee would be able to standardize practices that would lead to uniformity in government dealings with music industry groups. This standardization of practices never materialized as the government could not finalize its plans before the music industry developed its own standards and practices that it utilized for the duration of the war.

To deal with the problems brought on by the proliferation of such groups, subcommittees of music industry experts were formed to research copyrights, coordinate radio announcements, encourage songwriters across the nation in the quest for the "proper" war song, and meet with government officials to determine musical needs of those departments most concerned with the war: State, War, Navy, and Treasury. The OWI had National Wartime Music Committee members in New York, Los Angeles, and Washington, D.C. The National Wartime Music Committee did not initiate any programs or operate any music projects.

In an attempt to work with the OWI in its attempts to enlist Tin Pan Alley and Hollywood in the war music effort (and not content to wait for the federal government to act in the search for the Great American War Song), in May 1943 the American Theater Wing formed the War Music Committee, a group of independent Broadway businessmen, Hollywood and popular lyricists, and composers. They were separate from the National Wartime Music Committee of the OWI. Almost immediately it was decided that the names of the Theater Wing's War Music Committee and the Office of War Information's National Wartime Music Committee resembled each other too closely, and so the American Theater Wing changed its music committee's name to the Music War Committee.[3]

The American Theater Wing's Music War Committee sought to promote the composition and marketing of "proper" war songs, declaring, "Forget about 6/8 tempos and WWI. Today's songwriters should stop writ-

Above, The Savoy Ballroom, Chicago. (Library of Congress Prints & Photographs Division, FSA-OWI Collection, LC-USF34-038795-D DLC). *Below*, Dancing to the music of Duke Ellington at New York's Hurricane Ballroom. Library of Congress Prints & Photographs Division, FSA-OWI Collection, LC-USW3-023941-C DLC).

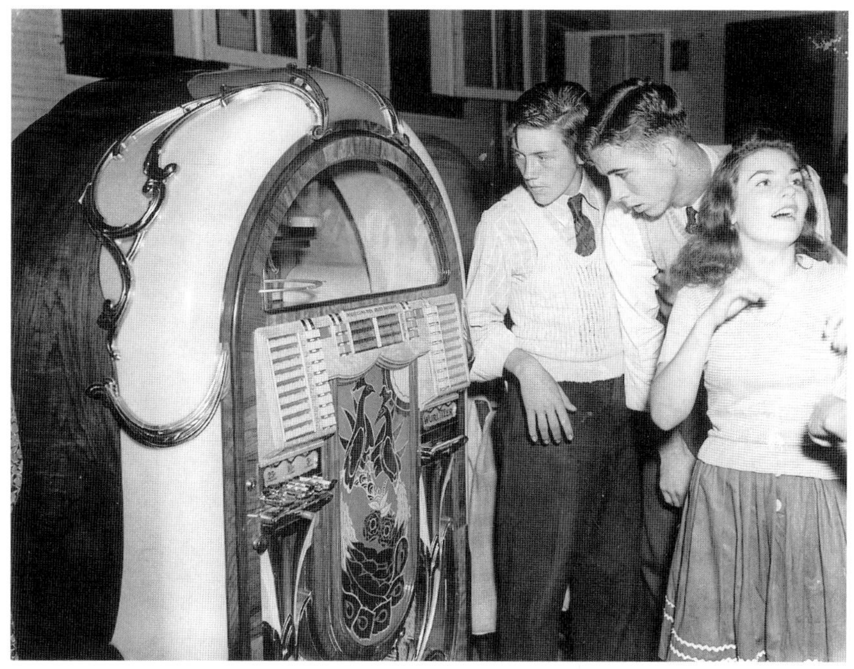

A dance hall in Richwood, West Virginia. (Library of Congress Prints & Photographs Division, FSA-OWI Collection, LC-USF34-083984-C DLC).

WE DID IT BEFORE
AND WE CAN DO IT AGAIN
By CLIFF FRIEND
CHARLIE TOBIAS
A.S.C.A.P.
Valley Forge
Bunker Hill
Jackson at New Orleans
Perry at Lake Erie
Dewey at Manila
The Argonne Forest
Featured by
EDDIE CANTOR
in the new Musical Comedy
"BANJO EYES"
M. WITMARK & SONS
NEW YORK

Praise The Lord
And Pass The Ammunition!!
Words and Music
by FRANK LOESSER
FAMOUS MUSIC CORP., • 1619 BROADWAY, New York City, N. Y.

THEY STARTED SOMETHIN'
(BUT WE'RE GONNA END IT)
Music and Lyrics by ERNEST GOLD • ROBERT SOUR • DON McCRAY
BUY DEFENSE BONDS AND STAMPS NOW!

WHEN THE LIGHTS GO ON AGAIN
(ALL OVER THE WORLD)
By EDDIE SEILER
SOL MARCUS
BENNIE BENJEMEN
CAMPBELL, LOFT & PORGIE, INC.
music publishers

WE'LL WIN THROUGH - WE ALWAYS DO
Lyric by
IRVING TAYLOR
Music by
VIC MIZZY
SANTLY-JOY-SELECT, INC. · 1619 BROADWAY · N. Y. C.

THERE'LL BE BLUE BIRDS OVER
THE WHITE CLIFFS OF DOVER
Words by
NAT BURTON
Music by
WALTER KENT
SHAPIRO, BERNSTEIN & CO.

WE MUST BE VIGILANT
Words by
EDGAR LESLIE
Music Adapted by
JOSEPH A. BURKE
Adapted from
F. W. MEACHAM'S—"AMERICAN PATROL"
Featured by
PHIL SPITALNY
and his ALL GIRL ORCHESTRA
on the "HOUR OF CHARM"
BVC

ANY BONDS TODAY?
words and music by IRVING BERLIN
THEME SONG OF THE
NATIONAL DEFENSE SAVINGS PROGRAM
U. S. Defense Savings Bonds
and Stamps
COPYRIGHT BY HENRY MORGENTHAU, Jr.
SECRETARY OF THE TREASURY, WASHINGTON, D.C.
SOUVENIR COPY
NOT TO BE SOLD

IRVING BERLIN'S BUGLE SONG
OH! HOW I HATE TO GET UP
IN THE MORNING
IRVING
BERLIN

American Patrol
March
by F. W. MEACHAM
PIANO SOLO, SIMPLIFIED
by JOHN W. SCHAUM
PRICE 30 CENTS IN U.S.A.
THE WILLIS MUSIC CO.
CINCINNATI, OHIO
FOERSTER MUSIC HOUSE
WISCONSIN

MacArthur's Here Again
(Dedicated to Lt. Alice Zwicker)
U.S.
RALPH F. BRAGG
LT. ALICE ZWICKER

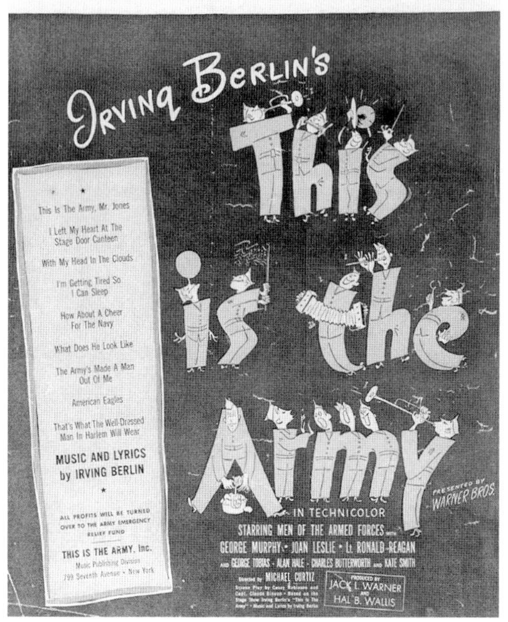
How About A Cheer For The Navy
Irving Berlin's
This is the Army
This Is The Army, Mr. Jones
I Left My Heart At The Stage Door Canteen
With My Head In The Clouds
I'm Getting Tired So I Can Sleep
How About A Cheer For The Navy
What Does He Look Like
The Army's Made A Man Out Of Me
American Eagles
That's What The Well-Dressed Man In Harlem Will Wear
MUSIC AND LYRICS by IRVING BERLIN
ALL PROFITS WILL BE TURNED OVER TO THE ARMY EMERGENCY RELIEF FUND
THIS IS THE ARMY, Inc.
Music Publishing Division
799 Seventh Avenue • New York
PRESENTED BY WARNER BROS.
IN TECHNICOLOR
STARRING MEN OF THE ARMED FORCES
GEORGE MURPHY • JOAN LESLIE • Lt. RONALD REAGAN
AND GEORGE TOBIAS • ALAN HALE • CHARLES BUTTERWORTH AND KATE SMITH
Directed by MICHAEL CURTIZ
PRODUCED BY JACK L. WARNER AND HAL B. WALLIS

IRVING BERLIN'S BUGLE SONG
OH! HOW I HATE TO GET UP IN THE MORNING
BY IRVING BERLIN

ARMY Hit Kit OF POPULAR SONGS
FEBRUARY • 1944
CONTENTS
Paper Doll
No Love, No Nothin'
Till We Meet Again
Hinky Dinky Parlay Voo (NEW STUFF)
The Marseillaise
My Ideal
Deep in the Heart of Texas
Put On Your Old Grey Bonnet
Issued Monthly by SPECIAL SERVICES DIVISION, ARMY SERVICE FORCES, UNITED STATES ARMY
For use by the U. S. Armed Forces only. NOT FOR SALE

ARMY Hit Kit OF POPULAR SONGS
NOVEMBER • 1943
CONTENTS
I Can't Give You Anything But Love
Pistol Packin' Mama
If You Please
We're Shovin' Right Off Again
The Marseillaise
I Heard You Cried Last Night
Let Me Call You Sweetheart
Issued Monthly by SPECIAL SERVICE DIVISION
ARMY SERVICE FORCES, UNITED STATES ARMY
For use by the U. S. Armed Forces only. NOT FOR SALE

ARMY Hit Kit OF POPULAR SONGS
"GIRL OF MY DREAMS, I LOVE YOU!"
AUGUST • 1943
CONTENTS
Stein Song
Sunday, Monday or Always
Put Your Arms Around Me, Honey
I've Been Working On the Railroad
Paper Doll
Meadowland
There Is A Tavern In The Town
My Melancholy Baby
Issued Monthly by SPECIAL SERVICE DIVISION
ARMY SERVICE FORCES, UNITED STATES ARMY
For use by the U. S. Armed Forces only. NOT FOR SALE

ARMS FOR THE LOVE OF AMERICA
BY
IRVING BERLIN
ORDNANCE DEPARTMENT, U.S.A.
THE ARMY ORDNANCE SONG
Dedicated to Major General C. M. Wesson
Chief of Ordnance
ARMY ORDNANCE ASSOCIATION
Washington, D. C.
IRVING BERLIN INC., 799 Seventh Ave., New York
SOLE AGENTS

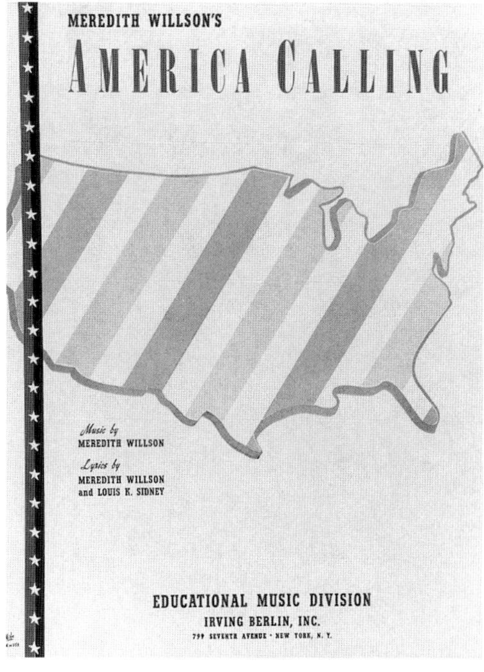
MEREDITH WILLSON'S
AMERICA CALLING
Music by
MEREDITH WILLSON
Lyrics by
MEREDITH WILLSON
and LOUIS K. SIDNEY
EDUCATIONAL MUSIC DIVISION
IRVING BERLIN, INC.
799 SEVENTH AVENUE • NEW YORK, N. Y.

EV'RYBODY EV'RY PAYDAY
Lyric by TOM ADAIR • Music by DICK UHL
Copyright 1942 by HENRY MORGENTHAU Jr., Secretary of the Treasury, Washington, D. C.
International Copyright Secured Made in U. S. A.
All Rights Reserved Including the Right of Public Performance for Profit

FIGHT·FOR·AMERICA
PRICE 25 CENTS
WORDS & MUSIC
BY
CECILIA
ELLERBE
SMITH
1942
©
PUBLISHED BY
CECILIA E. SMITH
SHREVEPORT, LA.

Low in D
(A to B)
Medium in F
(C to D)
High in B♭
(F to G)
GOD BLESS AMERICA
by
IRVING BERLIN
First Performance by Kate Smith
Armistice Day, 1938
IRVING BERLIN Inc.
Music Publishers
799 SEVENTH AVE., NEW YORK, N.Y.

KATE SMITH Sings
"WE'RE ALL
AMERICANS
(ALL TRUE BLUE"
WORDS AND MUSIC
By
JAMES T. MANGAN
AS FEATURED REGULARLY
By
KATE SMITH
COLUMBIA RECORDING ARTIST
ON
KATE SMITH HOUR
COLUMBIA NETWORK
FRIDAY EVENINGS
BELL
MUSIC CO.

MOLLY PITCHER
IT'S NEW!
IT'S PATRIOTIC!
Jolly Molly Pitcher
COPYRIGHT BY
HENRY MORGENTHAU JR.
Secretary of the Treasury
WASHINGTON, D.C.
Souvenir Copy
NOT TO BE SOLD
Words and Music by
TOM ADAIR
and
SGT. DICK UHL
as Introduced by
HJALMAR HANSON
and
THE GREAT LAKES CHOIR
DISTRIBUTED BY THE INDEPENDENT RETAIL GROCERS OF AMERICA

The Song Of The
SEABEES
Lyric by
SAM M. LEWIS
Music by
PETER DE ROSE
SEABEES
Dedicated to the SEABEES
Construction and Fighting Men
of the UNITED STATES NAVY
Printed for complimentary distribution by Bureau of Yards and Docks, United States Navy, by
ROBBINS MUSIC CORPORATION

HATS OFF TO MacARTHUR
AND OUR BOYS DOWN THERE
Words and Music by
IRA SCHUSTER
PAUL CUNNINGHAM
LEONARD WHITCUP
PAULL-PIONEER
Music Corporation
1657 BROADWAY, NEW YORK

Shout! Wherever You May Be
I AM AN AMERICAN
by
IRA SCHUSTER A.S.C.A.P.
PAUL CUNNINGHAM A.S.C.A.P.
LEONARD WHITCUP A.S.C.A.P.
MERCER & MORRIS, INC.

Official Song of the United States Army Air Corps
THE ARMY AIR CORPS

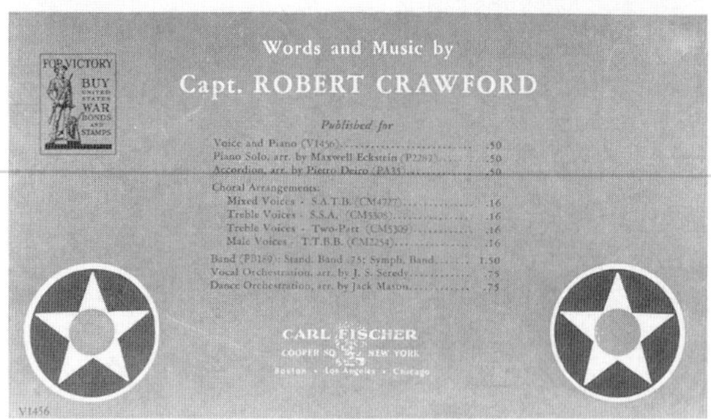
Words and Music by
Capt. ROBERT CRAWFORD
FOR VICTORY BUY UNITED STATES WAR BONDS AND STAMPS
Published for
Voice and Piano (V1456) .50
Piano Solo, arr. by Maxwell Eckstein (P2287) .50
Accordion, arr. by Pietro Deiro (PA35) .50
Choral Arrangements:
Mixed Voices - S.A.T.B. (CM4727) .16
Treble Voices - S.S.A. (CM5308) .16
Treble Voices - Two-Part (CM5309) .16
Male Voices - T.T.B.B. (CM2254) .16
Band (PB189): Stand. Band .75; Symph. Band 1.50
Vocal Orchestration, arr. by J. S. Seredy .75
Dance Orchestration, arr. by Jack Mason .75
CARL FISCHER
COOPER SQ. NEW YORK
Boston · Los Angeles · Chicago
V1456

WHAT DO YOU DO IN THE
INFANTRY
by
FRANK LOESSER

Make Uncle Sam Your Banker
EASY PIANO SOLO
With Words
by Virginia Pearson
WAR STAMPS
THE WILLIS MUSIC CO.
Cincinnati, Ohio

THIS IS THE ARMY, MISTER JONES
UNCLE SAM PRESENTS
"THIS IS THE ARMY"
WORDS AND MUSIC BY IRVING BERLIN
THE NEW ALL-SOLDIER SHOW
PRODUCED FOR
ARMY EMERGENCY RELIEF
American Eagles
That Russian Winter
This Is The Army, Mr. Jones
How About A Cheer For The Navy
The Army's Made A Man Out Of Me
I Left My Heart At The Stage Door Canteen
With My Head In The Clouds
I'm Getting Tired So I Can Sleep
My Sergeant And I Are Buddies
THIS IS THE ARMY Inc.
MUSIC PUBLISHING DIVISION

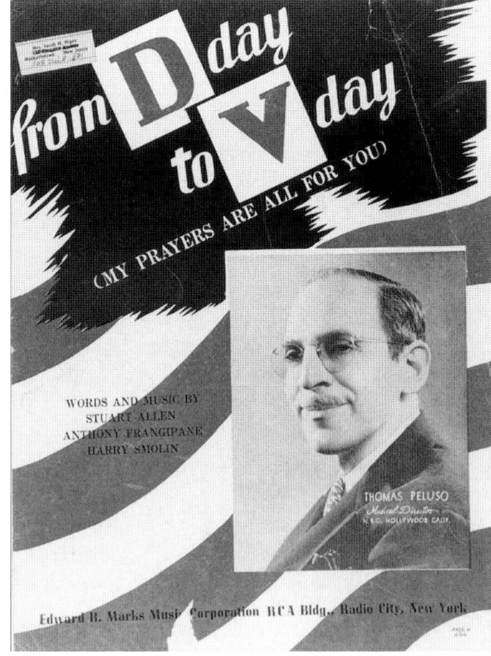
from D day to V day
(MY PRAYERS ARE ALL FOR YOU)
WORDS AND MUSIC BY
STUART ALLEN
ANTHONY FRANGIPANE
HARRY SMOLIN
THOMAS PELUSO
Musical Director
Edward B. Marks Music Corporation RCA Bldg., Radio City, New York

ing for the 1917 war. They should adapt their patriotic and military ideas to the 1943 pattern of show business and showmanship."[4] The popular music industry echoed the sentiments of others who believed the United States had to turn from the thinking of World War I, when fewer sacrifices and less participation in winning the war were required of American society. During World War II, this "total war" thinking was to encompass all of society—every phase of American life was to be connected in some way, however small, to winning the war. Popular music was no exception. The OWI was insistent on dedicated participation and the musicians of Tin Pan Alley were more than happy to give it.

The Music War Committee's (MWC) instructions to its fellow members of the popular music industry were in tandem with the OWI's approach to wartime melodies: The MWC urged members to assume a positive approach to their writing. "Forget the frustration of the 'Maybe I will lose my girl' or 'Is my girl back home two-timing me?' songs." Also, songwriters were not to fret about the "lights going out all over Europe, but sing of victory."[5]

Prior to this time, Oscar Hammerstein II, president of the American Theater Wing's Music War Committee, had been soundly criticized by the OWI for his song "The Last Time I Saw Paris." Although the song was released in 1940 before the United States entered World War II, it was deemed "far too pessimistic." Despite the criticism, "The Last Time I Saw Paris," dedicated to the English songwriter, Noel Coward, won the Academy Award in 1941 for Best Song and became a best-selling record by Kate Smith.[6] It was an immensely popular song, but with the formation of the Music War Committee a change of musical direction was espoused at the highest levels of Broadway and Tin Pan Alley. Hammerstein and his fellow MWC members were primed to write and encourage war songs that were positive and uplifting, not sad or wistful like "The Last Time I Saw Paris."

Other writers such as E.Y. "Yip" Harburg and Ira Gershwin tried to rally the troops and the civilians with "If That's Propaganda (Make the Most of It)." Irving Berlin led the search for relevant contemporary songs as previously mentioned. He also wrote patriotic numbers for the movie *Holiday Inn*, including the "Freedom Song," whose lyrics are a listing of the Bill of Rights. This was a direct inspiration not only from the war, but also from President Roosevelt's "Four Freedoms," which had been immortalized in song as well as in a series of paintings by Norman Rockwell that graced the cover of the *Saturday Evening Post* and were later made into propaganda posters for the home front.[7] It was the film *Holiday Inn* that first introduced "White Christmas," often mentioned as the ideal wartime song, to the American public.

The American Theater Wing's Music War Committee was a group

of composers who considered themselves a musical melting pot that, through song, idealized American democracy for its ability to eliminate racial and ethnic discrimination. In the eyes of the MWC, all Americans participated in this musical society on an equal basis, leading to the eradication of class differences. Two meccas of entertainment for servicemen, founded by the American Theater Wing and aided by the Music War Committee, were instrumental in fostering the notion of an idealized America—at least musically. The Stage Door Canteen in the basement of Broadway's Forty-fourth Street Theater in New York City was founded in 1942 by the American Theater Wing,[8] and the Hollywood Canteen was founded by Bette Davis and John Garfield in early 1943.[9]

The canteens were constantly in the news because entertainers and other show business luminaries came nightly to entertain the crowds of servicemen and servicewomen. The venues, open every night from nine o'clock until midnight, charged no admission; everything was free to a person in uniform. Female entertainers danced with anyone who asked them, served coffee and donuts, and listened to the men's stories. Both the Stage Door Canteen and the Hollywood Canteen represented stellar democracy. Music at these canteens reinforced the democratic message. The most popular tunes of the day were always on the agenda, and any musical request a serviceman made was honored. Men of all races, all branches of the armed forces and all ranks, officers and enlisted men alike, were welcome. The music, designed to appeal to the young servicemen, included no marches, patriotic tunes, or religious music, making it very difficult for any of the "proper " war songs supported by the OWI or the Music War Committee to gain support. What they wanted was music to dance to, and the bands supplied plenty.[10]

The Billboard was of the opinion that "our current pops are far removed from the boys' present experiences and our 'war songs' have no reality to lads who are learning how to annihilate Fascists, so they get their belts from the solid stuff [swing and jazz]."[11] *Billboard* speculated that the musicians in the service who had been members of lesser-known dance bands—the so-called "Mickey Mouse bands," sometimes called "sweet bands" such as Sammy Kaye's, Kay Kyser's, and Guy Lombardo's—before the war might be "indulging themselves in forbidden fruit and are off on a jazz kick and pushing it for all it's worth." And although servicemen were content with such music, the OWI and others prominent in the war effort on the home front did not think swing tunes and love songs conducive to high morale and a strong fighting spirit. Tabulating the number of swing tunes favored by servicemen on *Billboard's* popularity charts, it is evident that servicemen thought swing well-suited to sustaining their morale. Swing was the music they wanted to hear, whether live, on the radio, or on records.

Why was it so difficult to find a war song that filled the requirements of the OWI and the public? First, it is necessary to take a closer look at the revolution in the music business between the two world wars and the changing technology that stimulated a profound alteration in America's musical environment. Improved technology, such as the electric phonograph and radio, made musical innovations instantaneously recognizable and commonplace. An American with a radio could hear new songs and new musical styles as soon as these were introduced from Tin Pan Alley, Broadway, or Hollywood. Americans who had access to one or more of these musical conduits found themselves at the forefront of any invention in the music world. The extraordinary became a daily occurrence. Musical artists, whose appearances were usually limited to large cities, were available to network radio listeners across the nation. The most popular dance bands and orchestras could be heard regularly on the radio—for "free."

Both of these innovations, the phonograph with the record changer that allowed more than one song to be loaded on the player at a time and the radio, had the capacity simultaneously to expand the market and to introduce "fresh material" to supplant that which had been "recently" introduced. As a result, the turnover of new songs became a rapid-paced phenomenon.

Following World War I, thanks to the radio's ability to reach a massive audience, the music business boomed. New songs were continually entering the music marketplace and the listening public was constantly primed to hear them. After World War I, songs from the years 1914–1918 were available on phonograph records, and songs dating back to the onset of the twentieth century were available as sheet music, thus preserving virtually an entire generation of music. Americans knew and sang the songs from World War I, and the OWI and the music industry expected the same popularity and longevity for songs of the Second World War. But long before the war was over, the family sing-along had been replaced by the radio and *Your Hit Parade*.[12]

Despite the apparent contentment of the listening public with popular music offered on the airwaves, in the jukeboxes, and in music stores, the lack of a wildly popular war song was lamented in the popular press and show business tabloids. The search for one became a sacred crusade for the music business. The monetary rewards for publishers and performers of the Great American War Song were not mentioned in the press. But the royalties from best-selling songs could make performers and publishers wealthy.

In the September 1943 issue of the *American Mercury*, Mina Lederman wrote a lengthy analysis of the reasons behind the dearth of war songs. She recalled how past American wars "have given us songs that are touching, gay, spirited or deeply moving, and many of enduring vitality."[13] She reminded the reader that the biggest group of war songs such as "Rally Round the Flag, Boys," "Dixie," "Battle Hymn of the Republic," and "When Johnny Comes Marching Home" were written during the time of the Civil War. Lederman recounted the glories of American wars in songs from the ragged armies of the Revolution making a victory tune out of "Yankee-Doodle," and "at an exalted moment in 1814, Francis Scott Key pour[ing] out the words of the 'Star-Spangled Banner.'" Fighting with Spain revived the bawdy, bubbly "Hot Time in the Old Town Tonight," and in 1917 everyone sang "Over There," "Oh, How I Hate to Get up in the Morning," and "Mademoiselle from Armentieres." Lederman said, "World War II is already older than World War I, but to date its songs have been uniformly trivial, their mood lugubrious, even maudlin. Dance music, sweet and hot; swing-jump, scat and jive; boogie-woogie; hill-billy tunes; crooning ditties; torch songs and blues roll off our assembly lines in unprecedented quantity to reach Broadway and Port Darwin simultaneously. Many items are opulently scored, and have rhythm for which American jazz is famous. Yet among them all there isn't a single stirring song that identifies our feeling with the present day."

Lederman charged that the songs of World War II were indistinguishable from those Americans had known for twenty years. These songs "moan of times gone by, of home and the girlfriend and they mention the war only as in 'The White Cliffs of Dover' and 'When the Lights Go on Again,' to yearn for the day it will be over, over there."

But wanting the war to be over, longing for the comforts of everyday life, returning to their homes and all the other familiar things home implied were exactly what the American servicemen said they were fighting for. They had some vague ideas about "freedom," "democracy," and "the American Way of Life," but all could understand the concept of "home." Home meant a number of things: "It was home in the broadest sense they were fighting for: their families, their girlfriends, their growing up, their childhood hopes and ambitions, their very identities."[14] Is it any wonder that the GIs preferred music that reminded them of home and comfort and security? If there was one place the soldiers could escape the war, if only for a little while, it was while listening to a favorite song.

According to top ten popularity charts, servicemen definitely did not want patriotic songs or war tunes of any kind—except the humorous—to intrude on their listening time. Surveys of their musical preferences compiled by *Billboard* in both 1944 and 1945 found that American servicemen preferred the same type of music as did their civilian counterparts. In September 1944 their top three favorite tunes were "I'll Be Seeing You," "Long Ago and Far Away," and "I'll Get By." In July 1945 the favorites were "Don't

Fence Me In," "Rum and Coca-Cola," and "Sentimental Journey." This "GI tune report" proved one thing, according to *Billboard*: "The reason why there hasn't been a 'great war song' is that they don't want war songs . . . [in a] foxhole or training course—they like the same tunes . . . the pattern doesn't change."[15]

Lederman had no patience with those who made the excuse that the present struggle was "too grim, impersonal, and global for the boys to sing about."[16] She pointed to the songs of the Chinese with their brand new guerrilla music and the Russians with "Meadowland," the cavalry tune that became an international hit. Other examples included the French in Africa with their revision of "Madelon" and the British following bagpipers into battle. She argued that it was the Civil War, the bloodiest conflict in American history, that produced the best of our own songs. So, Lederman also wondered, why are there no American war songs spurring the fighting men on to victory?

In answer to such questions, army and federal government officials met in New York City's Town Hall and reviewed current musical practices with alarm. The Treasury Department and the United Service Organization (USO) sent songleaders from coast to coast to lift morale of the war workers and servicemen with a repertory designed to pep them up. The War Department even stepped in to bolster the effort for a proper war song. Through its Special Services Division, the army offered a prize for a new song, and, each month, beginning in March 1943, distributed to the soldiers in training camps a million copies of pocket-sized *Hit Kit* songbooks of patriotic and popular numbers carefully chosen by a group of writers, composers, and show business men and women known to the OWI as the "Committee of 25." These committee members included Goodman Ace (Easy Aces), Fred Allen, Jack Benny, Edgar Bergen, Maj. Edward Bowes, Bob Burns, George Burns, and Gracie Allen. Others were Eddie Cantor, Freeman Gosden and Charles Correll (Amos and Andy), Bing Crosby, Nelson Eddy, Clifton Fadiman, Jean Hersholt, and James Jordan and Marian Jordan (Fibber McGee and Mollie). Also participating as committee members were Andre Kostelanetz, Chester H. Lauck and Morris Goff (Lum and Abner), Frank Morgan, Harold G. Peary (the Great Gildersleeve), Edward G. Robinson, Lanny Ross, Kate Smith, Kay Kyser, Bob Hope, and Red Skelton.[17]

The *Hit Kit* was the Army's own version of *Your Hit Parade*, patterned after the already successful armed forces radio show, *The Army Hour*. After some grumbling about cost and profits, music publishers agreed to donate many of the songs they owned, minus their usual royalty fees. The publishers did, however, charge for orchestral arrangements of the *Hit Kit* tunes. The *Hit Kits* generally incorporated two songs from the ballads and novelty category and four from the marching song category. Songs selected for the first *Hit Kit* were "This Is the Army, Mr. Jones," "Praise the Lord and Pass the Ammunition," "I've Got Sixpence," "Move It Over," "I Had the Craziest Dream," and "There Are Such Things."[18]

The War Department was surprised at the insistence of Bing Crosby and Kate Smith that "There's a Star Spangled Banner Waving Somewhere" be included in a future *Hit Kit*—thinking that these radio stars were much too sophisticated for hillbilly music. But Kate Smith argued that a song selling over one million copies without Tin Pan Alley publicity behind it must certainly be a song Americans cared about.[19]

When composers failed to write the stirring tunes so desired by the War Department, the private sector offered a remedy: a war song contest. On February 7, 1943, a nationwide contest to obtain a patriotic song of "outstanding merit," which would "hypo [boost] public morale and aid the nation's war effort," was sponsored by the NBC radio network and the National Federation of Music Clubs. The judges included Leopold Stokowski and Fred Waring.[20] This competition met with little success. Mina Lederman stated, "Fighting songs are seldom written for prizes, nor can people be led to sing by appealing to their instincts for social service."[21]

Still, the army wanted a rousing war song immediately. The most recent military song, "Over There," did not fit the language of this war. Before World War II, singing had been a traditional outlet for wartime exuberance. But in the Second World War people did not get together as frequently for singing. Lederman also asked, "How often do we hear singing today as troops go marching down the streets? Parades, it's true, are not a big feature of this war. But soldiers and sailors still gather in great numbers, and with them civilians, in theaters and churches, in railroad stations and parks, in dance halls, in night and service clubs, in all places where in earlier wars the air echoed with their voices."[22]

Lederman claimed that inhibitions once dissolved in barbershop harmony were violently released by swing, as could be seen in the jitterbug kids dancing in the aisles of metropolitan movie theaters, the conga lines of posh night spots, or in the "steak joints" of army towns where "the radio blares and the jukeboxes bray."[23] She did not find many songs worth the paper on which they were printed or the shellac on which they were pressed.

The decline of group singing of popular songs can be attributed chiefly to the advance of the machine age upon the music world. Twenty-five years before World War II the music business was a comparatively closed community consisting of the men who ran Tin Pan Alley and later the members of the American Society of Composers, Authors, and Publishers [ASCAP] who sought to professionalize the music business (and also to protect themselves from young, upstart composers).

ASCAP was founded in 1914 in an attempt to force restaurants, theaters, and other establishments featuring live music to pay fees for its public use. Before 1914, copyright protection covered only the purchase and mechanical reproduction of published compositions. Composers, lyricists, and publishers received no compensation from live performances of their music. After a series of legal battles eventually reaching the Supreme Court, ASCAP won its case on January 22, 1917. The ruling stated that all hotels, theaters, dance halls, cabarets, and restaurants were required to obtain a license from ASCAP—for a fee—before they could play a piece written by a composer or published by a publishing house belonging to the ASCAP organization.[24] In time, similar rulings were handed down in cases involving radio stations and motion picture studios.

ASCAP membership increased dramatically in the 1920s, eventually including all important publishing houses and almost all of the leading composers and lyricists of the day, and by the mid-1930s some $10 million in licensing fees were paid annually. Most of the money was distributed to the membership according to a complex rating system. The recording industry was already obliged to pay fees to composers and publishers under the "mechanical reproduction" clause of the copyright law of 1909, which had fixed a fee of three cents per disc or cylinder to be paid to the copyright owner.[25]

The overall effect of these developments in the music business was that each of the new media—the phonograph record, the radio, and the sound movie—obtained its music from ASCAP composers and publishers, whose chief concern was with the type of music already being produced, rather than with new styles of music perhaps more appropriate to the new technology. The ASCAP members did not want to trifle with success; they knew what sold and how to write it. The songs performed on radio and in the movies were written in a style born in vaudeville and other forms of musical theater in the late-nineteenth and early-twentieth centuries.[26]

The style of Tin Pan Alley remained constant, even in the face of these astounding technological changes. There were two reasons for this constancy. One was political (meaning the control of power and leadership in the music business): ASCAP membership was the exclusive property of the men of Tin Pan Alley. The other reason was musical: the style was not that old.

The dominant reason for the persistence of a single musical style in popular songs of the Tin Pan Alley era is simply that this musical style was vibrant, successful, somewhat flexible, and relatively new in the history of popular song forms. Changes in musical style, in popular songs as in other forms of music, happen when the dominant style has been in use for a considerable period of time and composers think that it is beginning to be exhausted, when audiences get bored, and when a style has lost its "cutting edge," in the words of Virgil Thomson, noted American composer and music critic.[27]

The first third of the twentieth century saw a large number of extremely talented songwriters exploiting a song style that was not yet dated and that could still be modified so that each of the composers was able to craft a distinctive musical personality. Thus, the first half of the twentieth century experienced a conflict between two cycles—a musical one, still in its strong formative stages, and an emerging technological one that made possible, at least in theory, some radically new concepts in song. In this instance, musical impulses proved to be stronger than technology.

The Tin Pan Alley song, with almost no exceptions, was in the verse-chorus form; the verse sketched a dramatic situation or an emotional vignette, and the chorus followed as a "set" piece. The chorus was a more lyrical section, usually elaborating on the situation outlined by the verse.[28] The verse-chorus form of Tin Pan Alley songs functioned in much the same way as the recitative-aria pattern in opera. A single verse became standard by the 1920s, and even this was often omitted in non-stage performances. Within a decade, Tin Pan Alley composers began treating the verse as an optional part of a song.

Although most songs of the 1930s and 1940s continued to be written in verse-chorus form, the verses were seldom performed or recorded, appearing only on the published sheet music. The chorus of Tin Pan Alley songs was almost always arranged in four sections of equal length. The chorus was usually thirty-two measures in length, making each of the four sections eight measures long. The only exceptions came from a doubling of chorus measures in songs of lively tempos (to sixty-four measures) or from extensions of the last phrase. The four sections are usually in AABA or ABAC patterns, with occasional variations such as AABC and ABCA.[29] Thus the talent and versatility of Tin Pan Alley composers and lyricists was repeatedly demonstrated by what could be accomplished within a strictly determined formal structure. Of course, the cleverness of Tin Pan Alley composers could also be seen as formulaic writing, which would eventually cause the name—Tin Pan Alley—to become synonymous with mass produced, "canned" music.

The 1920s and 1930s were an era of specialization in popular song. There were composers, lyricists, performers, and publishers; it was rare for a person to be involved in more than one of these areas. This period saw the rise of the lyricist to a place of importance equivalent to composers. At the turn of the century, the average price paid a writer for a song lyric had been five dollars, with no further claim on a song's earnings. But as the popular music business moved into a period of unequaled prosperity, there was greater appreciation for the importance of a good lyric to the success of the song. With the formation of ASCAP, lyricists were regarded as the equal of composers and shared both publishers' royalties and the annual ASCAP fund from licensing fees.[30]

Initially, the verses the lyricists produced dealt with a wide range of situations and emotions. As America moved into the 1920s and 1930s, the expressive range of popular song narrowed. Texts began dealing almost exclusively with personal emotions, almost never with outside events. An increasingly large percentage of most popular songs was concerned with various aspects of romantic love. A glance at the titles on any representative list of the most popular songs of the period between 1915 and 1935, such as publisher Chappell & Company, Incorporated's list of major hits songs, is enough to verify this generalization. Observers of trends in popular music were quite aware of this shift. The sentimental ballads before 1920 were often about babies, separation, and death: "After the Ball," by Charles K. Harris ("Long years have passed child / I've never wed / True to my lost love / Though she is dead"), and "In the Baggage Coach Ahead," by Gussie L. Davis ("Never a word said the man with the child / As he fondled it close to his breast / 'Where is the mother go take it to her,' this a lady then softly said / 'I wish I could,' was the man's sad reply / 'But she's dead in the coach ahead.') The theme of the sentimental songs two generations later was "the impotence of the male. . . . They celebrated sadly the failure of the man to keep his woman."[31]

And a songwriter of the period suggested that the preoccupation with personal love was a mirror of the times: "The Twenties sang of carefree nights and the frenetic days that rushed headlong into the nightmare and fantasy of the Thirties. Both had their reality, both voiced it. This was a score of years in which love grew from an idle and pleasant pastime into a vital avocation—romance."[32]

It is nearly impossible to find popular songs from the 1920s and 1930s that connect with or comment on in any way the great social and political issues of the period. Popular music generated by Tin Pan Alley did not mention the acute economic and social situation of African Americans; the struggle of working class citizens to unionize and their exploitation by owners and managers; the worsening situation of ethnic minorities, most notably the Jews, in Central and Eastern Europe; or the rise to power of totalitarian rule in many of these countries. These topics were left to "folk" singers, composers affiliated with the American Communist Party, union organizers, and African American blues singers.

A few popular songs dealt with the Great Depression, such as "Brother, Can You Spare a Dime?" and "Ten Cents a Dance." They stand alone in their subject matter: poverty. Other songs written with the Depression as a background were completely unresponsive to the plight of a large number of Americans. Instead these songs included cheerful, bouncy numbers like "Beyond the Blue Horizon," "Get Happy," "On the Sunny Side of the Street," "Life is Just a Bowl of Cherries," "Smile, Darn Ya, Smile," "Let's Have Another Cup of Coffee," "Let's Put Out the Lights and Go to Sleep," "We're in the Money," and "Who's Afraid of the Big Bad Wolf?"

These songs invited listeners to "leave your worries on the doorstep," "forget your troubles come on get happy," or, if faced with "no more money in the bank," just "put out the lights and go to sleep." Is it any wonder, then, that the United States produced so few war songs during World War II? Outright war-theme songs such as "Praise the Lord and Pass the Ammunition," "We Did It Before and We Can Do It Again," and "Comin' in on a Wing and a Prayer" made up a small percentage of the songs written during the war years.

In 1942, American's first full year in the war, 17 percent of all popular songs reaching the top ten charts were war songs. During the four years of World War II, twenty-seven war songs reached the top ten charts, but most lasted only a few weeks.[33] They did not have staying power. War songs were not what Tin Pan Alley specialized in, and as a result the view of the world offered to the American listening public was that of a small group of songwriters in New York City and a burgeoning group of transplanted ASCAP composers in Hollywood.

Tin Pan Alley's stance on the content and style of American popular song was a deliberate one. These songwriters were tied directly to the most powerful elements of the Broadway musical stage and the Hollywood film musical. The "Moguls" who ran Hollywood and Broadway were mostly Jewish Americans (Samuel Goldwyn, Louis B. Mayer, William Fox, the Warner Brothers, the Selznicks, Marcus Lowe, Nicholas and Joseph Schenck), described by Irving Howe in *World of Our Fathers* as, "Often vulgar, crude, and overbearing . . . fully attuned to the needs of their business . . . with a profound instinct for the common denominator of taste."[34] These men left a deep imprint on American culture; they knew when to appeal to sentiment, "which twirl of fantasy, which touch of violence, which innuendo of sexuality" to use to capture American audiences—natives and immigrants alike. The entertainment moguls believed that these media were best used to entertain people, to take their minds away from personal and national problems—not to remind them of such things.

American popular song moved toward urbanization, much as the United States itself did, beginning in the late nineteenth century. This transference of popular song from its rural roots was effectively completed in the 1910s and 1920s. By the 1930s and 1940s the field was monopolized by composers and lyricists born and trained in New York, who wrote songs for publishers based in New York City. "The style of the music and of the lyrics had become a New York style, [and] general attitudes as to what a song should be and where it should fit into American culture were also shaped by [the] taste of New York."[35] There was little effective cultural input from the rest of America into New York in the time leading up to World War II. Tin Pan Alley songs reflected American culture in the first half of the twentieth century because the rest of the country was willing to accept a uniquely urban, New York view as representing all of America. Hollywood music was a West Coast extension of New York. The songs of Kern, Gershwin, Porter, and their contemporaries were cosmopolitan, sophisticated, and fashionable, and they were aimed at people who could be described by one or more of these adjectives—or people who hoped to be.[36]

The result of all this was a product accepted all over America. Tin Pan Alley songs were written and produced for white, literate, urban, middle- and upper-class Americans. The songs remained practically unknown to large groups of Americans, especially in the rural areas, until the 1920s and 1930s. The new technology that established commercial radio, along with wide dissemination of the phonograph record, brought popular music within reach of the majority of Americans.

Just as the popular music of the first thirty years of the twentieth century was written for a limited audience, the music industry's writers, composers, and publishers thought of themselves as an exclusive group. ASCAP was a closed society with membership restricted to those who had a proven track record of compositions and successes. Prior to ASCAP the music business was a hit-or-miss proposition with a wide-open market. In the years between the wars, the music business expanded to the dimensions of a large-scale industry, thanks to the radio, the phonograph, the jukebox, and the sound film.

Mass distribution of music brought about by technological innovations was widely praised, though there was another side to the musical revolution. The American public had little understanding of the degree to which every musically productive source was controlled. Broadcasting and recording companies even influenced the repertories of the symphony orchestras whose deficits they helped to defray. For nearly twenty years before the war, broadcast companies, together with movie corporations, shaped the range of popular music's output.[37]

According to Mina Lederman, as a result of this control of the music business by the broadcasters, some of the dubious effects incidental to mass merchandising finally came to light in the years preceding World War II, "effects which neither the customers—the vast and generally inert public—nor the music industry itself has yet learned to counteract."[38] For

Lederman, the most flagrant violation of public trust by the music business was its failure to produce a good militant war song.

> Producing a good war song was not the most difficult task composers faced; getting it before the public offered a real challenge. The pattern of life and promotion for a popular song hit had changed radically from the days of World War I. Before 1917, a song would go from the stage directly to the people listening in the theater and from there it would spread across the country through sheet music sales. It lived until people stopped singing it. The music business was still fluid; its outlets were sensitive to the changing mood of the time. Spontaneous hits were possible and frequent.[39]

During World War II thousands of songs were written and recorded, but only a small percentage were promoted by the publishers. If a song was not given time on the radio or played by dance bands, it had little chance of survival. In uncertain times publishers preferred to stay with known composers and successful formulas.

Lederman determined that eighteen months after Pearl Harbor the popular music industry was still solidly embedded in its pre-war pattern as "composers, writers, publishers, arrangers, bandleaders, networks and jukeboxes give us for nightly consumption 'Moonlight,' 'That Old Black Magic,' and 'Taking a Chance on Love.'"[40] She was particularly incensed that a ten-year-old number, "As Time Goes By," was revived and promoted to the number one place on *Your Hit Parade*.

Another reason for the lack of a war song was that radio, as a mass purveyor of musical goods, had to keep the songs moving at a fast pace. It was, in effect, a killer of good songs because the turnover of popular songs was so rapid that a likely candidate for the top spot lasted a relatively short time on the popularity charts. A pre-radio "smash" hit usually lasted from one and a half to two years, sometimes longer. After the introduction of the radio into American homes, rather than a tune being spread gradually across the country, millions heard a popular song simultaneously, and generally it was "played to death within three months or less."[41] This rapid turnover also had a positive effect: songs that were topical or were part of a fad mercifully left the airwaves almost as rapidly as they came.

Another obstacle in the path of a hit war song was the fact that the radio, record player, and jukebox enforced the habit of passive listening. The commercial message was the lifeblood of the radio station, so the radio broadcasters, in choice of material and style, sought to have the listener in a receptive state. The use of recordings tended to develop listeners with an acute preference for a special type of music that usually involved passive listening. The jukebox might elicit physical response in the form of dancing, but active participation by playing or singing along was not encouraged. As Lederman pointed out: "Lawrence Tibbett, [an opera star] . . .visits Army and Navy Camps, . . . he finds the waiting boys always gathered around a radio or phonograph. In the last war, they sang loudly and lustily. Now someone does it for them, so why should they?"[42]

In the broad repertory of war music, nostalgia has a special place. Every war produces new songs about home and sweethearts. According to Lederman, if World War II songs followed this historic pattern, nostalgia would, in time, assume larger dimensions. It usually combined with lost buddies and scenes of battle to give the public songs with tragic overtones. But "songs of deep longing, melancholy, exultation, even of simple high spirits" could not easily break into Tin Pan Alley's structure.

This Is the Army, the government's own show written by Irving Berlin, was a monumental effort to shift from musical low gear to militant high gear. Designed, produced and plugged for "morale," it included a number of march tunes, including "This Is the Army, Mr. Jones." But the big hit of the show turned out to be "I Left My Heart at the Stage Door Canteen," a love song of the boy-meets-girl variety. Lederman, noting the contrast with the morale-raising aim of *This Is the Army*, was stumped by the success of Irving Berlin's "White Christmas," also a 1942 creation, but one designed to bring "a lump to the throat of every doughboy from here to India." She even wondered why Berlin would write such a song as "White Christmas" in wartime. In her view, this song, along with Cole Porter's "You'd Be So Nice to Come Home To," ran counter to the job that the popular music business should be about in a wartime setting.[43]

The popular music business claimed to be doing its mightiest to produce "proper" war songs. But by tabulating record sales, the popularity of radio broadcasts featuring the current dance band favorites, and the requests for current hits by Americans in the armed services, it is apparent that Mina Lederman's complaints about popular music and the lack of a war song did not seem important to the men and women in uniform.

Music publishers did not take any chances, either. The boys in the armed services wanted something that sounded just like the radio they left behind: "Hot, heavy, and with a heart-throb."[44] As *Billboard* expressed Tin Pan Alley's case, why risk any changes when you have a system that "rings the bell every time?" Broadcasters claimed to be ready to take a chance on war instead of love, if only the publishers, arrangers, bandleaders, and singers would cooperate.[45]

Chapter 10

"From Cantata to Outright Corn"

From the beginning of the United States' involvement in World War II, it was apparent to the music business that the American public was not overly interested in bloodthirsty martial songs. Although the American Society of Composers, Authors, and Publishers president, Gene Buck, urged members on December 8, 1941, to "do their bit" for the crisis by writing "fighting songs,"[1] others in the music business doubted that the American public was inclined toward war songs. Publishers declared that the only way to find out was to put such songs into circulation. Marching melodies in manuscript form were dusted off and given to competent lyricists, and publishers waited for the fighting songs to roll in. Tin Pan Alley cited the experience of London's music business following the beginning of the war. At first the British had a flurry of fighting songs: "We Must All Stick Together," "Wings Over the Navy," and "We're Gonna Hang out the Washing on the Siegfried Line," but then the mood shifted, and they were interested mainly in popular tunes with themes of nostalgia and the anticipation of peace: "Wishing," "We'll Meet Again," and "Wish Me Luck."[2]

In the United States, music consumption followed much the same pattern. Prior to the attack on Pearl Harbor, the best-selling sheet music roster in America for the week ending December 6, 1941, listed simple, cheerful, and romantic songs such as, "Tonight We Love," "Shepherd Serenade," "Chattanooga Choo Choo," "I Don't Want to Set the World on Fire," and "Why Don't We Do This More Often?" These same tunes were listed in *Variety*'s "10 Best Sellers on Coin-Machines" for the same date.[3] This would seem to indicate a pattern similar to the British musical trend.

By mid-December 1941, U.S. music publishers started to reappraise some of the war songs that had come out of England. To maintain neutrality, they had been staying away from any British war songs. They also looked for songs to cheer the public; one publisher kept a list of what he termed as "smile" songs, including "A Smile Will Go a Long, Long Way," "Smiles," "Let a Smile Be Your Umbrella," and "Smile, Darn Ya, Smile."[4] The idea was that the war was going to be gruesome and Americans would need cheery diversions. Publishers also realized they could not make a living selling war songs only. People would need some variety in their choice of entertainment, and Tin Pan Alley proposed to offer its patrons an assortment of tunes.

As early as January 7, 1942, *Variety* reported that the English public's sentiment was definitely negative toward war or patriotic songs of the "There'll Always Be an England" type. Abel Green, editor of *Variety*, said, "The majority of people feel that they get enough of the war in the newspapers and they don't want it in their music."[5]

American publishers blamed others for the failure of war songs to sell; their main targets were dance-band leaders. Publishers said there was a change in the musical taste of Americans, but the bandleaders were not aware of it because they were too immersed in their own egos and "swing fantasies" to give the public the type of patriotic songs it wanted. Jack Robbins of Robbins Music Corporation stated, "Leaders are still living in a world of their own and are loathe to yield themselves to playing music of the times."[6]

The lack of interest on the part of the bandleaders had "discouraged wider acceptance and publication" of these tunes. And, according to *Variety*, "The average jumparoo band, they hold, feels that such tunes are corny and if they play them their followers will drift away from them."[7]

Leo Feist, of Leo Feist, Incorporated, recalled with other publishers the advantages they had enjoyed in World War I when a song's popularity did not depend on dance bands but on vaudeville singers who were closer to the "temper of the times" and were quick to respond to songs that reflected the "current thoughts and feelings of the people."[8] This observation indicates that even music publishers had not realized the full extent of the changes in the music business brought about by advanced technology and the rise in popularity of dance bands since World War I.

Feist seemed to think that music publishers had lost control of song promotion and longed for the days when vaudeville performers plugged the publishers' work. In his observation, Feist neglected to mention that vaudeville singers might possibly have had a financial interest in promoting a song to best-seller status. Vocalists' pictures usually appeared on the covers of sheet music with which the singers had (or hoped to) become identified. Often the words "As introduced by," "As made famous by," or "As sung by" were printed on the front cover. Sheet music acted as advertising for both the song and the singer.

Publishers also offered singers a percentage of profit on sheet music sales in payment for their song-plugging services, so it would appear publishers had more control of their product when vaudeville was the primary mode that Tin Pan Alley used to sell songs. When the music industry changed from vaudeville to recorded music as the primary means of reaching the public, the emphasis changed from the actual song to the performance. Rather than singing the songs themselves (using sheet music), people sought out particular recorded performances of a song.

By March 11, 1942, W.H. Lewis, former CBS vice president and then Federal Radio Coordinator for the Office of War Information, had had enough of what he termed "prima donna" behavior and began chastising the music business for its petty jealousies, frequent squabbles, and noisy bickering. He said, "Unless all pull together to smite the common enemy the desired ends cannot be achieved."[9]

Music publishers were not alone in their skepticism about the first flood of war melodies being turned out in early 1942. Coin-machine operators (the men who serviced jukeboxes and provided the recordings for them) closed their machines to most of the war tunes. *Variety* said, "They shrug off new tunes with quick . . . bored dismissal . . . adding pointed remarks about the quality of the majority of the numbers."[10] The coin-machine operators thought that too many tunes had been written and that few of them would make money. One operator said that most of his machines were in barrooms and similar venues, and that he had had requests to "remove war tune discs he had inserted." Standard numbers like the "Marines' Hymn" were acceptable, but all of the music written after December 7, with the exception of "Remember Pearl Harbor," was unsatisfactory. Very few jukebox operators went against their customers' wishes, and the war songs were removed from the machines.

In order to bolster the impression that the music business was actively doing its part for the war effort, the Music Publishers Protective Association began encouraging its members to print patriotic slogans on the title page of sheet music. "Buy U.S. Bonds and Stamps," "Let's Go U.S.A.," and "Keep 'Em Flying" were just a few of the slogans that graced sheet music in the ensuing years.[11] By April 15, 1942, just four months after the attack on Pearl Harbor, the Music Publishers Protective Association's title registration division announced that it had not had a new war song added to its files in weeks. Music publishers stayed away from war songs unless there was a novelty or romantic twist to them, claiming that Americans would not take to a fighting song until the United States had rung up "a few resounding victories." As one put it, "Apparently this is one war that American people don't want to sing about until it's won and over."[12]

There was a tremendous amount of discussion in Tin Pan Alley regarding the lack of a good war song. Composer Isham Jones, the bandleader who wrote "You're in the Army Now" during World War I, thought that "America is too mad about this war to do much singing. There won't be any warblin' until we're winnin.'" He continued, "You see, we never took a licking before. . . . In fact, we never have known the taste of defeat until now. We don't like it and we don't feel like singing as long as that taste is still in our mouth."[13]

What were people singing? Old war songs, those written during World War I, were the most popular at the military training camps in the weekly community sings. Maj. Harold A. Vorhees found that "K-K-K-Katie," "Goodbye Broadway, Hello France," "Tipperary," and "Yankee Doodle" were preferred over the more modern songs.[14]

The U.S. naval victory at the Battle of Midway, June 4, 1942, and the accomplishments of the Allies in Western Europe and Africa boosted music sales, proving the publishers correct in their assertion that there was nothing wrong with the industry that a few victories couldn't cure. Sheet music sales soared by 40 percent in the week following the U.S. Navy's defeat of the Japanese at Midway. The upsurge in sales was not boosted by a "hot" song. There were no new hit songs introduced at this time; the best-sellers had been on the list for over a month.[15] The boom in sheet music sales was paralleled by the public's general outlook on the war. The OWI's "Surveys of Public Attitudes" showed an increased confidence about winning the war against Germany and Japan. When five thousand Americans were asked in August 1942, two months after Midway, "Which of these four statements comes closest to the way you feel the war with Germany and Japan is going?," they replied:

1. We have practically beaten them	4%
2. It may take time but we cannot lose	63%
3. Unless we work harder, we will not win	28%
4. It looks as if it is too late	1%
5. Do not know	4%

When this same question was asked in December 1942, the confidence level of Americans had risen even higher:

1. We have practically beaten them	8%
2. It may take time, but we cannot lose	72%
3. Unless we work harder, we will not win	17%
4. It looks as if it is too late	less than 1%
5. Do not know	3%

By the following June, after a year of difficult fighting, the American public's optimism had reached new heights. The same questions were asked of five thousand people with the following results:

1. We have practically beaten them	8%
2. It may take time, but we cannot lose	73%
3. Unless we work harder, we will not win	15%
4. It looks as if it is too late	1%
5. Do not know	3%[16]

Despite the bolstered confidence of the American public, the dearth of war songs persisted. The public still preferred sentimental or romantic songs. If by chance a war song caught the public's attention, it was usually a topical or novelty song. According to the OWI, "The only fighting tunes that have clicked since Dec. 7, even in a moderate fashion, are 'We Did It Before and We Can Do It Again' and 'Remember Pearl Harbor,' and these had their run months ago."[17]

Professional show business managers, once again, contended that the industry's failure to "sell" a fighting song was due more than anything else to its principal source of exploitation: radio. For a martial song to produce a real emotional impact, they pointed out, it was necessary for the listener to see the song actually performed and to be part of a crowd where proximity to others generated the reaction. In the last war, there had been a steady, slow procession of war songs because vaudeville audiences served as the chief determinant of a war song's life. But *Variety* concluded that the First World War's crowd psychology was missing from the Second World War, which contributed to the lack of good war songs: "It is easy to assume . . . that one or two persons . . . listening to the same radio aren't likely to get the same emotional lift from even a patriotic tune as . . . these same two persons [as] part . . . of several hundred or several thousand. . . . the spirit of the people may not have changed, but the channel for getting at this spirit is certainly different and in no small measure a handicap to the business of selling war songs."[18]

Immediately after its formation, the OWI urged songwriters and music publishers to pay more attention to the war tunes they were producing and to try to avoid what the OWI called "tactless" war songs. The government suggested that songs of the "Slap the Jap" and "Goodbye Mamma, I'm Off to Yokohama" variety that belittled the size and power of the enemy were "unwise." The "peace-and-ease" songs about the future like "The White Cliffs of Dover" also annoyed the OWI at a time when there was still "a war to be won and hardships to be endured."[19] One of the few songs that the OWI pointed to as properly serious and morale boosting was "This Is Worth Fighting For." But it did not sell.

Clearly the production of war songs had not gone as the government thought it should in 1942, and propagandists in Washington, especially William B. Lewis of OWI, were anxious to remedy the situation. He announced plans for a series of conferences between OWI officials and representatives of the music industry. Lewis wanted songwriters and publishers to concentrate on songs that would both boost morale and sell. The OWI perplexed and sometimes amused the music business. As *Variety* editor Abel Green noted, "Song hits are not easily picked nor are artificial selections easily put over on the public."[20]

A preliminary meeting was held in New York City, July 15, 1942, between popular music publishers and a representative of the OWI, Domestic Radio Bureau coordinator Elmer Davis, who was acting for William B. Lewis. At this meeting Davis stressed that the OWI wanted more "fighting" songs and "less boy-meets-girl roseate stuff" to better prepare the public for the "glum long war" ahead.[21]

The music publishers agreed that the runaway success of a war song like George M. Cohan's "Over There" was inexplicable and that "the wrong kind of slushy stuff unsuitable to tough times should be kept in the publisher's safe until after the war as a matter of patriotism."[22] In short, the OWI wanted to encourage lyrics that supported the war, or, failing that, to at least check the kind of "drivel" that might handicap fighting and winning it.

The music industry leaders at this meeting were some of the most powerful men in publishing and broadcasting. They should have been able to solve the problem of a war song, but even the best informed and most powerful people in the music industry had difficulties finding a war song for the country. At this meeting were Edwin Hughes, president of the National Music Council; Harry Fox, general manager of the Music Publishers Protective Association, whose function was to guide the publishers toward "correct" war songs; Sigmund Romberg, who helped set "correct" guidelines for the songsmiths; Manie Sachs, recording director of Columbia Phonograph, who was liaison to the recording companies; Philip Carlin, program director of the CBS Blue Network, who would lead the radio networks; Lloyd Egner, manager of Thesaurus Transcriptions, who programmed recordings with the "proper" war song material; John O'Connor, president of the Music Contact Men's Union, a "songplugging" (music advertising) agency that was an important go-between in the propagation of war songs; and Ralph Peer, the music publisher (Southern Music and Peer International, San Antonio, Texas) who was also on Nelson Rockefeller's Latin American coordinating committee. These men were to set the tone for the music industry's cooperation with the federal government's "morale planners."[23]

On July 28, 1942, W.B. Lewis, the Federal Radio Coordinator of the OWI's radio division, came to New York from Washington to speak at the Songwriters Protective Association dinner. This was part of the OWI's drive to stimulate a war idiom in American popular song. The campaign against "tactless" songs was reiterated to the songwriters, along with the prime objective of the OWI: "The need for a new high standard in the U.S. pop [songs] standard so as to best get across the cause of Democracy to America and our Allies."[24]

At the July 28, 1942, meeting, Sigmund Romberg, noted composer of operettas and president of the Songwriters Protective Association, stated: "The need is for songs to be sung by the fighters rather than at them," and Lewis said that a little extra effort would lead to the publication of "worthier" fighting songs that would result in getting the message across to the American public.[25]

Despite these congenial meetings there were grumbling voices in the music industry, many of which preferred to remain anonymous. One such publisher wrote *Variety* to complain that not only were "tactless" war songs a problem, but there were also shortcomings in the catalog of war songs. The most notable seemed to be the fact that "the bulk of our published war songs are not really war songs at all, but the old boy-girl songs re-staged in a war setting, or rehashed with a bit of military terminology."[26] He also noted that some of the most competent lyricists and composers were ignored by the music business when they offered a song that did not present the war in boy-girl terms.

One songwriter, Bernie Grossman, complained that he and others faced many obstacles when they attempted to sell war songs. The first was finding a title that would garner attention so that artists would record or perform a song. The second hurdle was finding a music publisher. The publishers, already wary of war songs, wanted tunes that would sell. Grossman added that "the bandleader, the broadcaster and recording artist . . . will tell you (as they have told me), 'We don't want any war songs, there is enough war talk on the air by commentators and the newspapers are chuckful of it. We are not interested.'"[27] The American people did not need or want a war song to motivate them, and war songs simply did not make money.

There was another problem. American servicemen were not particularly interested in war songs. Entertainer George Price said that in traveling to the various military camps, he had discovered "the soldiers don't want any war or patriotic songs. They want old favorites and gang songs . . . they don't want to be reminded of the war in song."[28]

Gracie Fields, an English comedienne who had just returned from a ten-week tour of the battlefront in Europe, explained why war songs failed to catch the attention of the soldiers: there were "too many tanks and planes and trucks. . . . Soldiers are on the move . . . never do enough of them stay in one place long enough for a tune to sweep [through] divisions and armies."[29] On one hand, Fields told *The Milwaukee Journal* that the soldiers knew as many of the new popular songs as any civilian; they learned them by radio. On the other hand, she said that the soldiers requested old songs and always asked for "Ave Maria" or "The Lord's Prayer." But the absolute favorite of the men wherever she appeared was a little ditty about army life:

> Don't be angry with me, sergeant,
> Don't say what you're going to say—
> Don't call me what you called me yesterday.
> Don't say rude things about my parents.
> Remember, they're the only ones I've known;
> And some day, tho you are a sergeant,
> You might have some parents of your own.[30]

An OWI survey of army camps throughout the United States found that soldiers wanted to hear dance music above all else, but a rousing patriotic number on the order of "Over There," though not necessary to win the war, would certainly be welcomed. In the meantime, American troops were singing "Jingle, Jangle, Jingle" while the British were belting out "The Beer Barrel Polka"—neither of which had much war flavor.[31]

In answer to the accusation that music publishers favored songs with a boy-girl sentiment and played down those with a martial spirit, Jack Robbins, music publisher, listed a number of patriotic songs his firm had issued. Further, Robbins proposed to publish any ten songs selected by the OWI or by a committee of the top ten dance-band leaders and outstanding vocalists such as Kate Smith, Dinah Shore, Bing Crosby, Rudy Vallee, and Barry Wood, and promised to donate his company's profits to the USO.

Robbins was quick to point out that the American public might surprise the music business by discriminating between patriotic songs and "rah-rah" war songs. By this Robbins meant patriotic songs in the same vein as "America," "Battle Hymn of the Republic," and "God Bless America," and not simple-minded, cheerful tunes of bravado such as "Cranky Old Yank in a Clanky Old Tank," "Nimitz and Halsey and Me!," "Gee, Isn't It Great to Be an American!," "Hey, Tojo! Count Yo' Men!," "I'm a Son of a Son of a Yankee Doodle," "Shout Wherever You May Be—I Am an American," "You'll Be Sorr-ee!," and "Thank Your Lucky Stars and Stripes."

The following song titles, from the Metro-Robbins syndicate of music publishers, were only a few of the hundreds of war-theme songs that failed to appear on *Your Hit Parade*: "Ballad for Americans," "Uncle Sam Gets Around," "I Hear America Singing," "Uncle Sam Stands Up," "The American's Creed," and "Me and My Uncle Sam."[32] Most of these songs were never recorded, or if they were, they had a limited release. Minor artists and studio bands were usually called on to perform. Not one of these songs was recorded by a well-known artist. That fact alone meant these tunes would yield low sales figures. The best of these tunes sold only a few thousand copies of sheet music.

Music publishers continued to blame the bandleaders for not exposing the public to war songs. Jack Robbins contended that some bandleaders were only interested in their own publishing houses and "seemed to think the war has no connection with their lives."[33] People were interested in hearing inspiring patriotic tunes, he thought, but the bands would not play them. Robbins's solution was to put pressure on bandleaders, by way of a committee of publishers, talent agency executives, and star performers empowered to force performances of worthy war songs. In his words, "Only when you force selfish people to co-operate will you get any results."[34]

Robbins had a vested interest in performance of "worthy war songs," as his publishing company had a large stock of patriotic tunes but very few current popular hits. Bandleaders used their own publishing houses to supplement their incomes, so it was natural they would play tunes they owned or had recorded.

The U.S. military circumstances up to this point had been discouraging. The war started with a series of defeats and stalemates, leading government officials to worry that the people might become demoralized or impatient for peace. As *Time* magazine observed, during the first six months after the Japanese attack on Pearl Harbor, the United States had not "taken a single inch of enemy territory, not yet beaten the enemy in a major battle of land, not yet opened an offensive campaign."[35]

The government was especially concerned that a significant portion of Americans would be anxious for a compromise settlement with Germany. A mid-1942 survey indicated "three out of every ten Americans would view favorably a negotiated peace with the German army leaders."[36] With nearly a third of the population willing to settle for a compromise peace, the government's demands and commitments to meet the stated war aims seemed threatened. The government went on the offensive. And so did the OWI.

By August 25, 1942, it was clear to the OWI that every branch of the entertainment business would have to be involved in a comprehensive government plan "to aid in and encourage the writing of rousing war songs." W.B. Lewis said it was important to "sell Federal officials the importance of not neglecting" this major psychological need of the war. Lewis's theory was that everyone who had an interest in songs, from the writers and composers to the sales clerk in the music store, should participate in whipping up public enthusiasm, since, in Lewis's words, "a nation that sings can never be beaten."[37] The nation was singing, all right, it just was not singing "proper" war songs.

Following Lewis' initial talk to the songwriters in July 1942, a secret trade (music business) committee designated by Lewis and described as "a group of disinterested publishers" began sifting through hundreds of compositions looking for the "right kind" of war songs. Those songs deemed worthy by the Lewis committee were returned to the authors with a list of publishers who insisted they were interested in good war songs.[38]

Some music publishers were angered by the OWI's tendency to exclude them from meetings with composers on the war song problem. One complained, "The government has made no requests to us, but has wasted time talking to the songwriters. . . . It's up to us to interpret public tastes, and if the government had only come to me I would have set it straight." The publisher continued, "I know for a fact that the public doesn't want fighting songs . . . you can't write songs to order." He warned readers that "Somebody Else Is Taking My Place" was voted most popular song among the soldiers, and "This Is Worth Fighting For," a good war song, was not selling. "Until such time as the Government is ready to foot the bill I'm not going to lose money printing fighting songs. If you want to quote me, say that I am all for fighting songs, tho!"[39]

This publisher's attitude was typical. They were first and foremost in business to make money, and the government was not going to reimburse the publishers for their losses. If war songs flopped, the publishers were out the expenses of printing, promotion, and payment of fees or royalties to the songwriters. But these men did not want to appear greedy or uncooperative and so continued to insist they were eager to help find the Great American War Song. Walter Douglas of the Music Publishers' Protective Association said, "We can't write the songs. All we can do is publish them, if we think they're worth publishing. The Office of War Information has spoken to the songwriters and the rest is up to them."[40]

Some of the publishers might have feared losing control of the music industry to the government. After all, music publishers were the most powerful part of the industry. Without their approval, no song was published. They were also in a battle with record producers to obtain the first rights to songs. Any move that threatened music publishers, such as consulting with composers and performing artists without the publishers, too, concerned them. Government interference in the established method of song production was not popular on 42nd Street.

Joe Davis, head of a small publishing firm, believed that the government was wrong—that there were many good war songs available, but bandleaders simply would not play them in the belief that people would not like them. Davis also echoed Jack Robbins's argument that many bandleaders were more concerned with the success of their own publishing ventures than promoting war songs. Bandsmen, writers, and even some publishers thought that if the music industry put as much energy behind good songs as it did bad ones, the good songs would inevitably catch on and perform the desired morale-building job the OWI and others were so concerned about. These people believed that neither songwriters nor bandleaders were going to cooperate until the publishers (who supported the writers and supplied the leaders) indicated that they were ready to pitch in.[41]

One music publishing firm that did turn out a remarkable number of war songs—almost on an assembly line basis—was Fred Waring's company, Words & Music, Inc. It published songs for every branch of the armed services, and most of these were then recorded by Decca. Some of these war songs included "Look Out Below (Song of the Paratroopers)," "Roll, Tanks, Roll," "Song for the Unsung: The Men of the Merchant Marine," "Cadets of the Army Air Corps," "Sky Anchors (Naval Aviation Song)," "Song of the M.P.'s," "High Away (With the Air Transport Command)," "Man to Man (Infantry Song)," "The Flying Marines," "A Toast to the Army Air Corps," and "Army Hymn."[42] "Fire Up! (A Marching Song of the Chemical Warfare Service)," by Meredith Willson, is typical of the march-type songs published by Words & Music, Inc., and recorded by Fred Waring's Pennsylvanians:

It's hip, hip, hooray!
For the CHEMICAL WARFARE SERVICE ev'rywhere,
On the sea, in the field and in the air,
It's FIRE UP! Carry on to victory. . . .

It seemed as if no area of military service was to be overlooked by Fred Waring and his stable of writers. Even the military police were given a musical tribute, also in march tempo with a forgettable tune by Fred Waring and Jack Dolph, in "Song of the M.P.'s":

When artillery is blasting and equipment's moving up,
And a traffic jam would do a lot of harm,
Who is working under fire
And who never seems to tire?
He's the man with the band around his arm
He's an M.P., M.P., M.P., M.P.

The thinking behind many of these "service" songs concerning war-related jobs considered less than glamorous or not as worthy of musical tribute as pilots or combat infantrymen was that all jobs were essential to the war effort and each area of service deserved to be recognized as worthy of praise. One of the most popular ways to single out a group for praise was by commissioning a song in its honor. For example, Charles Hamlin of the Civil Aeronautics Authority asked Fred Waring to write a song for transport pilots. Hamlin thought transport pilots had received "little credit for the work they are doing," despite facing "just as much danger as the combat pilot." A song dedicated to them would be a "deserved tribute and a morale-builder" for the transport pilots.[43]

Just when Tin Pan Alley and the OWI despaired of finding a great war song, Frank Loesser's "Praise the Lord and Pass the Ammunition" appeared on the best-seller charts. *Variety* thought the song might become the "Over There" of World War II because it was "different from the other war tunes in that it is not a ballad. It's out-and-out war propaganda, yet it has a lilt and a touch of genius which may give it immortality."[44]

The song caught on so rapidly that the publisher, Famous Music, with the approval of the OWI, asked radio networks to air it once every four hours in order to prolong the normal six-to-eight-week life span of a typical popular tune. The networks, however, insisted that neither the publisher nor the government could tell them how to run their business. Many radio stations played "Praise the Lord and Pass the Ammunition" as often as they wished. After begging for a war song, the OWI was afraid that "Praise the Lord" would not last. And it did not. The American people bought enough records and sheet music and networks broadcast the tune so many times that it quickly catapulted onto *Your Hit Parade*. It sold over a million records for Kay Kyser and a total of two million records by various artists. It was the tenth-ranked song of 1942's top ten tunes.[45] During the first week of November 1942, other songs on the best-seller list included songs lacking war themes such as: "White Christmas," "I Got a Gal in Kalamazoo," "Strip Polka," and "Mr. Five by Five." These songs and hundreds of others with similar titles caused the Office of War Information to reinforce its efforts to get war songs before the public.

Meeting in Columbia, Missouri, on November 10, 1942, the Association for Education by Radio heard Charles A. Seipmann of the OWI (by way of the British Broadcasting Corporation and Harvard) stress that what Americans needed was more of the "Yankee Doodle spirit of 1776." Seipmann continued, "Propaganda can win the war, and must. Armed victory alone cannot . . . music is . . . our strong morale builder." He acknowledged that entertainment programs were valuable "morale maintainers" that helped Americans relax from the strains of war, but he stated that "until 'Praise the Lord and Pass the Ammunition' we have had no songs with which to march away to war."[46]

Hoping that Loesser's song would be the Great American War Song, the U.S. Treasury Department commandeered the tune and rewrote the words to help sell war bonds. The lyrics became "Raise the cash to buy the ammunition," but even this did not satisfy the OWI.[47] The U.S. Treasury Department and the OWI wanted Tin Pan Alley to do more to raise war bond sales. Every one of the war loan drives was oversubscribed. But most of the money came from banks, corporations, and other businesses. Despite all the gimmicks the government tried—offering items such as Betty Grable's stockings or Jack Benny's violin to the highest bidder or having Hollywood movie stars sell bonds—the individual bond quotas were never met. A concerned government looked for every means possible to boost individual bond sales, not only to curb inflation by siphoning excess cash from the economy, but also to ensure that Americans' hearts and minds would stay close to the war effort and their pocketbooks.

The Music Publishers Protective Association took the OWI's suggestions for song topics that would promote morale and boost pride and passed them along to association members. Paul Fussell says that one way of generating morale, or "Pride in Outfit," was to write songs "for the troops . . . especially songs that glorify such hopelessly unromantic branches of the service as the infantry and the construction battalions, or Seabees."[48]

With this concept in mind of rewarding or giving credit to lowly occupations, mundane duties, or commodity rationing, the OWI recommended during the first week in December 1942 that songs backing the government's current campaign on transportation conservation could be helpful. The OWI letter even suggested a title, "Wrap It Up and I'll Take It Home." This song's name was meant to suggest to Americans that they could do their part to conserve gasoline, tires, and automobiles by taking their purchases home with them instead of expecting the stores and shops to deliver to private homes, as had been the custom in many places before the war began. The OWI's communication concluded with these thoughts: "Some . . . important themes . . . are the war worker (including the woman war worker); the fundamental rationing theme, which is a theme of sacrifice; the theme of conservation. This last means taking care of what we have, making the things last, making things do. . . . Cheerful treatment of the theme of doing without, of getting along with what we have, helps keep us rolling toward victory."[49]

Music publishers commented that the writer of the OWI letter obviously was unaware that many songs already published dealt with conservation, rationing, war workers, and the sacrifices that all Americans were being called on to make.[50] Some of the most obvious choices were "American Women for Defense," "Back the Red, White and Blue with Gold," "Knit One, Purl Two," "Making Hay for the U.S.A.," "Seeds for Victory and Peace," "Buy a Bond Today," and a song that spoke of American women's new roles working outside the home: "Rosie the Riveter," by Evans and Loeb. The latter song, with its lively meter and bouncy tune, was intended to boost the morale of and pay tribute to the women working in defense industries, although the lyrics insisted that "Rosie" was still a "little frail" (a 1940s term for "female") who was doing a man's job in order to "protect" her boyfriend. The lyric "There's something true about / Red, white and blue about / Rosie the Riveter" referred to her devotion to the nation or her boyfriend or both. This song reinforced two important war time messages: hard work for the war effort and loyalty to those serving in the military:

> All the day long,
> Whether rain or shine,
> She's a part of the assembly line.
> She's making history,
> Working for victory,
> Rosie, Brrr (Imitate noise of riveting machine), the Riveter.

Much more typical of the tunes sponsored and approved of by the OWI was Perry Alexander's up-tempo, though forgettable tune, "Pluggin' Jane":

> Oh, Pluggin' Jane keeps pluggin' every day
> She has no time to play
> Just plugs along all day
> ....
> When it's over—"Over There"
> We'll say that you're O.K.

The third verse of "Pluggin' Jane" is notable for its not-so-subtle suggestion that when peace comes, women should be ready to vacate their wartime jobs so that men returning from the war could have employment. The OWI, already concerned with the country's postwar conversion to a peacetime economy, wanted to make sure that people did their jobs while being ready to return to prewar society. Those who kept their morale for the duration would be rewarded with "our Liberty":

> Now when this war is over
> And the boys come marching home

She won't delay to make a way
Her job will be his own.

It was suggested that since a plea from the Office of War Information for stronger morale songs had not accomplished much, the publishers might be required to submit their songs for approval (as was the case with the film industry's movie scripts following the Motion Picture Bureau's transfer to the Foreign Bureau of the OWI) before publication.[51] When the cry of "censorship" went up from the music industry, the OWI was quick to point out that "clearance is not censorship or a means of holding your [song] up. Clearance is—a way to make your [songs] better."[52] Since the broadcasting networks already had a strict code of censorship that forbade any mention of sex, alcohol, or profanity on the air, this threat from the OWI could have amounted to an even more repressive system than the one already in place.

Despite the efforts of the Office of War Information and Tin Pan Alley, the American public was not interested in war songs, at least not the type of war song that the morale builders were pushing. In December 1942, one year following the Japanese attack on Pearl Harbor, a look at the best-selling records in jukeboxes and on the radio networks revealed few songs that could be classified as war songs. The "10 Best Sellers on Coin Machines" listed in *Variety*, December 2, 1942, were

1. "White Christmas"
2. "Praise the Lord and Pass the Ammunition"
3. "When the Lights Go on Again"
4. "Daybreak"
5. "Mr. Five by Five"
6. "Dearly Beloved"
7. "Manhattan Serenade"
8. "My Devotion"
9. "Why Don't You Fall in Love with Me?"
10. "There Are Such Things"[53]

Jukebox favorites included "The Strip Polka," "Der Fuehrer's Face," "Here Comes the Navy," "I Had the Craziest Dream," "Brazil," "There'll Never Be Another You," "Sweet Dreams," "For Me and My Gal," "This Is the Army Mr. Jones," and "Moonlight Becomes You."[54] By the end of December 1942, none of the latter tunes remained on the hit list. Only two of the top ten tunes were related to the war, while the two most popular songs, "White Christmas" and "Mr. Five by Five," had lyrics with absolutely no connection to the war.

Previously, the only march-type song to make *Your Hit Parade* was "Remember Pearl Harbor," and its popularity had lasted only a few weeks. Since *Your Hit Parade* reflected public taste, in the form of what was being bought, it was apparent that the American record-buying public had not yet found a lasting martial war song. "This Is Worth Fighting For," a war song by Edgar DeLange and Sam H. Stept of the inspirational, non-escapist type, made the number ten spot on June 27, 1942, but it never rose above that, and by August 8, 1942, it had disappeared from *Your Hit Parade*.[55] Despite its ballad tempo and the sentimental theme of the lyric, the message of the song was clear and to the point:

I saw a peaceful old valley,
With a carpet of corn for the floor,
And I heard a voice within me whisper,
This Is Worth Fighting For.

The war song that remained in *Your Hit Parade*'s first place for the longest period, from October 1942 through January 1943, was "Don't Sit Under the Apple Tree." To categorize it as a "war song" meant assuming that the lyrics referred to war-parted lovers; the clearest war-related idea in the song is the phrase "Till I come marching home." Maybe all that was necessary for a song to catch the public's favor was just a hint of the military. "Don't Sit Under the Apple Tree" was also a song of parting, so in that sense it qualified as a war tune. The bright melody and bouncy rhythm, combined with the performance by the Andrews Sisters, put the song on the popular music top-sellers charts. It was in first place for five weeks. "He Wears a Pair of Silver Wings" held first place for four weeks, after battling with "Jingle Jangle Jingle," an escapist "cowboy" tune that revealed a cowboy's joy that "there'll be no wedding bells for today." "Johnny Doughboy Found a Rose in Ireland" never hit first place, but it was among the top ten for sixteen weeks.[56]

Other songs with some war connotation that made *Your Hit Parade* were "I Left My Heart at the Stage Door Canteen" (a soldier on leave falls for a canteen hostess but must return to his unit), "I Wonder When My Baby's Coming Home," "When the Lights Go on Again (All Over the World)," "I Came Here to Talk for Joe," "Gobs of Love (The Sailors' Love Song)," and "Three Little Sisters" (about three girls in love with three boys in different branches of the services).[57]

At the close of 1942 "Praise the Lord and Pass the Ammunition" was becoming the most popular war song, and many in Tin Pan Alley and the OWI had hopes that it would become the "Over There" of World War II. "Praise the Lord" was different from the other war tunes in that it was not a ballad. It was out-and-out war propaganda. Its tune had a peppy lilt, and the refrain was simple and had frequent word repetitions so that anyone could hear it once, pick up the tune, and remember it. The simplicity of the song helped boost it onto the popularity charts briefly, but then it disappeared from the best-sellers' list. Repetition on the radio and live performances all over the country made Americans soon grow bored with the song. They were ready for the next hit.

By 1942 standards a song that was not a ballad rarely zoomed into popularity, unless it was a novelty number or had a catchy refrain. Occasionally, tunes like "Jingle Jangle Jingle," "Beer Barrel Polka," "Daddy," "A Tisket, A Tasket," and the "Woodpecker Song" caught the public's ear, but based on the best-selling songs of *Your Hit Parade*, it was plainly the love ballad that was the perennial favorite. Apparently, despite the OWI's and Tin Pan Alley's best efforts, Americans on the home front could not be dissuaded from their preference for the nostalgic, romantic, or yearning song. The OWI was interested in songs that would instill "hatred for the enemy" and a "hardy determination to win" in Americans. William Lewis, of OWI, stated, "If we expose the American people to enough worthy war songs, it's a certainty that some of them should take, just as they've already cottoned to the drivel about 'Slap the Jap,' 'Goodbye Mama, I'm Off to Yokohama,' 'Remember Pearl Harbor' and the like."[58]

As Abel Green, editor of *Variety*, reminded Lewis, "You can lead the American ears to the microphone or the jukebox, but you can't make 'em like it or buy it."[59] The list of 142 World War II songs published in the *Variety 37th Anniversary Issue*, January 1943, demonstrates the truth of Green's statement: fewer than ten made it onto any best-seller list. Some of the songs approved of by the OWI but not the buying public were "America to Victory," "Bang 'Em One for Me," "On the Old Assembly Line," "That's Sabotage," "All Out for Freedom," "A Dash of the Red, White and Blue," "Freedom Ring!," "Here's to the Flag! (Keep It Flying Over Here—Over There—Everywhere)," "They Started Somethin' (But We're Gonna' End It)," "The Time Is Now," "We're In to Win," and "There's an 'FDR' in Freedom."

The lack of a popular war song and internal struggles over policies and fee payment eventually led to the demise of the National Wartime Music Committee. It disbanded following disclosure of its failure to come to terms with music publishers on uniform agreements covering performance, recording, and reproduction rights.[60]

The end of the committee came just when success began to seem possible. Only a few days before the committee dissolved itself, the members of ASCAP had stepped forward to offer full cooperation with regard to uniform agreements for publishing, recording, and distributing war-related music. Before this time, the federal government had had to negotiate separately with each publisher, performer, or recording company, and the OWI thought a uniform contract agreement would simplify matters. Agents representing artists and songwriters were not as enthusiastic about the government's plans for a single contract for the music industry.[61]

Chaper 11

Tin Pan Alley's Music War Committee

At first the music industry was shocked at the demise of the National Wartime Music Committee, and at the accusations the committee aimed at Tin Pan Alley, faulting ASCAP and Tin Pan Alley for their tardiness in supplying contracts and agreements for copyrights. The music industry asserted that it had always cooperated with the government and would willingly cooperate further if the government would only explain what it wanted done. In reply, the committee, according to Abel Green, "gasped in surprise, stuttered that it didn't want nothin' from nobody, and that it had been misquoted—and then scuttled itself."[1] The committee voted itself out of existence in Washington, D.C., on April 13,1943.

The government immediately announced that a new committee would be formed with more than advisory power to push through the standard contract forms which the OWI desired. The National Wartime Music Committee could actually do nothing but advise and recommend. In late April 1943, the OWI set up a new, streamlined version of the National Wartime Music Committee, with Jack Joy of the War Department as chairman. This new committee, called the Wartime Music Committee, undertook the task of setting up uniform contracts between government agencies and the music industry, talent agencies, and various music-related unions and guilds.[2]

In May 1943 the OWI once again attempted to mobilize the music business into a "psychological fighting force" in the war effort. Abel Green, the editor of *Variety*, was named as special consultant and advisor to the Office of War Information's newly created Performance Division, with instructions to set up a Composers' War Council of Tin Pan Alley and Hollywood songwriters. The purpose of the council was "to harness the talents and resources of America's songwriters to further the war effort"[3] by putting patriotic popular music to stirring wartime use. The committee was to parallel the OWI's messages on "rationing, button-your-lip, etc." Green prophesied that certain types of tunes might become a part of regular propaganda messages, with suggestions to broadcasters and other media that such songs could "ideally fit the pattern of what we are trying to project."[4]

Abel Green relished his role as special consultant to the OWI and immediately began making recommendations for songs. He bemoaned the failure of a solid song on behalf of the Army nurses who were "right up there at the fighting front." And he pointed to the fact that there was still no satisfactory song supporting the Women's Auxiliary Army Corps. "The WAAC Is in Back of You," written by WAAC lieutenant Ruby Jane Douglas was acceptable, but most WAAC songs, in his opinion, had been "too wacky."[5] Songs from Tin Pan Alley were not what the women wanted for marching music: "I've Got a WAAC on My Hands and a Wave in My Hair," "I'm Wacky over Something in Khaki," "I'm Doing the WAAC, WAAC, WAAC Walk," "Sally WAAC," "He's Got a WAVE in His Hair and a WAAC on His Hands," and "Nimitz is the Limitz" (supposedly a sentiment of the WAVES).[6] "In My Little G.I. Shoes," included in the *WAC Song Book*, was typical of these songs:

In my little GI shoes
I walk along the street.
In my little cotton hose,
I give the boys a treat.
My skirt looks like a barracks bag,
My hat just like a pot.
But I am in the Army now
And glad with what I got.

Atypical of the songs written about women in the military was Meredith Willson's "Yankee Doodle Girl," which did not poke fun at the WAAC or belittle women's service:

'Ten-shun, you Americans,
The Yankee Doodle Girl has gone to war,
And when you mention,
True Americans,
You'll mention ev'ry woman in the Corps.

The prolific Fred Waring and his lyricist Jack Dolph produced an earnest song for the WAVES, but its message was controversial. In essence the song said that by joining the WAVES a woman could release a sailor from a safe stateside job and send him into combat. To many women, with men in the navy, this was not a particularly appealing thought.

A different standard applied to women in the military who released a man for combat, as opposed to one man taking another man's place. Servicemen in clerical jobs did not always appreciate being replaced for combat; mothers did not want a daughter to enlist if it meant that a son would be sent to his death; and a woman whose husband or sweetheart was killed overseas did not like to think that but for her or some other woman he would have been safe at a desk job.[7]

The idea that by joining the military a woman might send a loved one, hers or someone else's, to the front lines made the choice more complicated for some women. Although its title might suggest otherwise, "(WAVES) In Navy Blue" by Fred Waring and Jack Dolph did not promote Navy service by telling how flattering the Waves uniforms were:

For every WAVE in Navy blue,
There's a sailor on the sea.
And for ev'ry hand at the WAVES' command there's
a mighty fist against the enemy.
HAIL WAVES, NAVY'S FOR YOU!

The Composers War Council tried to point songwriters to the subjects that needed a boost from music. The OWI, knowledgeable of possible morale problems (public complacency was damaging the war effort through absenteeism, job switching, strikes, decreasing voluntary enlistments, and the growing reluctance of civilians to sacrifice material goods),[8] supported the Composers War Council. The music industry was perfectly willing to be coached on the matter of wartime morale. As William Burke Miller, the War Program Manager of NBC's Public Service Department, stated in a letter dated February 17, 1943, "In Washington they know where the morale problem is most crucial at a given time, and it is to these points they would prefer to direct entertainment and programs rather than the 'hit or miss' fashion that appears to be the present practice."[9]

Green thought the OWI might even become more involved with popular songs than merely casually endorsing them if some suitable piece of song material were to come along. He hinted that the OWI might "throw the force of the federal government" behind a song with material suitable to OWI's efforts.[10] This meant production, distribution, and promotion of a song would be paid for by the government.

Another reason the OWI gave for wanting "name" composers involved with the new Composers War Council was the fear of Nazi propaganda. Morale experts in Washington, D.C., pointed to the example of the German song "Lili Marlene," which had been adopted as a favorite tune by Allied soldiers. According to Green, "'Lili Marlene' [is] No.1 on the Nazi hit-parade, to which *Time* magazine and *March of Time* both gave wide publicity." He added, "Unofficially, D.C. fears that the Nazis may turn the situation around; DX [radio] our troops in North Africa, and elsewhere, that 'Lili Marlene' is a good enough song to get wide magazine and national network publicity in America, that, 'what's the matter, can't your American songwriters turn out as pretty tunes as "Lili Marlene," and you see, we're not so terrible if we can give the world such pretty music.'"[11]

Abel Green's advisory position with the Office of War Information did not last long. On May 24, 1943, the Tin Pan Alley and Hollywood composers preempted the federal government's control and formed the previously mentioned voluntary association, the Music War Committee of the American Theater Wing, with Oscar Hammerstein II as president.[12] The songwriters, of their own volition, formulated a practical Music War Committee, primed to do its share in the all-out victory effort.

The new Music War Committee was a broad cross-section of the music business. The MWC included not only songwriters but also interpretive artists, recording executives, music publishers, conductors, newspapermen, music critics, labor leaders, educators, and civilian groups. The latter was composed of public school music teachers, band directors, community orchestra leaders, and church choir directors.

The Music War Committee decided at its first meeting, May 24, 1943, that all the negative focus on the quality and quantity of war songs would come to an end. The approach was to be positive: "No matter the hurdles (publishers' tepidity toward war songs, radio listeners' aversion to martial 6/8 tempoed songs, etc.)—these are being ignored." The committee saw as its task exposing Americans to a new idiom in popular song, regardless of the fact that World War I saw a marching army, or that ballads of the "My Buddy" type were popularized by vaudeville headliners, whereas dance bands and radio dominated the current music field. The committee concluded that songwriters should stop writing songs that fit World War I; they should adapt their patriotic and military ideas to the 1943 pattern of show business and showmanship. Tin Pan Alley would write war songs that would "swing" or were "hot." Musical style did not matter; the Music War Committee looked for a song that every American would recognize as a symbol of the war.

At the committee's first formal meeting, invited guests included the OWI's William B. Lewis and Jack Joy of the War Department (and also host of *The Army Hour* on NBC). Lewis had what he called "a few private opinions" about what was wrong with the new war songs. He counseled members of the committee to forget the "frustration of maybe-I-will-lose-my-girl, or is-my-girl-back-home-two-timing-me" and instead write "positive, assertive songs." He cautioned composers not to "fret about the lights going on all over the world; let's sing about victory to come—the Gay White Way display will take care of itself." Lewis could not resist a criticism of the Music War Committee's president, Oscar Hammerstein II, when he said, "Even though great is the song, 'The Last Time I Saw Paris' . . . maybe now we should sing of 'The Next Time I See Paris.'" Lewis also insisted that songwriters stop their narrow view of the war by focusing solely on Tokyo and Berlin: "Let's inculcate the idea as strongly as possible that this is a global war, not restricted to any one capitol. From the Aleutians to the South Pacific, from the Lowlands to the Balkans, there's more bitter warfare and hatred manifested right now than around the immediate geographical Axis capital."

Still, a song with a fighting, positive declaration would not matter much if the public refused to buy it. Bandleader-songwriter Eddie DeLange's "This Is Worth Fighting For," an OWI-favored song, was briefly popular in the latter part of 1942. But DeLange said that whenever he played it, somebody in uniform would invariably step on the dance floor and yell at him, "Yes, then why aren't you in uniform?" Understandably, bandleaders like DeLange often had an aversion to playing such tunes no matter how much the OWI liked them. And, after all, he explained, "The band's major task on a hotel or cafe job is to get 'em up on the dance floor—and war songs haven't been able to do it." According to DeLange, there was also a problem for composers, "We can't get war songs played."

Other composers present at the Music War Committee's birth were Billy Rose, Richard Rodgers, Charlie Tobias, Fred Ahlert, Allan Sloan, Buck Ram, Robert Russell, and Gladys Shelley. They, too, were vocal in their appraisal of war song hazards and agreed with Delange that it was nearly impossible to get a dance band to play war songs. Robert Russell stressed that publisher Jack Robbins was "literally screaming at the bands' embargo—unconscious as it was—on 'Comin' in on a Wing and a Prayer,' until Eddie Cantor with three broadcasts projected it into hitdom."

Despite these barriers, Oscar Hammerstein II pledged himself, along with many successful composers such as Ira Gershwin, Jerome Kern, Irving Berlin, Johnny Mercer, Arthur Schwartz, Vincent Youmans, Mack Gordon, Harry Warren, and Leo Robin, to keep writing war songs, although he emphasized, as did Rodgers, Rose, and the others that "publishers' shelves and safes are cluttered with war songs gathering dust because nobody will perform them." Lewis suggested that "worthwhile" songs could possibly bypass the dance bands and recalcitrant publishers by going directly to the greatest source of dissemination: radio. It was also suggested by Billy Rose that a Victory Music Committee be set up for nonprofit publication of these "worthwhile" songs if publishers refused to issue them.

As head of the radio division of the OWI, W.B. Lewis directed composers to include certain themes in their songs for the "best effect." Some song material was not particularly romantic, he conceded, such as the importance of salvaging fats or collecting scrap. But Lewis directed the Music War Committee to turn out songs that would get those ideas across in a manner that would entertain as well as educate. Fred Waring at least was willing to give Lewis's idea a try. Waring's publishing firm shortly thereafter produced "Save the Grease" by Joe Sanders for the federal government's campaign to conserve the use of household fats:

Save the grease from the potsy
It's for peace!
Make it hotsy
And we'll pour it on the Nazi
And the Nips,
Japs, Nips!
....
Let it sizzle, let it boil for the foe
Mrs. America, let's go!

Like the majority of the songs written to satisfy OWI directives, "Save the Grease" never became popular and had little play outside of Fred Waring's dance band, The Pennsylvanians, who, of course, premiered the song. But Waring's efforts did not go unnoticed; in a letter dated February 23, 1944, Wilder Breckenridge, chairman of the American Fat Salvage Committee, wrote to John Van Nostrand in the OWI's New York Deputy Chief's office: "Thanks so much for your help in getting the Fred Waring 'Save the Grease' song published. It's a peach and we can make awfully good use of it."[13]

Casting about for inspiration, the Music War Committee and the OWI suggested that composers visit military training camps and there become "indoctrinated with the proper spirit." The committee also observed that over seventy professional songwriters were currently serving in the military, and it was thought that "proper" war songs would come from these composers who faced "action-under-fire."[14]

The American Theater Wing also added its ideas to the search for war songs. It sponsored a new war song contest, with four categories designed to include all levels of songwriters from the amateur to the professional to be judged by the Music War Committee. With luck, perhaps the contest would yield a song or songs providing a "sufficient cushion" until the professional writers "get the ball rolling."[15]

The Music War Committee was confronted with the problem of getting "likely" tunes before the public. Hammerstein and others decided that the best plan was to spread selected songs throughout bands, theaters, nightclubs, schools, and radio programs, if necessary, bypassing those publishers who were unable (or unwilling) to exploit this genre of song. A subcommittee, meeting once a week, was organized to select likely songs for promotion (no professional songwriters were included on this subcommittee). This song-judging subcommittee comprised well-known music business celebrities, including Paul Whiteman, Paul Robeson, Olin Downes, W.C. Handy, William Morris Jr., Abel Green, Manie Sacks, Al Goodman, and Howard Dietz. The Music War Committee also hoped to have a commercial radio program use one selected song each week, and also to broadcast a "You Pick the Song" segment, with the general public invited to select the war song they liked best.[16]

With guidelines set, committees organized, and "name" musicians on both coasts pledged to the Music War Committee, a call was sent to all composers to submit unpublished materials: specifically, the Music War Committee asked for harmonized lead sheets, with lyrics clearly printed, the names of the composer and author, and the copyright number. Then the council waited for the war songs to deluge their offices.[17]

Not every Tin Pan Alley composer jumped on the OWI's bandwagon. Irving Berlin, one of the most respected popular music composers of the twentieth century (and a man who had written dozens of war songs), thought all of the directives from the federal government and the machinations of the various music committees would not produce the "great war song." He said, "I have never believed that the 'Over There' of this war will come through contests or specific rules laid down by the OWI. Important war songs just aren't written that way."[18]

Berlin thought Tin Pan Alley should be allowed to go on as usual, without any restrictions, and eventually the right song would come along if it had not already. Berlin also astutely pointed out an important job Tin Pan Alley could do to help the war effort. In line with the OWI's directives, he agreed that special songs presenting the country's point of view would be helpful, such as those praising democracy and liberty. Berlin reminded *Variety* readers that his composition "Any Bonds Today?" had done a good job for the Treasury Department, helping to sell bonds although the song was not commercial. "Any Bonds Today?" was printed, distributed, and handled in Washington by the Treasury Department. Berlin also signed over his royalty payments to the war bond drive, as he did with several of his songs during the war.

Berlin argued that music publishers (including himself) could not be expected to spend their money to publicize non-commercial songs. Berlin proposed that a publishing company be formed for the sole purpose of printing and exploiting these songs. And if the government paid for this enterprise, money could easily be raised through subscriptions from the music industry. Berlin envisioned minimum-wage civilian workers staffing this special publishing house. Then the OWI could tell the composers' committee what subjects it wanted addressed in song, and songwriters could be assigned certain song subjects. The main object would be to get ideas across to the public through songs. "A good song on a subject, not necessarily propaganda but an amusing idea, would do much more than reams of speeches."

Berlin seemed to agree with Abel Green's assessment of music's part in the war; in his December 17, 1942, *Variety* column "Show Biz's Role in the War,"Green wrote that contributions from show business and showmen might seem of less military importance than well-equipped regiments, but "lyricists and songwriters win battles, too. One Kate Smith broadcast of Irving Berlin's 'God Bless America' is worth a thousand recruiting speeches."[19]

Other composers also spoke out on the war song problem. Harold Arlen heartily agreed that as long as the war was mechanized there would be no rousing tunes, at least none with the chance of repeating the stirring success of "Over There." Arlen said, "It's very difficult for a songwriter to get excited about a jeep, or a plane, or a parachute jumper, or any other of the facets that go to make up the present war and put them down in song form so that everyone feels like singing or whistling it."[20]

Arlen thought the best possibility for a war song was one that dealt with the future and the "world we're fighting to preserve." The great song of the war would be one that would tell Americans about the "world of tomorrow" and give everyone a "clearer understanding of their rights." Arlen did not think another "Over There" was possible because "the idea of getting over there has lost its kick, in the sense of adventure." Instead of a martial air, Arlen believed the war song would "just pop up one day and be a simple, sincere effort about the world to come."

Arlen's ideas ran counter to the OWI's plans for a war song; the government was still worried about complacency and urged its agencies to keep the defeat of the Axis powers before the public at all times. Songs that spoke of the postwar world were strongly discouraged by the OWI.

Frank Loesser's "Praise the Lord and Pass the Ammunition" spent three months on *Variety*'s "10 Best Sellers" list, sold over 450,000 copies of sheet music in two months and was, for a while, the best hope of Tin Pan Alley to repeat the success of "Over There." But Loesser had his doubts that a best-selling martial song would be written during World War II. He did not think Americans really wanted a true war song, one that was martial and/or factual. And if such a song were written, Loesser doubted that Americans would buy it. He was aware of just how far a songwriter could go in portraying the realities of war, both on the battlefield and on the home front.[21]

When asked about his song writing methods by *Variety's* editor, Abel Green, Loesser was of the opinion that the current war songs, of necessity, evaded the unpleasant facts of war and death. He recognized the actuality that in order to sell a song to the American public, the lyrics could not reveal much, if any, of the realities of war. In Loesser's words: "You stay in the middle sort of. You give her [the housewife in the listening audience] hope without facts; glory without blood. You give her a legend neatly trimmed."[22]

On the one hand, Loesser compared song marketing with selling Jell-O. "If you want to sell a housewife Jell-O you don't tell her: 'Madame, it is highly probable that your son is coming home . . . totally blind. But cheer up, tonight choose one of the six delicious flavors and be happy with America's finest dessert." On the other hand, Loesser saw the danger in too much cheerful confidence in song composition. Composers should not deliberately lie to the American people by casting the war in glowing terms. For example, one should never say, "Madam, our army is so smart and well equipped that all your son does is sit in an impregnable tank and shoot down Japs like flies, and you can expect him home for Christmas in better health than ever." Both Loesser and Arlen saw the lack of a war song as stemming from the actualities of the war and not the failure of songwriters to produce.

Although reports from the battlefield were filtered through the OWI, the War Department's, and the navy's tightly controlled news coverage, by October 1943 (the date of Loesser's interview), the U.S. news media began printing explicit photographs of soldiers on the battlefields, including the first pictures of dead American soldiers. American policy makers feared people would react as Loesser, Arlen, and other songwriters evidently had. Until September 1943, the government purposely withheld pictures of American dead, fearing negative consequences on viewers, who might be led to favor withdrawal from the war before total victory was achieved. Fortunately for the War Department, the more open policy enabled the government to make use of the pictures to intensify public commitment to the war effort.[23] Unfortunately for the Great American War Song search, this policy did not have a similar effect on Tin Pan Alley. As more and more reports of the fierceness of the fighting found their way into the American media, it became more difficult for the Tin Pan Alley songwriters to glorify war—whether righteous or not—in song. It seemed frivolous and dishonest.

The Music War Committee of the American Theater Wing had cooperation from every branch of the music industry. Network radio shows offered air time for war songs, bandleaders and other performers agreed to perform the tunes, advertising agencies offered their services in the exploitation of war songs; the only thing that remained was for composers to turn out the songs.

Meanwhile, the American public was listening to "You'll Never Know (Just How Much I Love You)," "Paper Doll," "Don't Get Around Much Anymore," and "As Time Goes By." The only songs with war themes on the hit charts the summer of 1943 were "Comin' in on a Wing and a Prayer" and "Johnny Got a Zero."[24]

The first two songs selected by the Music War Committee for the U.S. Treasury Department's Third Defense Bond Drive of September 9, 1943, were "Swing the Quota" and "Get on the Bondwagon." Although bandleaders such as Ray Heatherton, Vincent Lopez, and Glenn Miller recorded and played these tunes, the songs died after the defense bond drive was over. Bing Crosby, who was the number-one male singer in America at that time, was unable to popularize "Get on the Bondwagon." Even "Der Bingle" could not sell a mediocre war bond tune.[25]

Other songs selected in the first rounds of Music War Committee judging were "One More Mile," "The Message Got Through," "Has Hitler Made a Monkey Out of You?," "We're Melting All Our Memories," "Voice of the Underground," "Yankee Doodle Ain't Doodlin' Now," "Have You Written Him Today?," "I Get That Democratic Feeling," "I Spoke with Jefferson at Guadalcanal," "In Business (Since 1776)," and "Unconditional Surrender."[26]

As with the previous Music War Committee selections, these songs remained buried at the bottom of the sheet music stacks and record piles. Meanwhile, copies of "Pistol Packin' Mama" by Al Dexter were so scarce that a black market developed around the recording and price gouging became common. Some stores charged as much as $1.25 per copy (35¢ and 50¢ were the regular prices of records). Many stores refused to sell a copy of a record in heavy demand unless the customer also purchased a slow-selling record that had been on the shelf for months.[27] By October 13, 1943, "Pistol Packin' Mama" was in the number-two spot on *Variety's* "10 Best Sellers on Coin Machines," and on November 10, 1943, it reached the number-one spot, where it remained on the top-seller list for twenty-five weeks.[28]

None of the Music War Committee's selections became hits. The top-selling songs of 1943 avoided any mention of the war. These songs included, in descending order of their popularity, "People Will Say We're in Love," "You'll Never Know," "Brazil," "That Old Black Magic," "As Time Goes By," "Sunday, Monday, or Always," "You'd Be So Nice to Come Home To," "I've Heard That Song Before," "Don't Get Around Much Anymore," and "It Can't Be Wrong." The only song in the first twenty best-sellers with a war connection was Jimmy McHugh's "Comin' in on a Wing and a Prayer," while the rest of the top twenty were love songs, good dance tunes, and novelty numbers.[29]

Tin Pan Alley did make a valiant effort to supply the Treasury Department with songs for the War Loan Drives. Eight campaigns to raise money to pay for the war relied heavily on radio and the music industry for promotion. The OWI, through its Domestic Radio Bureau, usually produced programs that were broadcast nationwide and appealed to all Americans to aid the war effort by purchasing war bonds. One of the functions of music was to get the point across to the American public in a pleasant fashion, so that people would purchase even more than their quota. The war loan drives were most often scheduled to coincide with important American holidays or events; these drives occurred twice a year (except in 1944 when there were three loan drives).

One of the most successful war loan programs was broadcast on Thanksgiving evening, November 23, 1944, from 8:30 until 10:00 P.M., Pacific War Time. Carried on the NBC network and titled "Let's Talk Turkey to Japan," the Sixth War Loan Drive aimed to raise $5 billion for the war effort. The program featured show business personalities, such as Robert Young, Jack Haley, Bob Hope, Joan Davis, Jack Benny, Amos 'n' Andy, and Kay Kyser and his orchestra, performing skits and scenes to encourage war bond purchases. Others with prominent parts in the show were Bing Crosby singing "Accentuate the Positive" and "White Christmas"; the Ken Darby Singers performing "Let's Talk Turkey to Japan" and "The Time Is Now" ("The time is now / The time is now / It's time to read the writing on the wall"); Dinah Shore singing "Always" and "Together"; Ginny Simms performing "The Man I Love"; Dick Powell singing "You Always Hurt the One You Love"; and Eddie Cantor performing a medley of George M. Cohan songs: "Yankee Doodle Dandy," "Harrigan," "Mary's a Grand Old Name," "Give My Regards to Broadway," "You're a Grand Old Flag, and "Over There."

The program concluded with the NBC orchestra and the Ken Darby Chorus performing "The Star Spangled Banner," while Eddie Cantor made one more plea for Americans to give "everything we have. We don't dare make it easy on ourselves . . . when by doing so, we make it harder on the men who are fighting for us!"[30]

There was something appealing to listeners of all ages and backgrounds in these bond drive shows, but the thrust of such programs was to invoke the listeners' emotions, to manipulate them into spending more money for bonds than they had planned. The shows were not-so-subtle forms of bribery. Robert Young asked Thanksgiving Day listeners, who probably had stuffed themselves with whatever holiday foods their ration coupons would allow and were lounging around the living radio, to visualize "What some Americans are going through . . . what some are giving to hasten victory . . . think how anxious you are to bring your loved ones home faster and then—when you're asked if you'll have another couple hundred dollars worth of the Sixth War Loan . . . take another helping."[31]

The war loan drives depended heavily on popular music to lighten the mood of the shows. There was concern that people would turn off their radios if they became bored with bond appeals, so favorite entertainers and popular songs were interspersed throughout the program to entice listeners to remain tuned in to the show. The idea was to continue the pattern set by pre-war variety shows, so that the listener would be familiar with the format: one that substituted commercials for war bonds in place of the usual advertisements for coffee and laundry detergent. The programs featured songs that were on the popular music charts, as well as patriotic standards plus a few songs calculated to boost bond buying.

The Seventh War Loan Drive, sponsored by the U.S. Treasury Department, relied heavily on the popular music industry to convince a war-weary population that there was still much to do to finish the war. This was an especially difficult task since the bond drive was to begin on May 14, 1945, a week after V-E Day, and end on June 30, 1945. The goal was to raise $14 billion dollars, with half the amount coming from individual subscriptions. This was the largest quota ever set for individuals, and with Hitler defeated Americans would want to know why such a tremendous sum was needed. Why should Americans dig into their savings accounts and current income when victory did not seem to be too far away?

The Treasury Department used radio to convince the American public of the necessity of this staggering loan drive. Radio pleas emphasized the fact that the war was not yet over and people must continue with their war jobs and give full support to all the home front activities that could "speed the final day of victory."

The Treasury Department counted on the fact that Americans' savings were at an all-time high. It was estimated that between January 1, 1940, and December 31, 1944, Americans saved $128 billion. Added to that figure was the $14 billion savings from January 1945 to May 1945, which brought the amount Americans had to invest in war bonds within the goals set by the Treasury Department.

As the Office of War Information told its Domestic Radio Bureau,

"The money is there, if people can be persuaded to invest it." To this end, radio utilized the themes that stressed continuation of the war and the responsibility of every American to "support this war until final victory is won on every front." Americans were reminded that their dollars were needed to pay the costs of the war. They would have to pay for moving the soldiers and their equipment from Europe to the Pacific; pay for fighting the Japanese, who were entrenched on hundreds of tiny islands; pay for creating a whole new air force for the Pacific war (Superfortresses were replaced with the jet-propelled combat planes, the P-80 or "Shooting Star"); and pay for the medical attention that the sick, wounded, and disabled would need, as well as the salary and benefits voted by Congress for service personnel once the war was over.

The Pacific war was to be an expensive one. Americans were encouraged to "back the attack" with personal sacrifice and buy more bonds than ever before. Radio planned to compare the hardships of the fighting men with the civilian hardship of buying another bond or an extra one.[32] Americans were asked to bear their "full responsibility" for the war effort just as the soldiers and sailors were bearing theirs. A "Fact Sheet" from the OWI encouraged radio stations to remind Americans that "We've promised our fighting men overwhelming superiority in weapons and equipment," and the only way to maintain this is to help "pay for the tools of victory" by investing every available dollar in war bonds. There was the inference that Americans must keep their promises to the military, because after all, the fighting men were really their fathers, husbands, brothers, sweethearts, and friends. Radio was encouraged to "give it all the dramatic impact that you can by reminding your listeners of the incomparable sacrifices our fighting men are making."[33]

Music was to play an important role in making every listener feel that he could not afford to refuse to buy an extra bond. Tin Pan Alley submitted songs for the Treasury Department's approval. The same guidelines that applied to radio programs were recommended for war loan songs. Songwriters were prompted to convey to Americans, in song, how urgently their dollars were needed to pay the cost of the war. And that personal sacrifice on the part of civilians was necessary. The American people should buy more war bonds than ever before. In 1945 songwriters responded with "Buy Plenty of Bonds" by Robert Miller; "Your Pot of Dough" by Robert Sour; "We're All in It Together" by Leonard Whiting; "This May Be Your Last Chance" by Vic Mizzi; "Let's Back Them with a Bond" by Nick and Charles Kenny; "Get Out and Buy Those E Bonds" by Herman Hupfeld; and "Idle Dollars, Busy War Dollars" by Andy Razaf, J. Rosemond Johnson, and Harold Rome.

A typical war bond drive song, Tom Adair and Dick Uhl's "Lend 'Til

It Hurts," was not only performed on radio but was also distributed free to schools to be used in conjunction with savings stamps promotions:

At the front, on the farm, on the factory run,
Or as the man behind the man behind the gun:
Oh, lend 'til it hurts the Axis;
Stand back of the boys who fight.
Let's win it. Lend 'til we win this war.

Another suggestion from the Treasury Department and the OWI for songwriters encouraged looking to the postwar world. Songs should stress the theme of financial security, in the form of bonds to be used in the future for education, home repairs or replacement, and for retirement. There was also the theme of buying bonds as a hedge against inflation in the postwar world when the government feared that prices for consumer goods would rise before the economy could convert to a peacetime one. Encouraging Americans to put more of their excess cash into war bonds would stall inflation since there would be less ready money for people to spend. Americans were to be encouraged to put "every penny over rock bottom expenses into the purchase of more war bonds." They were lending their money to the government at a "good rate of interest."

Tin Pan Alley answered the call of the Treasury Department in the spring of 1945 with "Ten Years from Now," "Lullaby of the Baby" (a lullaby about the great future in store because parents bought bonds), "Sergeant Housewife" (detailing women's roles and their ability to juggle household expenses to purchase more bonds), "Till the Last Beat of the Drum," "You Can't Be Here, I Can't Be There" (lovers who can't be together but can purchase bonds together so they will be reunited sooner), "Oh, What a Day That Will Be," and "Back Home for Keeps."[34]

As usual these war bond drive songs made little or no progress on the popular music hit charts. But these particular songs were written with a specific purpose in mind: to impress on Americans the importance of purchasing war bonds. At best, Tin Pan Alley would be able to send the message in such a manner that the radio listening public would be entertained and not switch stations on their radios. A bored public might not stay with a radio program long enough to be persuaded to buy bonds. Popular music and famous entertainers were as important to the war bond drives as the free air time donated by radio networks to broadcast the shows.

Chapter 12

Tin Pan Alley Still Seeks the "Proper" War Song

Other than the temporarily successful war bond drive songs, popular music was still in arrears when it came to war song production. By 1943 the press had noticed the failure as well. In a column titled "Tin Pan Alley Seeks the Song" in the *New York Times Magazine*, June 6, 1943, John Desmond asked why the same Tin Pan Alley that had produced two wildly popular war songs (each selling over a million copies of sheet music), "Over There" from World War I and "Hot Time in the Old Town Tonight" from the Spanish-American War, could not write another Great American War Song.[1]

Desmond believed there were a number of reasons why there had been no hit war song. For one thing, he agreed with other critics that the music industry had changed since WWI. The old method of spreading a song across the nation, through sheet music and phonograph sales, had been able to keep a song popular for as long as two years. A hit in World War I sold 500,000 copies; "Over There" sold 2 million, and "It's a Long Way to Tipperary" sold 6 million. In the Second World War, a "smash" hit lasted from ten to twelve weeks before it was played to its death on the radio and by dance bands, and a song that sold over 250,000 copies of sheet music and 50,000 to 100,000 records was considered highly successful. By the end of the war, sheet music sales of 1 million copies were common and with the end of shellac rationing, smash hit record sales jumped to 500,000–850,000.[2]

Desmond also pointed out that it was much more expensive to get a song "started on the road to success" than in the past. Advertising to put a song before the public cost between $10,000 and $25,000 per song. It was easy to understand why song publishers would rather invest their capital in songs they knew would make money: reasonably good, sophisticated love songs.

Desmond reported (accurately) that everyone in the music industry blamed someone else for the lack of a hit war song. Songwriters claimed they had the song but could not get it published. Publishers denied this and referred to several war songs they had backed with unsuccessful results. The publishers blamed the orchestras and dance bands for failing to play the songs, or they blamed the American Federation of Musicians' ban on recording new music (an issue eventually resolved with the recording companies). The bands blamed the public, saying that if the people asked for war songs they would play them, but the public wanted dance tunes, not march tunes. Desmond said there was the perception, or a stubborn refusal to think otherwise, that a "proper" war song had to be in march tempo. In his estimation all of these excuses actually pointed in one direction—the American public's refusal to accept war songs in the same old form in which Tin Pan Alley was writing them.

It was true that the public would not buy war songs. Olin Downes, music critic of the *New York Times*, suggested that war news was so censored and so meager (necessarily, he said) that by the time it reached the public and the composers in Tin Pan Alley, "It had been shorn of its drama and is 'cold.'" Evidently, "cold" war news was not enough to stimulate the imagination of songwriters. E.C. Mills, former chairman of ASCAP, wrote, "I don't think the emotions of the country have been roused. I've had twenty years' intimate relations with those fellows [meaning songwriters] and I know how they respond."[3] It is difficult to believe this statement—that Americans were not sufficiently aroused by the Japanese attack—could go unchallenged in August 1942, eight months after Pearl Harbor. But apparently, it did. The government's policy of suppressing all photographs of dead soldiers and shell-shocked GIs, or refusing to allow radio to air prerecorded news broadcasts from the battlefields (without passing through the government's filter), was in response to the fear that American military setbacks in 1942 would demoralize the public. At this time, most Americans did not know the full extent of the horrors American soldiers were facing, so why should the musicians of Tin Pan Alley be any different?

The Great American War Song, according to Downes, might have been the victim of the "unhappy difference existing between the state of mind of the nation in the last war and its consciousness of the present day." World War II's generation had to fight to overcome the "tragic misrepresentation" of the First World War. The outlook of soldiers going into battle in the Second World War differed from that of soldiers of 1918 when war had not yet lost its glory, and men thought they were fighting a war to end all wars. Downes blamed the "betrayal of our faith" (the disillusionment of many Americans following World War I) on men he called "self-interested demagogues, unscrupulous politicians, and tools of special interests," who had betrayed the peace and left surviving American soldiers with the "bitter . . . truth." The youth of America had died for "party politics and hypocrites and stuffed shirts at home." As a result, America had to convince young men that there were "good things worth fighting for" and that America was something other than "the noxious swarm that poisoned the thought of the whole nation after 1918." Downes said that America had to persuade its young men that the United States was truly fighting for "right and the four freedoms" and would not stop until "we have fulfilled our obligations as men and as a nation in the forging of a better world."

It was not solely triumphing in a war that concerned Downes; it was also winning back the faith of young American men. His conclusion was that if men had faith, they sang. It then followed that Americans had no war song because they lacked faith, which music could not fabricate for them. Only when there was a renewal of faith "born of crisis and need" might a "reality of feeling" do something in the "course of events for American music."

Downes had a point when he cited the disillusionment following the Treaty of Versailles as a possible explanation for the lack of a rousing war song in World War II. Americans were more jaded by 1940. They had lived through the "war to end all wars," and the restless, returning doughboys added to the colorful, sensational years of the twenties. The decade saw widespread disregard of the national law prohibiting the sale of alcohol, along with the birth of the speakeasy, the bootlegger, the flapper, the high-speed automobile, short skirts and bobbed hair on women, and uninhibited literature. Wide-open gambling, race riots, the Red Scare, Sunday sports, dance crazes, the introduction of jazz to musical America, movie madness, psychoanalysis, and the manipulation of credit flourished. Americans cheered "Lucky Lindy," followed with interest "the Monkey Trial," and were both aghast and titillated by the growth of organized crime. The twenties signaled a break from the old Victorian ways and a new attitude of looking forward to change.

The sophisticated thirties (as filtered through songs of Cole Porter and George and Ira Gershwin, plays and music of Noel Coward and Ben Hecht, writings of Robert Benchley and the Algonquin Round Table, and Hollywood screwball comedies such as *Bringing Up Baby*, *The Philadelphia Story*, and *His Girl Friday*) were one segment of the years of the Depression, which concluded with the outrage of the Nazi onslaughts. War could no longer be glorified with jingoistic slogans or softened with sentimentality. The younger generation was cynical, and their elders were disillusioned by the fact that their sacrifices had not brought about the new world they had fought for. But these facts did not keep American men from overrunning recruiting offices and offering themselves to help defeat the Axis.

Thoughtful Americans might have held Tin Pan Alley and, in particular, George M. Cohan, partially responsible for the enthusiasm whipped up for the Great War by march-like war songs. If "Over There" was as powerful a war song as the World War II generation seemed to think, then it is reasonable to deduce that a song of the same style and emotional power might have had a difficult time in gaining popularity slightly more than twenty years later. The young Americans of the World War II era were more worldly than the previous generation. They were embarrassed by shows of overt patriotism. For example, Kate Smith's performances of patriotic music earned her weekly radio show, *The Kate Smith Hour*, top ratings, but in the training camps and military bases, *Billboard* said, "The 'flag waving' hurt," since "the boys like to do their own" and any mention of a show or song with a "patriotic slant" apparently "chase[d] the trainees at camps far, far away."[4]

Some were even insulted by the notion that a soldier would not fight without a stirring song. Others resented being told what types of music they could and could not listen to. A soldier wrote *Variety* complaining that "slush tunes" had been banned from the Stage Door Canteen: "I see . . . bann[ing] tunes such as 'Dear Mom,' 'White Cliffs of Dover,' 'Miss You,' and 'My Buddy' on grounds they make the poor little soldier boy homesick and miserable." But, he argued that the soldiers like these tunes enough to "drop a nickel in the slot and play them all night long."[5]

It was apparent soldiers did not want their choice in music decided for them. Those asking for war songs for the Second World War were not the young men who were fighting the battles; it was the older generation who feared that unless there was an all-encompassing war song, American soldiers would not be inspired to fight and the home front would not rally behind the war effort. Very few articles in *Variety* or *Billboard* stated that soldiers wanted war songs. The exception was an editorial reprinted in *Variety* from *The Holabird Exhaust*, Holabird Quartermaster Motor Base, Maryland, in which the call for a forceful war song was issued by the editorial staff: "We're fed up definitely and thoroughly with these cute little plaintive songs. What we want are battle songs. Don't tell us there'll be bluebirds over the white cliffs of Dover. To hell with the bluebirds. Tell us there'll be vultures over Berchtesgaden."[6]

A poem by Captain Tom Payne claimed that servicemen wanted Tin Pan Alley to "Give us a song we can fight to," so they could "forget about the bluebirds over Dover," or wearing "a pair of silver wings" because "Johnny Doughboy's not there for fun." Payne claimed servicemen wanted songs that spoke of "things the enemy fears," like tanks and "big ships, torpedo boats, and subs." The poem concludes: "But a war is tough and it's mean— / Give us a song we can fight to."[7]

Irving Berlin strongly disagreed with Payne's sentiment. Returning from an eleven-week tour in London with *This Is the Army*, he said, "The American G.I. is getting the war songs he wants—something sentimental about home and love. He prefers this to the more martial tunes of the last war." Part of Berlin's theory for the lack of a martial war song was based on the American tradition of the citizen-soldier. He said, "After all, a war song is only a song popular during war, and who are these soldiers? They're just civilians in uniform." Since the songs most popular with civilians were love songs, it would logically follow that "the so-called sloppy, sentimental songs that are being sung reflect what the boys feel." And Berlin adds, "The boys like sentimental songs. They definitely do not like bragging, flag-waving songs."[8]

The majority of soldiers polled preferred dance tunes, and they wanted to hear them from jukeboxes, not military bands. The soldiers wanted the music they had left behind no matter where in the world they were stationed. And fears that the home front would not back America's armed forces without a song to bind the two together were unfounded. Civilians of all ages, races, and social classes contributed more to winning World War II than to any previous conflict. So many people volunteered to participate in civil defense programs, scrap drives, bond drives, and war-related activities that in many cases, the local, as well as the national, government was overwhelmed. The lack of a war song did not dampen the enthusiasm as the country closed ranks against Germany and Japan.[9]

There are other explanations for the scarcity of war songs. One of the most plausible is that music had become so sophisticated in melody and rhythm that the music industry gradually became insulated from the true mood of the American people. Swing had, through the war years, become too complicated and "difficult to dance to!" As smaller jazz combos began to influence the style and rhythms of the dance bands, there was often a crossover of musical styles and musicians who sometimes forgot the audience and played to showcase their own improvisational abilities.[10]

Jazz had become a cult for many intellectuals and rebellious teenagers.[11] Often the improvisational style became rhythmically impossible to dance to, and people who had once stopped dancing only to gather around a stage and cheer a soloist now stopped dancing completely. The tempos of the songs were either too fast or too slow for dancing, but there were many jitterbugs who made it a matter of pride and skill to be able to keep up with the fastest tempos of the swing bands. According to one dancer, "The bands seemed to be swinging faster every night and all the best dancers could follow them in new and different ways."[12] These dancers were the exceptions. Not every jitterbug had the skills to keep up with the increasingly rapid tempos, and eventually, the majority of the dancers would fall behind and leave the dance floor. The once infrequent solo improvisations of swing band musicians had become standard by the end of the 1940s. Jazz had grown so esoteric that it left most of its listeners behind.

David W. Stowe says in *Swing Changes: Big Band Jazz in New Deal America* that as early as 1940 swing music had begun to change the "cultural status of jazz" from the dance excesses of the jitterbugs into a form more closely associated with "art" music. The jitterbugs stopped dancing in order to listen (or because they did not find the rhythms danceable), and this freed the musicians and arrangers, according to Benny Goodman, to "create more musically inventive arrangements and musicians to engage in more creative expressive improvisation."[13] Whatever the reason was for the decline in dancing, one thing was certain: swing music was not conducive to war songs in the traditional sense, and apparently the American public was not willing to accept war songs in the traditional form: standard two or four beat measured tempos.

John Desmond's *New York Times* columns generated numerous comments, including one from retired U.S. Navy officer, Edward Price Ehrich, who thought that Desmond had omitted the one real reason there had been no war song: "This is not a singing war." In Ehrich's view World War II was "a very grim war—grimmer than the last one" and, furthermore, not a war where Americans stepped in (alluding to the U.S.'s late entry into WWI) "at the last minute to finish a job already well along." This was a war in which millions of Americans worked long hours in factories, bought war bonds, paid high taxes, and sent their sons and daughters to fight. Americans "are on the threshold of a frightening fight for survival—and they know it." Ehrich declared that the type of enemy with which Americans were faced—"fighting men who could do what they did to Pearl Harbor . . . men who carry out bayonet practice against Chinese prisoners . . . or Japanese nurses who hurl grenades at the backs of your troops"—these were not things that made the soldier sing as he went into battle. Maybe American soldiers did not feel like singing—except about their outfit, their loneliness, or their girlfriends. According to Ehrich, "They have nothing to sing about with regard to the war."[14]

The song titles on the best-seller lists demonstrate the validity of Ehrich's statement. American soldiers were not singing about the war, but they did sing about their loneliness and their girlfriends. Confirming this trend, "15 Best Song Sellers" for the week ending June 12, 1943, included the romantic ballads "You'll Never Know (Just How Much I Love You)" and "As Time Goes By," plus songs of loneliness and parted lovers: "Don't Get Around Much Anymore" and "Wait for Me Mary."[15]

Lieutenant Ehrich's letter is important: it was the first mention in the press of the realities of war in connection with Tin Pan Alley's efforts to write the Great American War Song. Until this letter was published in June 1943, there was little discussion of the horrors of war in the music industry trade papers and certainly no mention of killing or death in the songs. The government was always concerned that the public's morale would be affected if the truth about battlefield conditions were known. As a result the news media continued the government's policy, identical to that of World War I, of not showing photographs or news film of dead American soldiers. It was, however, perfectly acceptable to publish pictures of dead enemy soldiers or even Allied war dead.

This policy was in effect until mid-1943, when the OWI and the War Department reversed themselves and allowed wounded, dying, and dead American soldiers to be shown in published photos. Photos under the new policy were restrained. All identifying insignia were removed from the pictures, photos were cropped to remove soldiers' faces, and no mangled or dismembered bodies were shown. It was hoped these photos would spur home-front Americans to do more for the war effort. The government believed that most Americans had little concept of the war. And the OWI hoped to shock Americans out of what it perceived as public complacency.

Despite the new guidelines, the war pictured in the sanitized photos in *Life*, *Look*, *Newsweek*, and other news publications was far different from what most Americans imagined. It was "grim."[16]

Beginning in the fall of 1943, the government used photos of dead Americans in advertisements for its Third War Loan drive and public reaction was positive. An OWI survey of New York war plant workers showed 75 percent believed that photographs of dead Americans on posters would help sell more war bonds. And few thought the subject matter "too gruesome." In fact, the OWI found that the only messages able to reach war-saturated Americans were those pictures of American war dead that "make the people so mad they dig down deep."[17] But this new policy of openness did not affect Tin Pan Alley and the search for the Great American War Song. There was little change in the type of songs produced or the message or subject of those that made it onto the best-seller lists. Love and romance were the continuing interest of popular music consumers.

In conjunction with the censoring of newsreel footage and still photographs in the first two years of the war, the OWI cautioned writers and composers, along with radio broadcasters, to "avoid dramatic programs or music that attempt to portray the horrors of war." Sounds that simulated or might be mistaken for air raid alarms and sirens were forbidden. The

OWI reminded writers "war is not pretty. There's no point in rubbing it in or bathing in blood baths or having seamen fried in oil." The people on the home front could imagine the war and its terrible possibilities without show business adding to the strain.

The OWI seemed especially concerned that the "womenfolks" not be upset by maudlin or frightening songs, as they could "picture all too vividly the horrors that may befall their men without hearing . . . the possibilities in primary colors." Horror, in OWI's opinion, was unnecessarily harmful. The OWI was afraid listeners would associate a song of dying and death with someone "who is dear to them who may be serving under hazardous circumstances . . . it [a song] was not escapism but realism—something that's really happening in this war."[18] Reality was neither escapist nor entertaining, two of the primary aims (along with rousing a martial spirit in Americans) of the music business in the war.

The theory that the "grimness" of the war prevented any war songs from achieving popularity soon gave way to other excuses. Pundits excused the lack of a war song that would appeal to both soldier and civilian alike by pointing out that America's soldiers were spread over the globe and whoever composed a war song must cover the whole earth—a job that could not be done by order or prescription. If the song comes at all, wrote John Lardner in his *Newsweek* column, August 24, 1943, it would "come of its own accord, and no one can guess what sort of song it will be. It cannot be built to order." The war-song situation was beyond the control of the composers and the propagandists, he concluded, despite his belief that "no war is complete or respectable without a song or songs to represent it."[19]

The idea that the "grim seriousness" of the war precluded much singing about it on the part of soldiers was echoed in an article by Gustav Klemm, "The Fighting Man and His Music," published in the November 1943 issue of *Etude*. Klemm stated that American soldiers were so busy beating back the enemy that they had no time for singing. In addition, music was being provided for them in the form of portable entertainment centers—combined radio and phonograph sets—sent to soldiers overseas. Soldiers also had their own portable radios or access to them in the camp auditorium. Furthermore, concerts and other musical attractions in the camps helped to explain why soldiers did not sing much and had not singled out a particular song as the great martial song of World War II.[20]

Despite their many failures and the apparent indifference of the American soldier and American public, Tin Pan Alley and the Music War Committee of the American Theater Wing continued to push for war songs. Oscar Hammerstein II reminded the music industry that "the important point about a war song is that there is no virtue in its high purpose or patriotic intent. To justify itself it must stand on its own two feet as a really good song." The Music War Committee was trying to start a new cycle of war songs on a more positive note. It began the search for good songs with morale-building value by selecting forty-three songs as worthy of its recommendation. The choices varied, according to Hammerstein, "from cantata to outright corn, and the Committee is constantly reexamining them to discover whether the changing patterns of life in wartime have lessened the applicability or usefulness of any of them."[21]

Besides finding the Great American War Song, the Music War Committee took upon itself the job of analyzing the outpouring of war songs produced by its contests and calls for songs. The study of patriotic philosophy contained in war songs uncovered unsuspected complications. It would not be enough to find a song related to the war that was popular; the Music War Committee thought it could decide whether a particular song *should* be popular. "We must refrain from putting our stamp of approval on songs that might in anyway [*sic*] encourage complacency, disunity, or wishful thinking about how near we are to the end of the war."[22]

This sentiment certainly echoes the directives of the Office of War Information that discouraged songs written about the postwar world, along with love songs and songs that might divide the country by class, racial, or geographic lines. War songs also needed to present America's democratic ideology. The country could not be pictured as boastful, militaristic, or egocentric. The nation should be presented as a place where all people were free to decide their own fates, the traditional land of opportunity. The United States was a country in which the poorest boy could grow up to be president or at the very least be a success in his chosen field, if he worked hard enough and was willing to make sacrifices. And finally, Americans should be represented in war songs as a people reluctant to fight but willing to do what was necessary to preserve their freedom.

The attempt by the OWI and the Music War Committee to solve the problem—that of getting "correct" war songs—failed. Abel Green put it succinctly, saying, "Fact is nobody yet has been able to lead the nation to the musical trough and make 'em drink. . . . You can pound high-powered songplugging at 'em . . . but what they'll accept, one never knows till the songs move off the rack." Irving Berlin was also correct when he wrote *Variety*, in answer to the Music War Committee's idea of a songwriting contest, that nobody had yet "cooked up a song hit via a contest."[23]

The Pittsburgh Press finally suggested that it might be a good thing "if everyone would stop hunting for the perfect war song. They've got the boys in Tin Pan Alley pressing, and in Tin Pan Alley that's not good."[24] It seemed as if the nation's master songwriters could not perform under pressure, or perhaps they had been asked to do the impossible.

The drive for "correct" songs, even for use by servicemen, also failed. The Army's *Hit Kit* was a flop. Printed in pocket-sized folders for soldiers to carry with them, the *Hit Kit*s included at least one "oldie" and one patriotic song. They were published once a month and distributed around the globe. By the time soldiers in the field received the *Hit Kit*, it was usually several months old, and many of the songs had lost their popularity. The *Hit Kit* could not compete with live and shortwave radio broadcasts that allowed the men to hear the latest songs on *Your Hit Parade*.

After twelve months the army decided on July 22, 1944, to abandon the *Hit Kit* and concede to the soldiers' musical choices. In a nationwide poll of training camps both in the United States and overseas, GIs voted the *Hit Kit* as one of their seven least favorite periodicals. They would rather spend their money on commercial lyrics magazines such as *Broadcast Songs*, *Hit Parade*, or *Song Hits* than receive the free *Hit Kits*.[25] Evidently, American GIs did not want all of their decisions made for them. If a song was popular, it was because the soldiers decided so for themselves, and not because some committee told them which songs to sing.

Eventually, Tin Pan Alley began to promote the idea that the war song of World War II would appear with or without government aid or committees of composers and publishers. The American public would decide which songs it preferred and from those would come the "War Song." Music publishers admitted they were baffled by the public's indifferent response to martial songs. The popularity of nonsense songs, such as "Mairzy Doats" (which became the number one sheet music seller in less than three weeks with sales of over 450,000), proved what music publishers had been saying all along: "The song buying public gets enough of the big conflict in newspapers, magazines, and on the air, and that escapist material is preferred in musical form."[26] A few critics spoke out against "Mairzy Doats" by Milton Drake, Al Hoffman, and Jerry Livingston, fearing that its popularity was a comment about the mentality of the Americans who were singing and humming the tune.[27] Its words were said to have been inspired by the one of the songwriters' daughters. Apparently, he overheard his child talking to her dolls and saying something that sounded like, "marzie tweet an' cowzie tweet and liddle harskey doysters." This was then worked in to a bouncy song:

Mairzy doats and dozy doats and liddle lamzy divey
A kiddley divey too, wouldn't you? Yes!

The best-selling songs of February 1944 testify to the fact that the American public still was not interested in war songs. Of the top fifteen tunes, only two had any connections with the war. One was "Vict'ry Polka," a best-selling song written by Samuel Cahn and Jule Styne and recorded by Bing Crosby and the Andrews Sisters, with lyrics that proclaimed in polka style:

> There's gonna be a hallelujah day,
> When the boys have all come home to stay.
> And a million bands begin to play,
> We'll be dancing the Vict'ry Polka.

The "dream" aspect of "Vic'try Polka" could not have pleased the OWI, but the lyrics did mention war aims: freedom "across the sea" and a victorious "United Nations" on parade. Of the fifty melodies on the most-played list from the broadcast networks, only Jimmy McHugh's "Say a Prayer for the Boys Over There" actually mentioned the war in terms of battle and the accompanying danger to soldiers:

> Say a pray'r for the boys over there
> And tomorrow's sky will be brighter
> Bless them all as they valiantly fight
> And let your faith be their guiding star tonight.

Music publishers were beginning to think that World War II would never produce a war song comparable to those of World War I. Some publishers even claimed that if "Praise the Lord and Pass the Ammunition" had been published in early 1944, it would not have gotten more than "passing attention."[28]

The people who listened to jukeboxes in the weeks following the D-Day invasion of Normandy, beginning on June 6, 1944, did not register their opinions about the conduct of the war by song selection or by an increase in popular music sales as they did after other military successes (for example, Midway in 1942 and the surrender of Italy in 1943). "The Bells of Normandy," by Don Reid and Irving Miller, did not sell despite a large advertising campaign by Dorsey Brothers Music, Inc. It seemed that Americans did not care to sing that "The Bells of Normandy are ringing again / And hearts of Normandy are singing again."

The ten most popular songs had tenuous connections, if any, with events in either Europe or the Pacific. The "10 Best Sellers on Coin-Machines" in *Variety* for the week of June 21, 1944, included "I'll Get By," "I'll Be Seeing You," "Long Ago and Far Away," "San Fernando Valley," "I Love You," "Amor," "Goodnight Wherever You Are," and "Straighten Up and Fly Right." Only two songs had any connection with the war: "G.I. Jive" and "Milkman Keep Those Bottles Quiet," by Don Raye and Gene de Paul.[29] Both of the latter songs were based on current slang, and neither could seriously be considered "proper" war songs:

Milkman, keep those bottles quiet.
Can't use that jive on my milk diet.
Been workin' on the swing shift all night,
Turnin' out my quota, all right.
. . . .
Milkman keep those bottles quiet.

In the absence of hit war songs, music publishers turned to V-E Day songs. As early as October 1944, it was reported that music publishers were lining up songs to mark the celebrations that would occur when U.S. troops returned home. At least four Tin Pan Alley publishing houses had numbers using the back-home-again theme: "When My GI Guy Comes Marching Home," "Wish You Were Waiting For Me," and "Pretty Soon," and "When He Comes Home."

In view of the official government policy frowning on any premature celebration that might build undue optimism and lead to a drop in the war effort, there was a difference of opinion among publishers as to whether the "welcome-home" songs should be published. Leeds Music decided to withhold release of "When My GI Guy Comes Marching Home" until the situation really called for it. Other publishers said that the songs reflected actual public sentiment and they were going to publish and release these songs.[30]

In August 1944 Campbell-Porgie, Inc., published "Some Peaceful Evening (In Some Peaceful Town)," by Dewey Bergman, Carley Mills, and Ann Roberts. This song spoke of "Some peaceful evening / In some peaceful town" when "We'll be together again." In the meantime, "It's a Law-aw-aw-aw-aw-aw-aw-ong Way Back Home" by Collins Driggs told how "Step by step / Mile by mile / Tramp,tramp, tramping all the while /. . . How I long the whole day through / To hit that long, long way back to you."

Of all the premature homecoming songs, "When I Get Back to My Home Town" was one of the few actually to mention the war as a cause for separation and also to attempt to spread some war ideology. The verse rationalizes that the separation was necessary in order to preserve "freedom" and the American way of living in "home towns." Fearing reprisals from the MWC and the weakened OWI, publishers of "When I Get Back to My Home Town" printed a disclaimer on the front page of the sheet music noting that the song was "cleared thru NBC, Blue,[31] and CBS Networks," so it appeared to have official sanction, despite the OWI's discouragement of such songs.

Released in September 1944, Lew Berks's "When I Get Back to My Home Town" clearly looked forward to the end of the war:

> When I Get Back to My Home Town,
> There's gonna be a jubilee.
> And when the boys are homeward bound,
> ....
> And we'll have freedom everywhere
> When I Get Back to My Home Town.

Some of the radio networks also questioned the wisdom of playing V-E material before victory in Europe had actually been won. The Blue Network and CBS both decided to stress Berks's theme "There's still plenty to be done to beat the Nips," so publishers were unsure they would be able to get their V-E numbers played. Still, exceptions to the broadcasters' decision certainly existed, as evidenced by "When I Get Back to My Home Town" and other songs with a homecoming theme such as "Make Way for Tomorrow," "Sentimental Journey," and "When the Boys Come Home."

Despite the efforts of the OWI and the Music War Committee, the top tunes of 1944 continued to be those with romantic settings or those that touched on the war indirectly—but had added meaning because of the war. Even revivals of songs more than twenty years old found their way onto the best-seller list. Examples include Irving Berlin's "Always," first published in 1925, and an American folk tune, "Buffalo Gals," which was given new lyrics and made *Your Hit Parade* as "Dance with a Dolly (With a Hole in Her Stocking)." Others on the top-seller list for 1944 included "Don't Fence Me In," "I'll Be Seeing You," "I'll Get By," "I'll Walk Alone," "No Love, No Nothin'," "Paper Doll," "Swingin' on a Star," and, once again, "White Christmas."[32]

The Lucky Strike Hit Parade's Top Ten for 1944 included "I'll Be Seeing You," "Long Ago and Far Away," "I'll Get By," "I'll Walk Alone," "Amor," "Swinging on a Star," "I Love You," "Besame Mucho," "My Heart Tells Me," and "The Trolley Song."[33] None of these could be classified as war songs, but they had lyrics that could take on special connotations for wartime listeners. These songs spoke of love, of separation, and of faithful partners waiting to be reunited in the future. Listeners who were parted from a loved one could easily transfer the songs to fit their situations. The only restriction placed on popular music fans' musical fantasies was their own imagination or lack thereof. This association of lyrics with individual circumstances had the potential to make every song a war song.

Following Victory-in-Europe (V-E) Day, May 8, 1945, there was no holding back the "dream" songs or those that spoke of future plans with loved ones. Americans were just waiting for the time to pass and for their soldiers to return. Although the war in the Pacific was far from over, it would have been difficult to discern that fact from a glance at the popular music charts or the advertisements for new songs. Following V-E Day, the "Honor Roll of Hits" as published by *Billboard* in its May 19, 1945, issue was "There I Said It Again," "Sentimental Journey," "Laura," "My Dreams Are Getting Better All the Time," "Just Say a Prayer," "Candy," "Dream," "I'm Beginning to See the Light," "All of My Life," and "Bell-Bottom Trousers."[34]

"Bell-Bottom Trousers," a sea chantey of obscure origin, was introduced by bandleader Moe Jaffe—with sanitized lyrics—and for a while its popularity led the music business to believe that "Bell-Bottom Trousers" might be the "Mademoiselle from Armentieres" of World War II. "Bell-Bottom Trousers" was the last song with any military connection to make *Your Hit Parade*, and technically it fell in the novelty song category (with frivolous lyrics and a rollicking tune that was more conducive to toe-tapping than to marching) and was thus not the martial song for which the OWI had hoped.[35]

When victory did come in the Pacific, the popular music business made little note of the fact. Musical best-sellers were the same songs that had been popular for months: sentimental ballads and sweet dance tunes—not unlike the same songs that had been popular at the beginning of the war. There were some renewed efforts at homecoming songs, including "Now the War Is Over," "Victory Day," "Darkness Comes to Light Again," "The Lights Are on Again," and "Victory." Other songs of this variety were "You're Coming Home," "Back to My Country and You," "They're Coming Back," "They're Home Again," "Veterans on Parade," and "We've Won the War." Even Irving Berlin responded, sending "Just A Blue Serge Suit" to his publisher on August 18, 1945:

> Just a blue serge suit and a bright new necktie,
> A room of his own with a door,
> Just a bed with sheets and a home-cooked dinner—
> That's what he's been fighting for.

But these songs were the exceptions. Americans wanted to take that "Sentimental Journey" home "On the Atchison, Topeka, and the Santa Fe" to sit on "Saturday Night" with a "Rum and Coca-Cola"; they did not want to "Remember Pearl Harbor" or "Praise the Lord and Pass the Ammunition" any more than they had at the war's beginning. The songs on the hit charts in August 1945 were almost identical in subject and mood (romantic ballads and swing tunes) to those songs that were the leading record sellers of 1941: "I Don't Want to Set the World on Fire," "Green Eyes," "Beat Me Daddy, Eight to the Bar," "Chattanooga Choo-Choo," "I Guess I'll Have to Dream the Rest," and "Along the Santa Fe Trail."[36]

Chapter 13

Even Stale Music Sells Like Nylons

When the OWI created the National Wartime Music Committee, allied itself with the American Theater Wing's Music War Council, and called on all Tin Pan Alley songwriters to churn out tough-minded songs that would educate Americans about the realities of war, it hoped for better results than it got. The OWI never understood the function of talent and artistry in popular music production. To the government, song composition was a craft; songs were products to be manufactured. It assumed that if Tin Pan Alley tried hard enough and all its components cooperated, it would be possible to write the Great American War Song that would speak to all Americans and rally them behind the war effort. The OWI wanted a war song that would enshrine in the people's hearts the necessity of winning the war through every American's total participation.[1]

An unrealistic view of the American public hampered the OWI's thinking in regards to what type of song would become *the* war song. The United States was not a country of assimilated minorities, a contented working class, and small farmers, as might be supposed from listening to some of the OWI's radio scripts. According to William O'Neill, "Real Americans had conventional beliefs, few political ideas, and strong prejudices. They were delighted by commercial songs, movies, and radio programs—and the more sentimental, melodramatic, action-oriented, or comic they were, the better."[2]

American entertainment of the World War II years (like most American popular culture of any age) was superficial, mass-produced, and commercialized. Any attempts by the government to impose its guidelines on this national enterprise—show business—would have to accept these facts.

The OWI thought it understood this, and its unofficial policy of "business as usual" that allowed the entertainment industry to carry on as before seemed reasonable. Unfortunately, the OWI failed to comprehend the large extent to which the war effort would be defined by "advertisers and merchandisers." It was not prepared to admit that Tin Pan Alley could not be converted from manufacturing love songs to manufacturing war songs just as automobile plants had retooled to assemble planes or tanks. Selling merchandise, in the form of records and sheet music, was the first priority of Tin Pan Alley and the OWI never really swayed the music business from this course.

After an encouraging beginning in early 1942, war song production gradually slowed to a trickle. Even contests with monetary awards were unable to elicit a great war song to rally Americans. For example, in Chicago, *The Daily Times* offered $1,000 to the winner of its "War Song for America" contest, saying, "America is asking for an inspiring war song. America wants it badly."[3] As if $1,000 were not reason enough to enter, the contest sponsor asked aspiring composers, "How would you like to achieve undying fame as the writer of 1942's 'Over There'? . . . a stirring song that America would take to its heart . . . that the boys would whistle . . . along the path to victory?"

In marketing its contest, *The Daily Times* suggested the winning song would be played by leading bands, sung on the radio by renowned entertainers, and possibly used as the basis for a Hollywood motion picture. "There is no telling the extent of the glory and reward that will lie ahead of the winning contestant." The "War Song for America" contest drew over eight thousand entries from amateur and professional songwriters alike, but the winning entry, "Mud in His Ears" by Mac Weaver and Joseph C. Banahan, never received more than a few performances and was quickly forgotten. Still, Weaver and Banahan, the happy winners, declared that *The Times* contest had rendered a patriotic service and was of "immeasurable value to the morale of the country."[4] Winning the contest surely raised Weaver and Banahan's morale; one used the money to buy a house and the other used his to get married. *The Times* also explained that each of the winners was purchasing his full quota of war bonds through a payroll deduction plan and therefore felt no obligation to buy bonds with their prize money.

Although the National Wartime Music Committee and the War Music Council made a great show of backing war songs, their titles dropped from the popularity charts after 1943. Bands did not play marching songs, and the new swing band rhythms were not meant for marching.[5] People now heard music at home on their radios, not in theaters or dance halls, and the dominant type of music on the radio was the love song. Polls taken by the networks consistently reported romantic ballads as the first preference of listeners.[6] When a strike by the musicians' union, the American Federation of Musicians (AFM), stopped instrumental recording, vocalists were able to step out from the band and become highly visible entertainers in their own right. Thereafter, the popularity of the singer became an important factor in a song's fate. The cult of personality surrounding a musical star was often enough advertisement to boost a song into *Your Hit Parade*, but even the top male vocalist of the war years, Bing Crosby, could not boost a martial war song onto the charts.

Another factor in the change in the music industry was the ASCAP strike, which left the door open for other musicians to enter the music industry. Broadcast Music, Incorporated, was able to compete with ASCAP in the growing fields of swing, folk, blues, and country music.[7] Tin Pan Alley no longer controlled the market and, more importantly, the Alley no longer determined public taste in music. People were voting for their favorite songs with their nickels in jukeboxes and with their purchases of sheet music and records.

Although ASCAP had begun losing its choke hold on the music industry during the war years, it was far from being counted out in the race for America's entertainment dollar. Tin Pan Alley, like the rest of the entertainment industry, not only survived during World War II but also prospered beyond its wildest imaginings.

At the beginning of the war, the future did not look bright for the music publishing business. Following Pearl Harbor, sheet music sales went into a slump, but then staged a sharp comeback in the weeks after December 7, 1941. Especially profitable were sheet music sales of "The White Cliffs of Dover," "Elmer's Tune," and "Chattanooga Choo-Choo." The only war song with any noticeable sales listing in late January 1942 was "You're a Sap Mr. Jap"—advertised in *Variety* as "America's Greatest Novelty." There is nothing in the copy of the *Variety* advertisement to suggest that the country was at war, other than a slogan, "Buy Defense Bonds and Stamps and Lick the Other Side."[8]

Record sales never fell seriously; they continued on an upward spiral, most likely due to the Christmas gift-giving season. One tune associated with the war did stand out as a big seller in pre-Pearl Harbor 1941; "The White Cliffs of Dover" sold 43,000 copies as recorded by Sammy Kaye; 42,000 copies as recorded by Kay Kyser; 30,000 copies as recorded by Tommy Tucker; and 9,500 copies as recorded by Kate Smith. As a *Variety* headline boasted in its December 24, 1941, issue, "Socko Boom in Music Sales Sets In."[9]

By February 1942, *Variety* sensed that Americans were still "jittery" about the war, but they were "getting more accustomed to the situation and instead of staying glued to radios or newspapers [were] apparently breaking out in an amusement rash."[10] In fact all forms of entertainment were booming. In April 1942, the music publishing industry received record-high royalty payments for the business quarter ending in February 1942. RCA Victor distributed checks totaling more than $325,000, representing payments on copyrighted materials used on approximately 11 million recordings. One tune, "Chattanooga Choo Choo," was responsible for royalties of $35,000 to the publisher, Leo Feist, of the Metro-Robbins group.[11]

Dance bands also enjoyed prosperous times at the beginning of the war. Bands were booked for playing engagements throughout 1942, but some feared that restrictions on travel, most notably in the form of tire and gasoline rationing, would eventually force the "top outfits [to] hole up in theaters, hotels and major localities."[12] These predictions came true, and by the end of the war, very few dance bands toured the country as they had before the war. The draft also took its toll on the music industry.

Despite the blows the music industry suffered in the opening months of the war—the great reduction in record production, almost insurmountable transportation difficulties, and conscription of musicians—the industry "was in as good a shape as it [had] ever been at this time of year." Summer was normally the best time for dance band bookings, and 1942 was no exception. Agents and location managers all reported that business was "good." They were "cleaned out of open time on major properties and little unfilled time remains on the lesser names between now and August."[13] The number of one-night bookings fell, but those were compensated for by the increase in one and two week engagements.

Colleges were a major source of playing dates for dance bands. In 1942 many colleges conducted summer classes for the first time, and dance bands were eager to take advantage of playing opportunities never before available. Charlie Barnet's band was especially eager to play the summer college circuit and would often play one-nighters at schools within easy driving distance of a longer engagement. For example, the band took a side trip to Penn State College from Barnet's month-long job at Atlantic City's Steel Pier. Bands also found employment in military training camps, sometimes being brought in to play for special occasions such as air corps cadets' graduation at Maxwell Field, Montgomery, Alabama and similar ceremonies at the Naval Training Centers at San Diego, California, Great Lakes, Illinois, and Orlando, Florida.[14]

The war continued to mean good business for dance bands. Bandleaders found that they did not have to travel to make a profit. The practice of "taking a loss" to perform on the radio, instead of at a well-paying theater or ballroom, ceased during the war. Bandleaders demanded and got "location pay" that met or exceeded their "road" salaries, which also gave their musicians a chance to rest from the daily grind of constant travel. The war placed entertainment at a premium and at the same time the draft and recruitment reduced the number of bands, so that the ones that survived were highly profitable. The fees for bands increased by as much as 100 percent. One band playing a southern hotel in the summer of 1943 received a weekly fee of $3,000. Five months earlier, the same band had earned $1800 for a week's work.[15]

The music industry continued to post record-breaking sales during the war years. During 1943, alone, the recording industry expected commercial sales between 75 million and 100 million records. These figures are even more impressive when compared to the sales numbers for the years 1941 and 1942, the peak years for the industry when sales were between 100 million and 115 million. Although it was hampered by the loss of manpower to the armed services and civilian war work, and though it operated with 20 percent of its normal shellac supplies and donated about 50 percent of its commercial output to the OWI, the music business was able to generate high profits. But for 1943, the year's totals were not expected to be anywhere near the projected numbers.

The war also caused recording companies to reduce the number of new tunes they pressed, restricting new recordings to artists with a proven commercial following. Manufacturers and publishers were forced to drop their less profitable releases from small bands and singers with little name recognition in order to concentrate their efforts on the top bands that promised the greatest profit. And the top bands did produce. By spring 1943 several records had sold over 1 million copies; among these were "White Christmas" (the Bing Crosby version), "Chattanooga Choo-Choo," "Maria Elena," and "Green Eyes." Four recordings—"There Are Such Things" and "It Started All Over Again" by Tommy Dorsey and "I Heard That Song Before" and "Velvet Moon" by Harry James—were responsible for over 3,700,000 disc sales.[16] Harry James, with over 3,500,000 recordings sold in the first half of 1943, was said to have surpassed the earnings of an individual musician for one-year sales in the history of Tin Pan Alley. The recording companies maintained profitable businesses. For example, Decca reported profits for the first six months of 1943 that were $50,000 more than for the same period in 1942 and was able to pay its shareholders twenty-two cents a share more than the previous year. Many of the recording companies were able to pay higher dividends to their stockholders than in previous years.[17]

As the war progressed, sheet music continued to post record sales. *Variety* thought sheet music sales might go as high as 40 million copies in 1943. The total for 1942 was 25 million. Speculating on the reasons for this boom, publishers concluded that people had money to spend, and sheet music was one commodity that was not rationed. And families were evidently returning to home-based entertainment, such as singing around the piano. With gas rationing prohibiting families from much traveling, more Americans entertained themselves at home.[18]

The wartime prosperity of the music industry continued through 1943 with sales of eight hundred thousand and 1 million copies of a song no longer considered a novelty. Before the war, if a song sold over two hundred thousand copies it was considered a huge hit. One million copies in sales was almost commonplace during World War II. Publishers drew parallels with England's music business and the boom it enjoyed during World War II. Like the English, Americans found few luxury items to purchase with their extra money, so they spent it on sheet music, records, the motion pictures, and other forms of entertainment. People were paying what would have been considered exorbitant prices for sheet music (thirty-five cents) and as much as $5.00 for the Broadway cast recording of the new Rodgers and Hammerstein musical *Oklahoma!*[19]

By mid-1943, the Office of Price Administration (OPA) had become interested in the upward price shifts by the various recording companies. The major manufacturers had begun to move their more popular artists from the pre-war thirty-five cent labels to the fifty and even seventy-five cent discs. The OPA charged that the recording companies had failed to live up to their pre-Pearl Harbor promises to market a minimum number of thirty-five cent discs. The reasoning behind these price guidelines was to prevent inflation.

No formal charges were ever brought against any of the major recording companies, but a committee to study the problem was composed of OPA representatives and members of the executive committees of the various record manufacturing firms. This committee was to work out a plan whereby prices and artists' fees could be set at a reasonable level so that all companies could have a profit. The government continued to insist that recording firms make a certain number of thirty-five cent discs, but the record executives asserted that operating costs for artists, materials, and manpower had risen so dramatically that no firm could produce discs at the thirty-five cent price and stay in business.[20]

Although the government continued to insist that set amounts of records in all the price ranges be produced, the public demand for more discs allowed the manufacturers to ignore most of the government guidelines. The major record companies continued to produce the recordings that would maximize their profits.

Publishers and record manufacturers worried constantly during the first years of the war that the supply of paper and shellac, both vital to the music business, would be greatly reduced by the War Production Board. Faced with shellac rationing, the recording companies tried to solve the problem with "Shellac Drives"—having people turn in their old records to be melted down and made into new ones. The Joint Army and Navy Committee on Welfare and Recreation reported in September 1943 that it had distributed three hundred thousand new records to the fighting forces as a result of the November 1942–January 1943 scrap record collection instituted by Records for Our Fighting Men, and a second scrap record drive in May 1943 made an equal number of new records available for shipping. The use of drives was so effective that some record manufacturers were not able to keep up with the numbers of old records and had to call a halt to the promotion. One company reported its shellac drives were so successful that it had enough supplies for many months to come.[21]

On April 1, 1944, the government rescinded its rationing orders on shellac, and the recording companies were allowed to purchase 100 percent of their 1941 allotment.[22] Rumors circulated that the United States Navy had developed a synthetic shellac substitute and that an Illinois industrial manufacturer also had discovered a substitute shellac that would meet all the uses for which natural shellac was needed. But recording companies warned that this would not mean more records since their factories were still affected by the manpower shortage that most non-war material industries faced.[23]

Sheet music publishers were less fortunate than were record companies. At first sheet music production was unaffected by the shortages other industries faced, but rumors constantly surfaced regarding reduced paper allotments for music publishers. A new War Production Board order issued in June 1944 limited publishers to 75 percent of the paper tonnage they had used in 1941. Unfortunately, for music publishers, 1941 had been the year of the ASCAP strike, and they had not required their full allotment of paper since there had not been many new songs to print.[24]

In spite of the paper shortage, sheet music continued to sell, and by October music publishers were counting 1943 as the best year for sheet music sales in the last fifteen years. There were no seasonal slumps in 1943; people continued to buy, the good songs and the bad. Music publishers tried to analyze the trend and could only conjecture that the smaller number of records available had helped sheet music's profitability.[25]

By mid-December 1944, *Variety* reported that the music business was keeping pace with the "stratospheric earnings" of films, theater, radio, and all other forms of show business. Bonus earnings from sheet music sales alone for ASCAP members in 1944 were $1,700,000 higher than had been predicted, bringing the year's total royalty payments for ASCAP members to over $6,000,000. This was higher than any previous year's profit and about $1,500,000 higher than 1943.[26]

These revenues came at a time when sheet music salesmen had not expanded their inventory of sales racks;[27] people simply were buying more music. Such large first-round sales enabled publishers to recover their costs almost immediately and to apply the remainder of the sales revenue to the profits. Some music stores complained that they could not keep racks filled: customers were buying everything they could find. By April 1945 the music business was still highly profitable, even with the government-imposed paper shortage.

During the first week of April 1945, the War Production Board issued new orders limiting individual publishers to 75 percent of their consumption of either of the years 1941 or 1944, or five tons of paper, whichever was greater. Five tons of paper produced about 250,000 copies of piano sheet music, so the five-ton allowance was not an adequate supply. The year 1941 was not likely to be chosen as a base measure either, since during that year broadcasters and ASCAP were "at war and music sales were off." Publishers still were not pleased with the prospect of 1944 as a base year either, since by then paper restrictions had settled at a sub-normal level of "75% of what they used in 1941." And publishers who had had hit tunes in 1944 would fare better than those who had not.

This uneven distribution caused unrest among the publishers, for in the music industry a publisher could have a string of hits one year that would boost his paper consumption. In the following year he might be without a single hit and have more paper available than he could use, while other publishers would not have half enough to satisfy the demands of one or more hits. The music industry had no choice but to abide by the government's regulations and hope that the 1945 order would be rescinded as previous ones concerning paper rationing had been.[28]

Some publishers sold their old stock of sheet music with new covers (there was paper for covers) and marked up the price of the music. People still bought it. Retailers took advantage of the situation to clear out their inventory of old sheet music. Sometimes customers were required to purchase one or more old pieces of sheet music before they could buy a new one. In several New York stores, salesmen were instructed to ration sheet music sales. The number of purchases and the frequency with which they could be made were limited. The going rate was usually two new songs a week per customer, with no limits on purchases of older stock on the shelves or in the storerooms.[29]

It was not until July 1945 that the sheet music business noticed a slump in sales. Music salesmen and publishers stated that popular music sales had fallen as much as 25 to 30 percent in June and July. There were several reasons: (1) There was no strong top-selling song to pull the others along with it. (2) Record sales had begun to recover from the AFM recording ban. (3) Summer was always a slack time for sheet music sales.

There was general agreement among publishers and salesmen that the first and third reasons were valid, but there was controversy over the impact of the increased sale of records on the sheet music market. Most publishers thought that record manufacturers had not yet reached full production and so were not putting out enough records to hurt sheet music sales. Despite falling sales in mid-1945, business was still quite a few percentage points above pre-war figures. Experienced music businessmen maintained that "the music business since the start of the big battle has jumped 50%."[30]

Instrumental musicians, dance bands, and orchestra performers did not fare as well. When the American Federation of Musicians barred its members from making recordings in mid-1942, it removed a large portion of the income that was available to instrumentalists. Between 1942 and 1943, AFM members lost over $4 million.[31] The other factions in this dispute—recording companies, transcription services, and publishing houses—lost comparatively little money during the strike. Recording companies were forced by wartime shortages of materials and workers to reduce the number of new releases and to confine these new releases to the best tunes and the most popular performers. Million record sales became commonplace as a result of this selective recording. The only difficulty faced by the publishing companies was exploiting new tunes without the benefit of recordings.[32]

Musicians were also hurt by the government's restrictions on travel. James C. Petrillo had attempted to secure a special dispensation on tires and gasoline for traveling bands and orchestras on one-night routes. When the government announced gasoline rationing beginning in May 1942, many bands that had barely survived the Depression and were already in trouble from lack of manpower saw their livelihoods directly threatened. Bands that still had good tires decided to use their vehicles rather than let the rubber rot from disuse in storage. Other bands were not so fortunate. The lack of tires and charter buses and the prevalence of unreliable railroad schedules caused a "pyramid [of] travel grief." All of this tended to reinforce the decisions of band and orchestra leaders, who could afford to do so, to stay away from one-night schedules. Bands now preferred theater and "location" bookings; the latter were especially sought after for the radio time often available with this type of job. And bands and orchestras increased their fees to compensate for their higher travel expenses. The smaller, lesser-known groups did not survive and many musicians were thrown out of work. The lack of "name" bands on the travel circuit caused prices to rise when a name group was available.[33]

The restrictions faced by music businesses did not keep them from prospering. Although 1942 was the biggest year for the recording industry, with sales of over 132 million records—the years 1943 through 1945 continued to be profitable. Sales estimates for 1943 totaled 118 million records, and 1944 followed with 92 million.[34] Even though the sales figures diminished as the war lengthened, a direct result of the music boom of the early 1940s was that several large companies that had barely held on during the Great Depression were saved from bankruptcy. The twenty-seven month strike between recording companies and James C. Petrillo's American Federation of Musicians had made a dent in the production efforts of major record firms, but the shortage of manpower and raw materials had more of an impact on the business.

At the end of World War II, *Variety* boasted that 1945 had been "a year of years" for the music business. ASCAP reported royalty earnings of $10 million to be divided among the membership; this amounted to approximately $20,000 for each member. Publishing companies also had record earnings.

According to *Variety*, Santly-Joy Music Publishers reportedly grossed over $1 million, while the other major firms enjoyed profits ranging from $150,000 to $750,000. It was estimated that record production could go as high as six hundred thousand discs a year when all materials restrictions were lifted—especially if the new product from RCA-Victor, the $2.00 Vinylite (non-breakable plastic) disc was available in sufficient quantities to drive down the price. At the close of the war, there were approximately 130 record manufacturing companies in the United States, most of them looking to a postwar sales boom in plastic records. This new product, available for sale in racks like the sheet music then sold on newsstands, would decide which of these companies would survive.[35]

Chapter 14

Jitterbugs and Bobby-Soxers

The music industry's sales figures for the period December 7, 1941–August 14, 1945, also provide a clue to the mystery of why no great war song appeared. An analysis of who was buying the records and sheet music and what types of songs were preferred reveal that a new force had entered society and the marketplace: the American teenager, and more specifically, the teenage girl.

The 1940s introduced the age when the adolescent emerged as a social phenomenon and marketing target in America. The teen revolution, which would develop and flourish in the 1950s, was launched in the mid-1940s. Adolescence became an age to be carefully prolonged, intensely experienced, and profitably catered to by American manufacturers as never before. The American advertising business discovered the youth market, assigning a new name to this stage of development from child to adult.

According to some in the publishing industry, "teenagers," as adolescents were then popularly labeled, cared little about the war: "I think you should have more articles on dates and shyness," a girl wrote to *Seventeen*, "stories like those on atomic energy are very boring."[1] Another letter complained that a short story about the death of an older brother in the war was too horrible: "Who wants to read about it? It's enough to give one nightmares! Let's have more stories about lively teenagers."[2] The magazine itself was launched in 1944 to cater to the new fashions and fantasies of young girls.

Not all teenagers were bored with the war or as blasé as the young women complaining to *Seventeen*. The morale of teenagers, especially those boys who were or would soon be eighteen years old and eligible for the draft, was of great concern to the nation. Morale among high school students was a constant worry as evidenced by a number of studies undertaken to judge the reactions of high school youth to the war. Two education publications, *School and Society* and *Social Education*, published reports of their findings concerning student morale in March 1942 and November 1942, respectively. Stanford University Press published a monograph titled *Wartime Morale of High School Youth*, and the State College of Washington conducted a continuing investigation of the reactions of high school youth to the war.

In March 1942 four separate studies were undertaken. The fourth of these described a survey of morale at the end of the first full year of World War II, taken between November 23 and December 18, 1942.[3] Although the report was based on a small sample of high school students from Muncie, Indiana; Oakland, California; Longview, Washington; and Spokane, Washington, the findings of the study were suggestive of the possible morale throughout the nation's high schools. The study argued that the essential ingredient in good morale was confidence and optimism, tempered with a realistic recognition of the difficulties of war that were yet to be faced.

The study, titled "The Test on the Effects of War," required students to respond either "Yes" or "No" to seventy statements about the war. The test dealt with three periods: the present, the remainder of the war, and the postwar period. The test was also designed to gauge students' reactions to certain aspects of the war: the military seriousness of the war, the economic effects on civilians, and the restriction and discomfort of civilian life.

The results of the "Test on the Effects of the War" varied from school to school, but 90 percent or more of the students agreed with the following statements:

1. America has organized for this war faster than in 1917.
2. So far I have not suffered much from the war.
3. America will win the war.
4. The sacrifices civilians have made so far have really been necessary for victory.
5. After the war the United States will be more than ever the leading nation in the world.
6. Amusements and sports will be greatly reduced.
7. The government will set up a program to prevent poverty.

Ninety percent or more disagreed with these statements:

1. The war has caused no difficulty for the average business.
2. Inland cities like Chicago and Kansas City will be bombed.
3. Food will become so scarce that civilians will go hungry.

4. Because of rationing people will not have as much clothing as they need.
5. This country will have a complete dictatorship (before the war ends).

Nearly all of the responses to the statements above were of a cheerful, patriotic, confident nature. But on the following questions, opinion greatly divided the high school students:

1. If military affairs go badly, censorship will conceal the truth from the people. (Forty-four percent agreed.)
2. There will be epidemics of disease among civilians. (Forty-four percent agreed.)
3. Regular college work will be discontinued. (Forty-three percent agreed.)
4. A fair and lasting peace will be established. (Fifty-six percent agreed.)
5. All young men will be required to take military training after the war. (Forty-nine percent agreed.)

The results of this test of high school students' morale alarmed some educators. The mistrust of the government implied in the questions about censorship and epidemics showed, in the opinion of the testers, a lack of confidence in the government. There was also a strong tendency on the part of students to exaggerate the dangers and hardships brought by the war. Mistrust of business profiteering, misinformation about the rise in the cost of living, and the success of the American military, particularly in regard to shipping convoys to England, were also areas to be addressed so that the students' misconceptions of the war and the government could be corrected. But, the crucial questions concerning war mobilization, a successful conclusion to the war, civilian sacrifices for the war effort, and the United States' leadership role in the world were all answered in extremely positive terms.

From these questions two results concerning wartime morale of the high school students seemed apparent. The first was that students had good morale regarding wartime conditions, but not as high as the testers expected according to the United States' achievements thus far in the war during 1942. The second conclusion the researchers drew from the study was that a large minority held positions that could be "construed as detrimental to morale." The survey results also showed that students exaggerated the scope and danger of the war:

1. Thirty-three percent agreed that half of the American soldiers will be killed or permanently injured.
2. Thirty-three percent agreed that if a community is bombed repeatedly, one-fourth of the population will be killed

3. Eighty percent agreed that most American men will be in the Army or the Navy.
4. Thirty-three percent stated that they were "constantly worried" about their friends in the armed forces.

This set of questions and responses was alarming to the formulators of the survey because the apprehension that "half of the American soldiers will be killed or permanently injured" could only do harm to the morale of boys who would soon enter the military. Educators were encouraged to lead their students to realize that "the physical threat of war is small for any given individual" and that "war [is] a job to be done but only as a temporary part of their lives."[4] Patriotic "flag-waving" was discouraged, as well as the mention of heroic, "self-sacrificing" soldiers. The assurance that there would be a postwar future for them was supposed to make these students into "brave fighters."

It is apparent from the answers to the surveys that students saw their world changing. Women were leaving the home and joining the workforce. Jobs in heavy industry opened up to women as more men were called to active duty. The increase of the students who thought most heavy industry work would be taken over by women (from 52 percent to 79 percent) was a negative gain because this type of work was regarded as totally unsuited to women. The war was forcing them out of their traditional roles of wife and mother. Heavy industry work was a signal to these students that there were not enough men to do the jobs. The questions also dealt with mobilization and manpower resources just when many young men and women were entering the workforce or about to do so as the necessity for using all workers in America became apparent during the first year of the war.

An entire year of the war, for Americans, had not altered high school students' perceptions and exaggerations regarding the personal danger faced by soldiers, the economic outlook for civilians, or the eventual successful outcome of the war. About half of those questioned were pessimistic about the conduct of the war. Many appeared confused or misinformed about many aspects of the war, and students had not become either more realistic or more confident than they had been at the start of the war. Of course, with the limited, censored version of the war presented by the news media and allowed by the War Department and the OWI, it is understandable why the students had these perceptions.

This survey (and similar ones) was also an indicator of the new status of American teenagers. Their morale and role in the war and eventually in the postwar world was of great concern to educators and to the government because these students and others like them would soon be taking their places in the factories and on the front lines.

World War II played a strong role in creating the cult of the teenager and changing the lives of adolescents. The war intensified the gap between generations, leaving the adolescents on the home front as separate entities with increased buying power and without young adults to serve as role models. Jitterbugs, bobby-soxers, and Victory Girls[5] were all identifiable groups within the American populace.

With young men eighteen and older in the service, younger boys stepped in as "heads of families," and as "big men about town." They picked up easy pocket money in a labor-poor workforce. Girls, too, earned money to lavish on themselves either by babysitting for parents working night shifts at war plants or, in many cases, working in factories or defense plants themselves. Boys and girls under the age of eighteen accounted for 1.8 million members of the workforce employed in factories and on farms by May 1943. By the end of the war, 2.9 million teenagers were employed, with four times more fourteen- and fifteen-year-old girls working than in December 1941.[6]

In 1944, the number of employed teenagers between the ages of fourteen and seventeen had risen to 4.68 million. Many were employed part-time, but more and more young men and women dropped out of school to work full-time. War demands for labor and new types of jobs brought great changes to industries. It also meant new occupations for teenagers. Jobs that had traditionally been held by fourteen- and fifteen-year-olds, such as delivery and errand boys, street vendors, newspaper carriers, and house workers, now were passed on to younger children. Fourteen- and fifteen-year-olds moved into employment in retail and wholesale establishments, previously occupied by sixteen- and seventeen-year-olds. Older teenagers were removed from trade and the service industries and placed in manufacturing and mechanical work. This reversed a long-term trend of decreased child labor.

The increases in teenage employment came despite the Fair Labor Standards Act passed in October 1938, which barred employment of anyone under sixteen in industries producing goods for interstate commerce. The wartime demand for labor shifted the teenagers who were sixteen years and older into industry and manufacturing and left their previous employers in retail and service jobs dependent on fourteen- and fifteen-year-olds. Most teenagers who worked did so out of choice, not necessity, and received wages that permitted them some sense of economic independence.

Wartime labor for teenagers put money in their pockets, gave them independence, and provided them the opportunity to share in the war effort, but it also meant a loss of education for American youth. United States Office of Education figures show school attendance fell from 9.1 million in 1940 to 7.9 million in 1944.[7] Illegal employment practices spread during the war. Child-labor law violations rose by as much as 14 percent in North Carolina between 1940 and 1943 and an astounding 400 percent during the same years in New York. The Children's Bureau found the federal government's violations of the Federal Fair Labor Standards Act with regard to child labor to be just as egregious as the states'.[8]

World War II helped aggravate generational conflict. To release emotions arising from the intense war stimuli surrounding them teenagers found ways like swing dancing and jitterbugging, ways that did not always meet with their parents' approval. Nor were parents necessarily happy about their children's opportunities for independence and self-reliance. The wartime demand for labor meant that almost any young person looking for work could find it. Teenagers took what previously had been "adult" jobs and received adult wages. These earnings often equaled or surpassed their parents' earnings during the Depression. It was hard for parents to tell teenagers how to behave when their salaries were helping pay the rent.[9]

Teenagers of German, Italian, or Japanese extraction had special problems with their parents. Many of the teens saw themselves as wholly American, while looking on their parents as being at best inept foreigners, from alien nations that were at war with the United States. And finally, teenagers not only accepted the new, they sought it: new ideas, music, dances, and clothing. Older people tended to prefer the status quo, looking on the past with nostalgia; at the very least they were cautious in accepting what was new. And the war accelerated change in complex ways that restructured much of American society.

During World War II, for the first time in American history, adolescents had a separate identity, and for the first time adolescents had their own money. Promptly, advertising firms on Madison Avenue moved in to channel some of that money toward themselves. Since the war halted production of most consumer goods or replaced them with goods of inferior quality, Madison Avenue created new markets for the products that were available by promoting clothing crazes, popular songs, and dances. Most Saturday nights, multitudes of jitterbugging teenagers dropped their hard-earned coins in jukeboxes to listen to the latest recordings. By 1945, RCA, Victor, and Decca were each selling 100 million records annually, and jukeboxes had blossomed into an $80–million-a-year industry, with four hundred thousand of the flashing players in soda shops and diners.[10] Home phonograph equipment became a status symbol essential for a teenager's social success.[11] With swing music the generational cleavage was established; "for the first time in American history teenagers were very much a social reality."[12]

Ladies' Home Journal inaugurated a section titled "Profile of Youth," and newspapers like the *Chicago Daily News* launched widely read columns on "Teen News" and "Teen Views." Unlike their counterparts in later decades, teenagers in the 1940s were still largely innocent, sexually naive, and relatively uncritical of adults and the world around them. Personal appearance became tremendously important in American society, and the newly empowered teenagers became a target of the advertising industry, which was primed to take their money in exchange for the modification, adornment, and camouflaging of their bodies.

Other changes in American society also signaled the rise of the teenager to prominence. During the Second World War, the new label "youth listening" began to appear in newspaper radio logs. Prior to this, music was classified only by genre: popular, classical, hillbilly, western, and blues, sometimes was denoted as "race" music. One study reported "the pleasure of 72 percent of radio listeners under 30 in popular music is shared by only 22 percent of those over 50 years of age." Conversely, one observer reported, "old, familiar music is more popular with older listeners."[13]

Chapter 15

"Meet Soozie Cue"

In *Wartime* Paul Fussell contends that there was a tremendous amount of social cohesiveness during the Second World War and that community spirit during wartime was "revealed by the all-but-universal knowledge of the same popular songs by all ages, classes, and genders." He claims that Americans knew all the popular songs and who had recorded them: "Not to have known them would have been not to have played the game at all."[1] But there is evidence to suggest that not all of America was pleased with popular music or was part of what Fussell calls "a shared culture." Serge Denisoff asserts that the older and younger generations were not reconciled to the same aspects of popular music. In the sixty years preceding World War II, Tin Pan Alley produced music that was acceptable for all of American society: men, women, and children.

The professionalization of songwriting and publishing led to music that was uniform in style and primly moralistic in content. Tin Pan Alley music was careful not to offend Victorian sentimentalities. Another characteristic of Tin Pan Alley music, before the advent of jazz and swing, was its standard form and content. In order to be accessible to the average piano player, popular music had to have simple tunes and standard rhythms of two, three, four, or six counts per measure. The most exotic rhythmic combination was the use of a dotted eighth note followed by a sixteenth note. This particular rhythmic pattern was commonly found in songs of the Civil War era and then in Christian evangelical hymns, which had their roots in the martial Civil War tunes of George Root and, before Root, the melodies of the master minstrel, Stephen Foster.[2]

Only jazz and hillbilly songs deviated from this form. Although jazz began to appear in some recordings following World War I and eventually became prominent in the 1920s, it was still on the fringe of popular music, and middle-class musical conventions were not directly challenged. As H.F. Mooney said, "Commercial orchestras of the period around 1920–50 followed more or less the 'safe bet'—the aesthetic aspirations of the middle class market—as did, indeed, most of the Negro big bands. They presented a music, which despite solo variations emphasized precise, lush, ensemble harmony."[3]

Song lyric content also changed. Music of the Depression concentrated on themes of love. A new outlet for popular music, the sound motion picture, did little to change this. Songs from the movies were traditional Tin Pan Alley fare in both content and style, because many New York-based composers took up residence, at least part of the year, in Hollywood and carried their songwriting form with them. By the Second World War, popular music was still considered good, clean middle-class fare, music that both the older and younger generation could share. There was, nevertheless, a generational conflict. Older Americans were drawn to popular dance-band songs by the modest, inoffensive lyrics, but it was the fast, syncopated rhythms that accompanied the tunes that appealed to the younger generation.[4]

Swing was a hybrid of jazz, with its roots in African American music, and a milder dance-band musical style that young middle-class whites would accept. Swing also was a music that many adults perceived as "garbage," a sentiment their children did not share. A Barnard College professor labeled swing music "musical Hitlerism."[5]

Those who objected to swing attacked the dances teenagers invented for the music. Jitterbugs, who danced in the aisles of the Paramount Theater and at Benny Goodman's Carnegie Hall appearances, were criticized by the press as engaging in rebellious, riotous behavior. In July 1942 at a Louis Armstrong and Charlie Barnet concert in Griffith Stadium in Washington, D.C., some of the eighteen thousand fans leaped over the fences and began dancing on the ballfield in front of the bandstand. Customers who had paid $1.10 for a ticket to sit up front complained they could not see. When the police tried to evict the jitterbugs by stopping the music, a near riot broke out, complete with flying pop bottles, some minor injuries, and several teenagers hauled away by the police for disorderly conduct. It took seventy-five policemen, with the aid of the servicemen present at the concert, to calm the crowd. Despite the police presence, the teenagers would not stop dancing. Eventually, the concert was halted and the jitterbugs sent home. The dance and its performers were condemned by clergy, teachers, and parents.[6]

The bobby-soxers' idol, the boy band vocalist, was another target of adult outrage. Psychiatrists and social scientists diagnosed the phenomenon as "mass trauma" induced by the absence of men, who were away serving in the armed forces. The "swooner-crooner" craze was created by Tommy Dorsey's young singer, Frank Sinatra, at the Paramount in 1942. What began as a publicity stunt, organized by Sinatra's manager, spread across the country until young teenage girls everywhere "swarmed into the theater and wept, screamed, peed in their panties, and yes, even swooned when their idol sang."[7]

In *The Big Bands* George Simon says, "Mobs would wait for them [boy singers] outside stage doors. In the theaters they'd howl and scream."[8] When Arthur Rodzinski, conductor of the New York Philharmonic Symphony Orchestra termed "boogie woogie" and swing music as "one of the greatest causes of juvenile delinquency today," and declared that the "'jive type' type of music leads to 'war degeneracy,'" the "King of Swoon," Frank Sinatra, replied, "Nuts!"[9]

Teenagers did not rule all of musical America in the first year of the war. In the Midwest, ballrooms reported the comeback of the waltz, apparently because the younger "jitterbug lads are now in the Army, thus leaving much of the danceries to the older, more conservative clientele."[10] According to the Midwest Ballroom Operators Association president Carl Fox of Mason City, Iowa, "We've discovered that older persons like to dance as well as the young, provided they have an opportunity to dance the steps they are familiar with."[11]

Old-fashioned dance nights were popular with patrons of a Sioux City, Iowa, ballroom, with whole families coming to town for an evening of polkas, schottisches, and circle two-steps. Quadrilles were favorites again. At most Iowa ballrooms every third dance was a waltz, and music, though "less hot," was "twice as sweet." In the East, the Empire Ballroom's proprietor, Andy Perry, noticed an increase in the attendance of older persons at dates played by name bands. Several of the popular bands at the time had built their reputations with recordings of old-time standards, and this was particularly attractive to the older people. For example, Harry James and his band's recording of "You Made Me Love You" was an older tune repopularized during the war years. In Boston's Roseland-State Ballroom, three nights a week were devoted to older music and waltz, fox-trot, and polka dancing.[12]

But the big growth was in music for the young. Tin Pan Alley, which was profiting from teenagers as a newly recognized portion of American society, did little to quell the fears of anxious parents. Swing music sold, and teenagers bought it almost as fast as the sheet music could be printed or the recordings could be pressed.

By far the most substantial consumer of sheet music and records was the teenage girl. She had extra money and very few consumer goods on which to spend it. She also had more free time and had fewer boys to date, since most of the older teenagers were in the armed forces.[13] As *Variety* said, "Publishers are pretty well agreed on the main reason for the current boom in sheet sales. . . . Substantial contributors . . . are the girls in the family who have the means derived from their war plant employment, but whose going-out habits have been sharply limited by the lack of beaux."[14]

Adolescent girls amused themselves with songs played on the piano or the phonograph, and what these girls preferred determined the type of song Tin Pan Alley produced during World War II. What teenage girls wanted were songs that spoke of love in sweet, romantic terms. These were the same kind of songs that had been selling to Americans before the war, but now the buying power of teenage girls made love ballads even more profitable than before.

Jitterbugs became a barometer for musical popularity in the late 1930s. When one of the most prominent dance bands, led by Artie Shaw, ignored the tastes of these adolescents, it rapidly slipped from being a top band to one that had to fight its way back "via the jitterbug route."[15] Following this, music business managers and others involved in scheduling bands and the music they would play dared not ignore the jitterbugs' favorites.

It seemed to Robert K. Christenberry, an expert in booking dance bands for hotels, that the teenagers knew "a hit band and a click tune when they heard one." Christenberry put their preferences to work for his own benefit by gathering a list of "1000 gals and their pals" who were dance-band fans and encouraging them to write to him expressing their opinions of current bands. He was also interested in their opinions of new bands (meaning bands that were not yet nationally known). Christenberry maintained that the "kids were right EVERY TIME." He claimed that long before Harry James's band had a national following, the jitterbugs were writing about the young trumpet player and his band. Christenberry also said that he never made a change without consulting the jitterbugs by way of a questionnaire. His poll, in September 1942, revealed that teenage girls were inclined toward softer music with string instruments in the bands and not the blaring brass music of past years.

The type of music the jitterbugs preferred was called "sweet-hot," meaning music that favored faster rhythms and louder dynamics but was also capable of tender melodies and sentiments.[16] Hit tunes of the week ending October 2, 1942, bore out Christenberry's findings. Among the best-selling records were "I Got a Gal in Kalamazoo," "Jingle, Jangle, Jingle," "My Devotion," "Just as Tho You Were Here," and "I Left My Heart at the Stage Door Canteen."[17]

Other music business insiders agreed that adolescents were the hot target market for civilian composers and publishers. Jimmy McHugh, one of the most successful Tin Pan Alley composers, cautioned that composers had to know "what the kids want" because "they sense musical changes before the composers do. They hear everything on that radio, and they analyze it as though they were working a mathematical problem."[18]

The buying power of American teenagers was officially recognized by the music business during the war years. Starting in June 1944, *Billboard* began its annual poll of the musical preferences of high school students. Student newspapers in four hundred high schools throughout the nation were invited to participate in the poll.

The 1944 poll showed an overwhelming trend toward sweet music (with more strings—a sentimental, overtly harmonious style that lacks the bite of true jazz) as distinguished from swing music. Sweet music was the preference in nearly two-thirds of the groups considered in the poll, and the top three bands and top soloists in every classification were "on the sweet music side." The top three favorite dance bands were those of Harry James, Tommy Dorsey, and Glenn Miller. Bandleaders with honorable mention were Benny Goodman, Duke Ellington, and Kay Kyser. Nineteen other bands were nominated but did not have enough votes to qualify for the listing, and sixty-one different "coming" bands, showing a wide diversity of opinion, were named by the students.[19]

The Billboard poll of high school students also ranked vocal performers. The most popular male singers, working without a band, were Bing Crosby, Frank Sinatra, and Dick Haymes. The difference in votes between Crosby and Sinatra was less than 5 percent. The youth market was not completely dominated by the "boy singers." The most popular male singer working with a band was GI Bob Eberle, a former Tommy Dorsey soloist; Kay Kyser's Harry Babbitt was second and bandleader Vaughn Monroe third.

The most popular "female singer not appearing with a band" was Dinah Shore, followed by Ginny Simms. Helen Forrest "drew top preference as warbler with a band"; Kitty Kallen of Harry James's band was second; and Helen O'Connell, singing with Tommy Dorsey, received the third highest total votes. Some of the singers were not actively working with bands at the time of the voting, but that was the way teenagers remembered them.

The most popular male vocalists, whether soloists or performers with bands, were Bing Crosby, Harry Babbitt, and Frank Sinatra. The most favored female vocalists were Dinah Shore and Helen Forrest. Vocal groups favored by the teenagers were the Ink Spots, the Andrews Sisters, and the Mills Brothers. Honorable mention went to the Pied Pipers, the King Sisters, Fred Waring's Pennsylvanians, the Modernaires, the Golden Gate Quartet, and the Merry Macs.[20] The vocal group category is noteworthy for the range of styles represented, ranging from African-American gospel harmony to a polka band turned into a dance orchestra for the duration.

According to *Billboard's* poll, the top records of the 1943–1944 school year and the artists who performed them included (alphabetically) "Begin the Beguine" by Artie Shaw; "Boogie-Woogie" by Tommy Dorsey; "Don't Get Around Much Anymore" and "Do Nothing Till You Hear from Me" by Duke Ellington; "Flying Home" by Lionel Hampton; "G.I. Jive" by Johnny Mercer; "Holiday for Strings" by David Rose; "I'll Be Seeing You" by Bing Crosby; "I'll Get By" by Harry James and also Dick Haymes; "Long Ago (and Far Away)" as recorded by Jo Stafford, Perry Como, Helen Forrest and Dick Haymes; "A Lovely Way to Spend an Evening" by Frank Sinatra; "Mission to Moscow" by Benny Goodman; "My Heart Tells Me" by Glen Gray; "Paper Doll" by the Mills Brothers; "Poinciana" by Bing Crosby and also David Rose; "Rhapsody in Blue" by Glenn Miller; "San Fernando Valley" by Bing Crosby; and "Stardust" by Artie Shaw. The song that received the most votes from the high school students was David Rose's "Holiday for Strings, followed by Tommy Dorsey's "Boogie-Woogie" and the Mills Brothers' "Paper Doll." A total of 139 different records were listed as being popular with high school students.[21]

In a parallel survey in September 1944, *Billboard* polled the preferences of GIs stationed within the United States. The same survey that was given to high school students went to all of the stateside military bases. *Billboard* decided to pass up the annual college survey because it said there were not enough "collegiates to be polled, musically or otherwise." Instead, *Billboard* "followed the boys and girls who would have been in college to their camps" in order to complete the survey. Hundreds of polls were conducted in camps and naval installations. The results were almost identical to those of the high school students.

One important difference was the GIs' inclination for bands that were "hot rather than sweet." GIs noted they liked their bands "loud and sending." They relished a band that "really blows when the brass lets go." The high school respondents wanted music "sweet and hot" with added strings in the dance orchestra, but it must be remembered that the high school ballots had a larger percentage of female voters than did the polls in the military camps.

The servicemen and servicewomen also stayed away from any music with a military flavor. For example, according to *Billboard* Ginny Simms ranked only third in the female vocalists category because her radio appearances had most often been in connection with "a service slant." Kate Smith's radio show was also one of the top-rated radio programs on the home front during the World War II years, but she was given a mere "mention" in the GI poll. *Billboard* thought "the flag waving hurt, the boys like to do their own, and while Kate's good job on the home front gets her a top dialing audience it chases the trainees at camps far, far away."

On the whole, the men and women in uniform had not drifted too far from their high school counterparts' taste in music. A second part of "*The Billboard* First Annual Survey of All Service Music Preferences" also confirmed that the music choices of the two groups were very similar. Seven of the top ten recordings were listed by both high school students and service personnel, including "I'll Be Seeing You," "Long Ago and Far Away," "G.I. Jive," "Holiday for Strings," "I'll Get By," and "Paper Doll."[22]

The only noticeable difference between high school students and armed service members in the popular music knowledge quiz was the superior ability of the students to identify record labels. "High school kids," *Billboard* guessed, "are able to spend much more time 'studying' everything about disks." On the other hand, "Once they don the khaki or blue these same kids, faced with the grim business of learning how to fight and kill, lose a little (but only a little) of their disk knowledge."[23]

GIs also overwhelmingly preferred Bing Crosby's vocals over those of Frank Sinatra. Five of the top thirteen tunes were Crosby tunes, while Sinatra was listed only as a vocalist on Tommy Dorsey's version of "I'll Be Seeing You." Crosby's version of the same tune was the number one favorite with the GIs. Again, this disparity can be traced to the fact that the GI poll contained far fewer female voters than the high school poll. The GIs were not as fond of Sinatra for another reason: Frankie, a young draft-free man, was home, making the girls "swoon," while the GIs were away training, fighting, and dying. Bing Crosby was an older, married man, with a large family. He was not nearly as threatening to the GIs.

Both the high school students and GIs heard the music in similar ways. Most teenagers heard disks by way of radio disc jockey shows and on jukeboxes. The GI survey showed that jukeboxes were the preferred method to listen to music on bases and camps; disc jockey programs were second. *Billboard*'s survey also found that nine of the top thirteen recordings featured a vocalist whose version was favored over a band's version of the same song. Possibly, the AFM strike was responsible for some of the popularity of vocalists over the efforts of the bands.[24]

United States forces stationed in Europe were also included, though informally, in *Billboard*'s survey. With few exceptions, the GIs stationed in European liked the same tunes at the front as their counterparts in the training camps. The number one song at the European front was "I'll Be Seeing You," followed by "Long Ago and Far Away" and "I'll Get By." The soldiers did not like marching songs, which, according to *Billboard*, illustrated a fundamental difference between World War I and World War II: "The absence of marching songs in the G.I. preferences is not surprising because the boys are just not marching to the wars—they're riding and when they ride they sing nostalgic or novelty tunes—not marches or military slanted songs."[25]

Billboard's poll revealed that overseas GIs differed from the high school students in the purchase of sheet music. The GIs stationed in training camps and in Europe relied more than students on sheet music for their entertainment. The best-selling sheet music in order of preference was "I'll Be Seeing You," "Long Ago and Far Away," "I'll Get By," "Paper Doll," "G.I. Jive," "Amor," " San Fernando Valley," "Besame Mucho," and "I'll Walk Alone."

GIs purchased music most frequently from local music shops, chain stores, the Post Exchange, recreation departments, or directly from the publishers. The GIs preferred music they enjoyed singing and were able to sing. As a result, some of the "hot" numbers, which required some musical finesse, were not among their favorites. As for the *Hit Kits*, published by the armed services for the servicemen, *Billboard* reported on September 30, 1944, that 52 percent of the GIs polled used the *Kits*, while 48 percent did not. Sixty-four percent of GIs said they preferred to purchase song folios, with collections of hit tune lyrics, as opposed to 36 percent who said they did not buy them. These figures were true only for servicemen in the United States camps. Men stationed overseas were dependent on *Hit Kits* for words and music of popular songs. *Billboard* came to the conclusion that "the boys in uniform haven't drifted too far away from the boys in mufti. They still know what they want—and how."[26]

"The Second Annual High School Survey," June 16, 1945, for *Billboard* was once again conducted with the cooperation of over four hundred of the leading scholastic newspapers and magazines in high schools across the United States. The report showed "a few music and personality yens of the kids who are wearing rolled pants and denim overalls this year. They still go . . . for the Bingle, the Shore, Andrews Sisters, and Harry James, Jo Stafford, Les Brown and a few others get plenty of attention, too."[27]

The 1945 poll showed that high school students still preferred "sweet and hot" tunes over swing, Latin American, and "corn"of the Spike Jones and His City Slickers' variety. The top ten favorite songs of the high school students polled in 1945 were, in order, "Rum and Coca-Cola" by the Andrews Sisters, "Don't Fence Me In" by Bing Crosby, "Candy" by Johnny Mercer, "Sentimental Journey" by Les Brown, "Ac-Cent-Tchu-Ate the Positive" by Johnny Mercer, "I'm Beginning to See the Light" by Harry James, "Hamp's Boogie-Woogie" by Lionel Hampton, "Cocktails for Two" by Spike Jones, "Boogie-Woogie" by Tommy Dorsey, and "Dream" by the Pied Pipers. A mix of "sweet" and "hot" music in the top ten, with "sweet" edging out swing by about 10 percent, contradicted older music listeners' views that anyone under age twenty-one was a "jump addict."

One important difference between the teenagers' favorite tunes and those songs that were currently on the top-ten seller lists kept by *Variety*, *Billboard*, and *Your Hit Parade* was the fact that four of the top ten songs favored by the general public were not among the teenagers' favorite records. These four tunes were "I'll Walk Alone," which was in the number two place on best-seller lists for June 1945; "My Dreams Are Getting Better All the Time," in eighth place, and "Laura" and "I Dream of You," which tied for tenth place.

Disc jockeys were still most important to the teenagers in building their enthusiasm for new music; home record players were second, and jukeboxes placed third. However, jukeboxes were only three points behind home phonographs as the preferred way of hearing popular music. *Billboard* concluded that teenagers might have changed their clothing styles, "going in for outside shirt wearing and long pants with the legs rolled up," but their musical tastes were steady, "still orthodox," and "what they yen sells."[28]

These polls had a practical use. They informed music industry leaders of who was buying records and sheet music, who their favorite musicians were, what types of music they liked, and how and where high school students listened to music. A new record label could become a success if teenagers approved of its musical offerings. For example, Asch, a label that featured hot jazz, jumped from a 15 percent recognition and acceptance level in 1944 to a 40 percent approval rating in 1945, "which just shows just how rapidly the soxers get to know a label—if it has what they yen."[29]

Billboard called high school students "the age group that admittedly forces more disk sales than any other—even if they spend their parents' dough." The teenagers knew the record labels and the artists and the "ones that get the votes are the toppers, the jazz, the original waxers, the polka crowd and some of the folk music platter pressers." If teenagers did not know a record label, the sales volume dropped because "no disk org[anization] that really gets up into the solid press run does so without having the Junior Prom gang rootin' for them." *Billboard* thought it was impossible for a record to succeed without teenagers' support, even with a label getting help from jukeboxes, disk jockeys, and other forms of songplugging.

The real test of high school students' buying power was shown in the results of an adult music preference survey conducted by *The Minneapolis Star-Journal and Tribune*. Ninety-five percent of the surveyed adults responded that they had heard Bing Crosby in person, on the radio, or on records; 89 percent had heard Frank Sinatra; and 49 percent had heard Enrico Caruso. Of those who replied, only 3 percent had not heard of any of these particular performers. The second question asked of adults revealed a reversal of fortune for Frank Sinatra. When asked which one performer they enjoyed the most, the respondents replied Bing Crosby (57 percent), Lawrence Tibbett (9 percent), John McCormick (7 percent), John Charles Thomas (6 percent), Enrico Caruso (6 percent), James Melton (5 percent), and Frank Sinatra (5 percent). It was noted that all age groups gave Bing Crosby the top rating, but Sinatra was second in the twenty-one to thirty age group and dropped in each successive group until the adults over sixty years of age ranked Sinatra in last place. This age group placed Caruso higher than the other age divisions. Also, the older the voters, the more likely they were to record their votes from their memories rather than from actual concert or radio listening or record buying. All singers were placed in the same category by both men and women, although women did rank Sinatra fifth.[30]

By the summer of 1945, the enrollment on college campuses had increased sufficiently enough for *Billboard* to include college students in its annual survey of favorite tunes and musicians. The results published in the July 21, 1945, issue again repeated the pattern established by the GIs and the high school students: "This year ballots came in strong and representative of the nation . . . the cap-and-gown contingent's musical yens hadn't changed much . . . compared to the G.I.'s and the denim, rolled-up pansters (high schoolers) the inmates of the institutes of higher learning were about as hep."[31]

Musical tastes proved to be almost identical. Whereas the high school student poll placed Harry James in the number one spot and the servicemen voted Tommy Dorsey in first place, the collegians "voted them a dead heat." James and Dorsey were both "big draws" on campuses, and Glenn Miller, though a war causality, was still a contender for the top spots. Benny Goodman's new orchestra was in fourth place with the college students and third place with the GIs. Woody Herman received the same ranking from both "the G.I.'s and the mortar board wearers."[32]

A comparison of the votes for favorite male singer showed Bing Crosby with a substantial lead over Frank Sinatra. High school students gave Crosby 250 votes and Sinatra 167; GIs favored Crosby 1,188 to 374 votes for Sinatra; and the college students voted 334 for Crosby and 234 for Sinatra. The favorite female vocalist, for the third year in a row, was Dinah Shore. She lead the nearest contender, Jo Stafford, with 196 votes from high schoolers, 902 from GIs, and 297 from college students. In the "singing groups" category, the Ink Spots took first place away from the Andrews Sisters by a thirty-point margin, a surprise as both high schoolers and GIs voted the Andrews Sisters in first place, with 200 votes and 682 votes, respectively. The college poll gave the Ink Spots 204 votes and the Andrews Sisters 174 votes.[33]

The highest rated songs by GIs, college students, and teenagers were "Don't Fence Me In," "Rum and Coca-Cola," "Sentimental Journey," "Laura," "Ac-Cent-Tchu-Ate the Positive," "Candy," and "I'll Walk Alone."[34] The reason for the survey's equivalent findings on both sides of the Atlantic, *Billboard* surmised, was that both college students and GIs got their music from records played on phonographs, radios, or jukeboxes, "whereas prom and dance dates contributed solidly to music faves in past years . . . under present conditions the tunes are made in denim, cap and gown, khaki and bell bottom trousers circles by disks, disks, disks."[35] In previous years, dance bands playing at colleges had a great influence on the students' musical choices, but during the war, with "band dates and all other college musical dates at a minimum, radio, disks, theater dates and other personal appearance stuff have a great deal more to do with what they like."

One of the few ways that college students could hear new bands and new music was at live concerts if their campuses happened to be adjacent to or part of an army or navy installation. Many colleges had students and military personnel sharing the same buildings, and students were able to take advantage of the opportunity to hear live music when the bands played for servicemen and women. Travel restrictions had kept most of the dance bands from playing college proms and dances, so it was not as easy for new bands to get a following or for songs that had not been recorded and played on the radio to gain much of an audience. The college poll tended to stay with the established bands and failed to pick any "new outfits" or "unknowns" as serious contenders for spots on the favorites list. *Billboard* thought this was due to the fact that college students "haven't had the opportunity of hearing any 'fresh' groups of sidemen. That's going to have to wait 'til V-J Day and after."

Billboard acknowledged the buying power of the older teenagers and their ability to boost a song or a band into prominence: "The boys and girls in camps and colleges are the cream of pop music fans. It's been in this group that most names have been built (this building starts in the soxers' classes but doesn't get solid until they graduate from secondary schools)." Music industry members were advised to follow the 1945 survey selections of college students and GIs: "Cut the survey boxes out—paste them in your next year's diary—date July 1946—and see how the colleges and camps have pointed the way for the music biz." *Billboard* concluded, "Since the colleges still train the future of America, what they 'know' about pop stuff is important."

Before December 7, 1941, *Variety* began a series of columns written by the staff of various college newspapers. These columns were really opinion polls of the current college students' taste in popular music. There was almost complete agreement on the types of music favored on American college campuses. *The Daily Californian* from the University of California at Berkeley stated that, "Sweet swing, the nation's favorite, is . . . the students' favorite." Big name bands like Tommy Dorsey and Glenn Miller were especially popular and "draw Californians like beer draws Betas." Those students who preferred "hot jazz" had to travel to San Francisco, particularly if their interest was "modern Negro jazz" from New Orleans.[36]

The Syracuse Daily Orange predicted that students would prefer bands that would play "sweet" music consistently. Donald R. Larrabee, the author of the column, cited as evidence the fact that students at the University of Syracuse emptied the dance floors when "the band broke into a killer such as 'Persian Rug,' but were quick to return 'en masse' when the boys struck up a romantic ballad."[37] Larrabee found this to be the trend on every eastern campus. Sweet music was favored for dancing and "hot and groovy jive" was best for listening. A poll of Syracuse sororities and fraternities found that the women unanimously preferred "Everything I Love," "This Love of Mine," and "Piano Concerto." The men also were partial to ballads, the number one tune being Harry James's version of "You Made Me Love You."

In the year following Pearl Harbor, *Variety* continued the "College Rhythm" column, but it was not a weekly feature as it had been before the war and was soon dropped from the schedule. In a January 14, 1942, column, Harley Bowers, editor of the University of Georgia newspaper, *The Red and Black*, stated that Georgia college students were the most critical group in the South whether they were listening to jukeboxes, radio, or orchestras. He also said that Georgia students would not accept an orchestra on reputation alone; the group would have to prove itself through a personal appearance. Bands that were popular in the East were not necessarily those popular in the South. For example, the only "colored orchestra that received any recognition [was] Erskine Hawkins, who had quite a few popular recordings in the jukeboxes."[38]

Georgia students favored music that varied from swing to fast jive. Of the leading bands making appearances at the Georgia campus, the following were favorites: Glenn Miller, Tommy Dorsey, Kay Kyser, and Charlie Spivak. Serious contenders for the favored spots were Benny Goodman and Bob Crosby. In the jukeboxes, Georgia students did not appear to be as fickle as the general public. When a tune reached one of the top spots, it stayed there for months. Favorites in the jukeboxes were records by Glenn Miller, Tommy Dorsey, Benny Goodman, and Kay Kyser. The fraternity and sorority houses also had their own jukeboxes, and the "jealousy between houses . . . keeps the record companies in business, because the record buyers get almost every record in an effort to please everyone." Glenn Miller was the favorite on the Georgia campus. Bowers thought that any of Miller's recordings would be welcomed and "if it should happen that the recording isn't tops, Georgia students are so prejudiced in his favor that they would still think it the best." Georgia collegians "love[d] their dancing . . . [took] their music seriously and really believe[d] in that thing called swing."

In late January 1942, students at Northwestern University, Evanston, Illinois, said in the *Daily Northwestern*, "War or no war, we like lots of dance music—not only one type but all types. The solid rhythms of Glenn Miller take the lead as the best all around favorite."[39] Every fraternity and sorority house on the Northwestern campus boasted a large phonograph and a fraternity record chairman who scouted music stores for sweet, swing, and jive. Sorority tastes were somewhat different, leaning almost exclusively to "sweet" with an occasional "hot" number. The girls favored Glenn Miller, Artie Shaw, Tommy Dorsey, and Jimmy Dorsey.

Since Northwestern was located so close to Chicago, students had many opportunities to hear and dance to the best in popular music. Students patronized the places that put the emphasis on the orchestra and not on the "swank atmosphere." At Northwestern, as with most schools, the real test of a band's popularity was the campus dance. Selection for the all-campus dance was a real sign of popularity. The Junior Prom in 1941 featured Benny Goodman, and it proved to be the "largest formal in the history of the University." Lionel Hampton played for the annual Navy Ball in the fall of 1942 and proved to be number one with the swing fans. At times Hampton's penchant to show what he and his orchestra could do with their own brand of music caused some confusion in his audience: "NU's smooth dancers were lost to the rapid-fire jive which the Hampton organization released late in the evening." By this time, most collegians either sat or stood around the bandstand and listened to the concert.

The Claw, UCLA Monthly Humor, from the University of California at Los Angeles, confirmed the trend that college students savored music "which is pleasing to the ear." Columnist Bob J. Thomas said, "This means that sweet can't be beat, novelties are short-lived, and swing no longer accelerates the blood in the student body."[40] In Los Angeles as well as New York and Chicago, Glenn Miller's was the highest-rated band, having recently played the Junior Prom at UCLA. Although some students may have thought Miller's tunes over-arranged and so sweet as to be "repulsive," the author regarded these students as "obviously eccentrics . . . to be shunned on campus." Other dance band favorites were Jimmy Dorsey, Artie Shaw, and Tommy Dorsey. "The way they like 'em is sweet and lovely, and hot only if it's clever."

In concluding this study of American popular music during the Second World War and attempting to discover the reasons for the failure of any martial war song or songs to ignite the country and become a nationally recognized battle cry as had George M. Cohan's immensely popular "Over There" in World War I, certain important points should be kept in mind. The first is that the search was misguided. The OWI, trying to influence what is essentially a process of artistic creation, had little concept of the role talent plays in song composition. The government approached Tin Pan Alley with an assignment much as it did manufacturers of household appliances who were told to, and did, convert their factories to war materiel production. The OWI assumed that Tin Pan Alley could do the same: convert from writing popular music compositions focusing on romance and light-hearted subjects to songs that would stir Americans' patriotism and unite the country to aid the war effort and "Back the Attack."

During World War II the music industry was run as big business (and still is). This fact had an impact on the production of war songs; if a song was not a potential money maker, music publishers and recording companies were not interested. According to William O'Neill in *A Democracy at War: America's Fight at Home and Abroad in World War II*, "The business of America was show business,"[41] and certainly Tin Pan Alley's many publishing houses and recording companies fit the corporate pattern of the 1930s and 1940s, so the business slant and the structured milieu of song writing cannot be discounted. But without the creative genius of men like Irving Berlin, Johnny Mercer, and Duke Ellington, Tin Pan Alley would not have been as successful as it was during the war. Although the Tin Pan Alley style certainly is formulaic, the government never fully understood that popular music could not be written to order. All music has form, but that does not mean anyone who understands a particular form will be able to write a successful piece.

The OWI also did not know how to cope with the refusal of Americans to be coerced into supporting songs they did not care for. The government did not seem to be cognizant of the fact that Americans' musical tastes had changed, and they no longer accepted every composition coming out of Tin Pan Alley as readily as they had before World War II. The variety of music on the radio and excess cash to spend on records and sheet music gave the people a wider knowledge of popular music and a stronger voice in what types of songs became popular. This is not to say that advertising and merchandising were not employed effectively by Tin Pan Alley to keep certain tunes before the public, but these ploys mattered little if Americans did not care for the songs.

The OWI and Tin Pan Alley compounded their misguided search for a war song when they insisted that the new "Over There" was just waiting to be written or discovered. It was not until 1943 that the OWI and Tin Pan Alley admitted both that World War II was a very different war from World War I and that the new generation had a musical style all its own that excluded martial tunes. Another factor is that during World War II, radios, record players, and jukeboxes made music available to more people than ever before. Almost everyone in America and Europe could hear popular music.

Because of the technological advances that made radios and portable phonographs easily transportable, the popular music of World War II did more to build morale, both on the home front and for the fighting man, than at any previous time. Popular music, often as close to home as a person displaced by war work or military service could get, was easily accessible and deemed to be a necessity by both civilians and the military alike. Unlike the majority of songs born of World War I, far fewer songs written during World War II dealt with propaganda, patriotism, and morale; songs written during the Second World War were more about sentiment than strength, more about romance than military victory.

Of the 150 best-selling songs from 1941–1945 listed in *Variety Music Cavalcade, 1620–1950: A Chronology of Vocal and Instrumental Music Popular in the United States*, only five specifically mention the war as a military endeavor: "Remember Pearl Harbor," "Praise the Lord and Pass the Ammunition," "This Is the Army, Mister Jones," "Comin' in on a Wing and a Prayer," and "What Do You Do in the Infantry?" This compilation includes songs closely associated with the war, but they are ballads—as opposed to martial-style tunes. Best-sellers in this category included "The White Cliffs of Dover," "I Left My Heart at the Stage Door Canteen," "When the Lights Go on Again (All Over the World)," and "The Vic'try Polka."

Ben Arnold, in *Music and War: A Research and Informational Guide*, writes, "Twenty-seven popular war songs reached the top ten popular charts. In 1942 . . . seventeen percent of all popular songs reaching the top ten were war songs."[42] A look through the titles of the songs on the top ten lists during the war years complied by *Variety* and *Billboard* confirms that the vast majority were love songs.

The strikes called by the ASCAP and the American Federation of Musicians suspended the production of new songs at a crucial time—the beginning months of the war. The combined work stoppage by these two groups lasted from the fall of 1941 until the last recording company settled with the AFM in November 1944. Popular music was not dormant during these years, but the possibilities for more "hit" records were diminished since publishers cautiously chose only those songs or performers that had a proven history of success. The chances of a tune from an unknown source getting recorded or published, much less gaining access to the "Best Seller" lists, was extremely slim. "Pistol Packin' Mama" was about the only significant exception.

Radio, phonographs, and jukeboxes made popular music accessible for a majority of Americans and also made it possible for American culture to become more homogeneous than it had ever been. People all across the country tuned their radios to the same programs, laughed at the same comedy shows, and listened to the same soap operas, music performances, sports events, and network news presentations. The radio and the jukebox were also increasingly the vehicles by which popular songs were spread and by which the public grew tired of these songs quickly, usually in less than twelve weeks. Radio became both a builder and a destroyer of hit songs. Songs rose to the top of the popularity charts and then disappeared in less than three months. The life of a popular song in the World War I-era had been one to two years. Radio also displaced vaudeville stages and musical stage shows as the purveyor of popular songs. Furthermore, before the electronic age, people gathered around the piano or in groups for communal singing as a form of entertainment. By the time of World War II, records played either on phonographs or in jukeboxes had replaced group singing. Entertainment could be had for a nickel, and Americans became unaccustomed to singing in public.

In addition, songwriters were just not writing war songs that caught the public's imagination. But it is also true that publishers would not take a chance on songs unless the tunes came from known composers with proven success records, and then they preferred songs that would sell—almost always either love songs or novelty songs. Record companies were reluctant to risk rationed shellac on anything less than a probable hit. The bands often refused to play war songs, not wanting to explain their civilian status when so many men were in uniform. Bandleaders preferred to play their own compositions and arrangements. And audiences did generally not want to hear war songs; they wanted to dance. All of this helps to explain the lack of a new "Over There."

World War II was a different war as well. Most Americans did not look at the Second World War (as they had looked on the First) as stepping in and "mopping up" the mess Europeans had made. This time the United States had been attacked. The war was so immense and caused such dreadful loss of life (perhaps 55 million military and civilian casualties) that it became impossible to see the war in romantic terms. Yet even in this global war, the United States was not invaded. American cities were not destroyed by bombs. People did not lose their homes. And except for rubber, sugar, and gasoline, there were no truly oppressive shortages. Certainly families with a loved one in the service had difficult times, but most Americans on the home front experienced the war at a distance. It came into their homes by newspaper or over the airwaves on their radios. As John Morton Blum put it, Americans fought the war "on imagination alone."[43]

On the whole, Americans at home did not suffer a great deal physically during the war. They were mobile and prosperous. New industries employed thousands who had been jobless or had never worked outside the home before. People who had been denied access to the American labor market were allowed into jobs that paid far above their former earnings. Confidence, lost in the Depression, was regained during the war. All Americans were encouraged to participate in activities to aid the war effort, and the national mood was purposeful and resolute. The most important of these factors was prosperity, which, more than any other element, contributed to the country's buoyant attitude. People had money for the first time in a decade, many for the first time in their lives. They were eager to spend, and with few consumer goods available, they looked forward to the day when they would be able to buy homes, automobiles, washing machines, and other household goods. An Elmer Roper survey for *Fortune Magazine* published December 22, 1943, asked Americans what they planned to buy first when the war ended. The number one answer was a car (21 percent), followed by a house (13.3 percent), furniture (9.2 percent), a refrigerator (8.6 percent), house repairs (5.3 percent), a washing machine (5.1 percent), and clothes (4.4 percent). But the largest group was those who had no specific buying plans (28.5 percent).[44]

In March 1944, a survey asked Americans what they planned to do with their war bonds. Twenty-four percent expected to buy a home, while 18 percent planned to use the bonds as income for living expenses. Seven percent wanted to buy a new car and 6 percent planned to start a new business or expand an existing one. Others expected to pay for their children's education or to buy household goods (6 percent).[45]

In the United States, "Things were better than ever, and the soldier was missing out."[46] The war opened up a whole new world. The defeat of the Depression was replaced by a flood of money and the added frenzy to have some fun. For many young Americans "there was just that feeling that maybe there would be no tomorrow and to hell with it!" One woman put it this way, "Everybody was dancing and they didn't really care to hear Caruso, they just wanted to dance."[47]

Of all the reasons examined for the failure of the music business to produce a popular war song, perhaps the most overlooked was the rise of the teenage girl as commanding consumer in the popular music marketplace. Music publishers were, first and foremost, in business to make a profit. The newly found purchasing power of American teenagers made them a primary target for all sorts of new merchandising schemes. Record and sheet music companies and their promoters attempted to appeal to young Americans with a product that would entice teenagers to part with their surplus funds. Songs of war and patriotism did not do this. Left at home with few young men to date, young girls spent their time listening to sweet love songs, romantic ballads, and an occasional zany novelty tune.

Since it was the teenage girl's money that contributed so significantly to Tin Pan Alley's profits, her musical desires became the focus of the music business. One of the most telling pieces of evidence for the primacy of the teenage girl's musical taste as the driving force behind Tin Pan Alley's marketing plans is a series of advertisements published both in *Variety* and *Billboard* during the years 1941–1945.

Columbia Records ran weekly half-page advertisements depicting a teenage girl and a jukebox. The girl was attired in the teenage "uniform": sweater, skirt, bobby-sox, and loafers. Her hair was curled with fluffy bangs held back with a barrette and on her left arm was the treasured "charm" bracelet. She appeared to be leaning on and dancing by the jukebox, which was pictured with musical notes issuing forth. There was a look of obvious enjoyment on the girl's face. But the salient part of the advertisement was contained in the large bold-lined letters over her head: "Meet Soozie Cue . . . she knows who's who!" The implication was that this figure represented American teenage girls and their strong preferences in popular music, songs, and performers.

Below the illustration were the current tunes and the recordings that Columbia was boosting that week. There were small photographs of the performers and a positive, upbeat sales pitch with each song, but the eye-catching part of the page was the teenager, "Soozie Cue." Her unfailing knowledge of what songs are "tops in her book this week" was a forceful signal to the music industry of the power of "Soozie Cue's" musical taste.[48] There were no similar advertisements aimed at any other specific age or sex group in either of these periodicals.

Tin Pan Alley publishers repeatedly told newspaper reporters, the OWI, and anyone else who would listen, that they were anxious and determined to publish war songs. Publishers and recording companies claimed to be on the constant lookout for the "proper" war song, but their actions suggested otherwise. With the exception of "Remember Pearl Harbor," "Praise the Lord and Pass the Ammunition," and "Comin' in on a Wing and a Prayer," no martial songs were strongly promoted by the powerful publishers, recording companies, or the radio networks. The latter two had brief appearances on "Best Seller" lists and *Your Hit Parade*, but no war song made a significant showing after 1943.

Amid all of the worry and concern about the morale Americans and the lack of a definitive war song, it seems as if the government did not analyze its own surveys or begin to understand the character of the American people during World War II. There was an extraordinary initiative on the part of average Americans who organized war support groups on every level of society and in their local and state governments: they volunteered for civil defense jobs; they conserved resources; they collected scrap of all kinds; they recycled materials needed for the war effort or those useful in everyday life; they bought war bonds—though not as many as the Treasury Department thought they should—or if, "like writers and entertainers, they had special skills, devot[ed] them to public service."[49] It was a war for the survival of democracy and the preservation of freedom as Americans had come to know it. The country was totally committed to winning the war both on the battlefield and on the home front.

Although opinion polls showed Americans were eager to aid the war effort far beyond what the United States government had ever asked of civilians, when it came to actually putting this willingness to work, the government was at a loss. Agencies like OWI were fighting a battle that did not exist. Once the bombs fell on Pearl Harbor, Americans forgot the isolationist versus interventionist divisions that had separated the country for several years. There was no need to convince Americans that the war was justified. They united against a common enemy in a just cause. They did not need a martial war song because Americans did not need to be convinced or coerced into giving their all for the war effort.

Love songs were the staple of the American popular music market before World War II, and they remained so during the war. Tin Pan Alley was conservative. It chose not to take chances with a proven song formula. People parted from loved ones during the war had a real affinity for love songs. Love songs were also the type of tunes that appealed to young women, whose surplus spending money spoke loudly and clearly to the burgeoning financial rewards reaped by America's music business during World War II. Americans—and teenagers—throughout the war got what they wanted and were willing to pay for . . . and that did not include war songs.

THIS IS WORTH FIGHTING FOR
Words and Music by
EDGAR DE LANGE
and
SAM H. STEPT
BUY UNITED STATES
WAR SAVINGS
BONDS AND STAMPS
HARMS

THERE'S A
STAR SPANGLED BANNER
WAVING SOMEWHERE
By
PAUL ROBERTS
and
SHELBY DARNELL
BUY WAR BONDS
AND STAMPS
FOR VICTORY
BOB MILLER, INC.
MUSIC PUBLISHER
1619 BROADWAY, NEW YORK CITY
MADE IN U.S.A.

JOHNNY ZERO
Lyric by MACK DAVID
Music by VEE LAWNHURST
Hirzel's Music Service
644 Main Street
LEWISTON, IDAHO
SANTLY-JOY, INC.

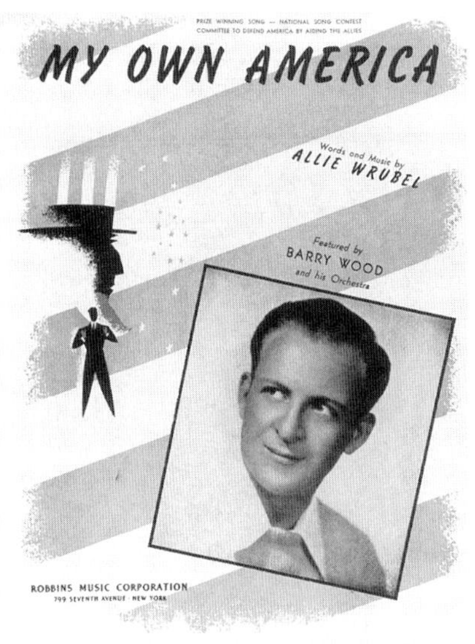
PRIZE WINNING SONG — NATIONAL SONG CONTEST
COMMITTEE TO DEFEND AMERICA BY AIDING THE ALLIES
MY OWN AMERICA
Words and Music by
ALLIE WRUBEL
Featured by
BARRY WOOD
and his Orchestra
ROBBINS MUSIC CORPORATION
799 SEVENTH AVENUE · NEW YORK

(There'll Be A)
HOT TIME IN THE TOWN OF
BERLIN
(When the Yanks Go Marching In)
By
Sgt. JOE BUSHKIN
and
Pvt. JOHN DE VRIES
FOR VICTORY
BARTON MUSIC CORP.

STARS and STRIPES on IWO JIMA
Words and Music by
BOB WILLS AND CLIFF JOHNSEN (CACTUS JACK)
Successfully Recorded by
BOB WILLS AND HIS TEXAS PLAYBOYS
for Columbia Records
Hill and Range Songs, Inc.

Vict'ry Polka

Words by **SAMUEL CAHN** *Music by* **JULE STYNE**

CHAPPELL
& CO · INC ·
RKO BUILDING
ROCKEFELLER
CENTER · N · Y · C
CHAPPELL
& CO · LTD · LONDON
MADE IN U. S. A.

HE WEARS A PAIR OF SILVER WINGS
Words by
ERIC MASCHWITZ
Music by
MICHAEL CARR
Johnnie "Scat" Davis
BUY UNITED STATES
WAR SAVINGS
BONDS AND STAMPS
PETER MAURICE, Inc.
MADE IN U.S.A.
SHAPIRO, BERNSTEIN & Co. Inc

From the COLUMBIA PICTURE "BEAUTIFUL BUT BROKE"
SHOO-SHOO BABY
by PHIL MOORE
Featured by
JOAN DAVIS ★ JANE FRAZEE ★ JUDY CLARK
in the COLUMBIA PICTURE
"BEAUTIFUL BUT BROKE"
Leeds Music

WAITIN' FOR THE TRAIN TO COME IN
By SUNNY SKYLAR and
MARTIN BLOCK
Introduced by
JOHNNIE JOHNSTON and JO STAFFORD
on
CHESTERFIELD'S SUPPER CLUB
MARTIN BLOCK MUSIC,
501 MADISON AVE., NEW YORK 22, N. Y.

TOGETHER
by B. G. DeSYLVA
LEW BROWN and
RAY HENDERSON
featured
in the motion picture
Since You
Went Away
A DAVID O. SELZNICK
PRODUCTION
Starring
CLAUDETTE COLBERT · JENNIFER JONES
JOSEPH COTTEN · SHIRLEY TEMPLE
MONTY WOOLLEY · LIONEL BARRYMORE
ROBERT WALKER
Directed by John Cromwell · Released Thru United Artists
CRAWFORD MUSIC CORP.
R.K.O. Bldg., Rockefeller Center, New York

OH! WHAT IT SEEMED TO BE
Words and Music by
BENNIE BENJAMIN, GEORGE WEISS and FRANKIE CARLE
FRANKIE CARLE
SANTLY-JOY, INC
Music Publishers
1619 BROADWAY - NEW YORK

WHO WOULDN'T LOVE YOU
Words by
BILL CAREY
Music by
CARL FISCHER
Featured by
KAY KYSER
AND HIS ORCHESTRA
Columbia Record
NO. 36526
MUSIC WORLD PUB. CO.
Sole Selling Agents
PACIFIC MUSIC SALES
HOLLYWOOD, CALIFORNIA

IN MY ARMS
By
FRANK LOESSER
and
TED GROUYA
Paper shortage getting worse,
Here is where we start the verse
IN MY ARMS
OVER

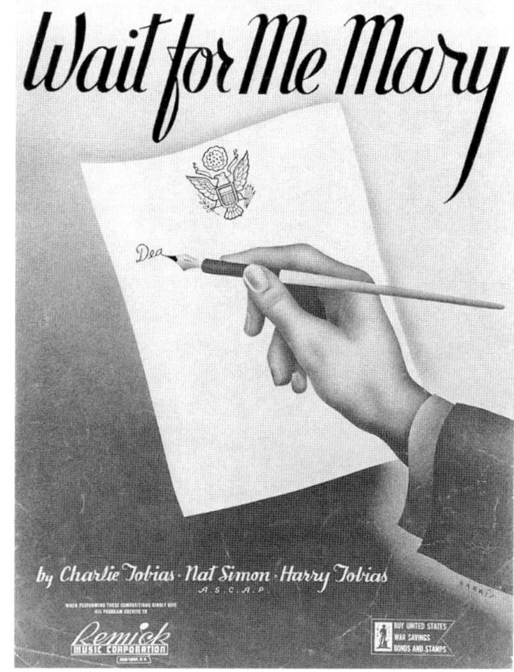
Wait for Me Mary
Dea
by Charlie Tobias · Nat Simon · Harry Tobias
A.S.C.A.P.
Remick
MUSIC CORPORATION
BUY UNITED STATES
WAR SAVINGS
BONDS AND STAMPS

MY DREAMS ARE GETTING
BETTER ALL THE TIME
Lyrics by Mann Curtis
Music by Vic Mizzy
Featured by
MARION HUTTON
SANTLY-JOY, INC.

I'LL WALK ALONE
Lyric by SAMMY CAHN
Music by JULE STYNE
Featured by
DINAH SHORE
"FOLLOW THE BOYS"
MAYFAIR MUSIC CORP.

RUM and Coca-Cola
Lyric by
MOREY AMSTERDAM
Music by
JERI SULLAVAN and PAUL BARON
TRINIDAD
Atlantic Ocean
South America
Featured by ANDREWS SISTERS with VIC SCHOEN and his Orchestra
Decca Record No. 18636A
Leo Feist inc

SIOUX CITY SUE
LYRICS BY
RAY FREEDMAN
MUSIC BY
DICK THOMAS
EDWIN H. MORRIS & COMPANY, INC.
MUSIC PUBLISHERS
NATIONAL MUSIC PUBLISHING CORP.

TEN LITTLE SOLDIERS
(ON A TEN DAY LEAVE)
Lyric by
SUE & KAY WERNER
Music by
ABNER SILVER
Introduced by
LANDT TRIO and CURLEY
LINCOLN MUSIC CORP.

G.I. JIVE
BY JOHNNY MERCER A.S.C.A.P.
Recorded by
JOHNNY MERCER
with
PAUL WESTON and his Orchestra
CAPITOL RECORD #141
HOLLEY
CAPITOL SONGS, Inc.
RKO BLDG • RADIO CITY • NEW YORK

WHITE CHRISTMAS

IRVING BERLIN'S

HOLIDAY INN

BUY WAR BONDS
AND STAMPS
FOR VICTORY

YOU'RE EASY TO DANCE WITH
I'LL CAPTURE YOUR HEART SINGING
BE CAREFUL, IT'S MY HEART
PLENTY TO BE THANKFUL FOR
WHITE CHRISTMAS
HAPPY HOLIDAY
LET'S START THE NEW YEAR RIGHT
SONG OF FREEDOM
ABRAHAM

IRVING BERLIN'S
"HOLIDAY INN"
STARRING
BING CROSBY • FRED ASTAIRE
A MARK SANDRICH
PRODUCTION
A PARAMOUNT PICTURE

IRVING BERLIN Inc.
Music Publishers
799 SEVENTH AVE., NEW YORK, N.Y.

DEEP IN THE HEART OF TEXAS
WORDS BY JUNE HERSHEY
MUSIC BY DON SWANDER
Featured by
BOB ALLEN
AND HIS ORCHESTRA
MELODY LANE PUBLICATIONS, INC.
1649 NORTH VINE ST. HOLLYWOOD, CALIF.
1619 BROADWAY NEW YORK, N.Y.

Dear Mom
By
Maury Coleman Harris
REPUBLIC
MUSIC CORPORATION
607 FIFTH AVE. NEW YORK

PISTOL PACKIN' MAMA

by
AL DEXTER

Recorded by
AL DEXTER
AND HIS TROOPERS
ON OKEH RECORD No. 6708

EDWIN H. MORRIS & COMPANY
INC.
music publishers
1619 BROADWAY · NEW YORK N

Don't Fence Me In
lyric and music by
Cole Porter
Warner Bros. presents
HOLLYWOOD CANTEEN
WITH
ANDREWS SISTERS, JACK BENNY,
EDDIE CANTOR, KITTY CARLISLE,
JACK CARSON, JOAN CRAWFORD,
BETTE DAVIS, JOHN GARFIELD,
ROBERT HUTTON, JOAN LESLIE,
ALEXIS SMITH, BARBARA STANWYCK,
JIMMY DORSEY & HIS BAND,
AND OTHERS.
CORNS FOR MY COUNTRY
DON'T FENCE ME IN
HOLLYWOOD CANTEEN
SWEET DREAMS, SWEETHEART
WHAT ARE YOU DOIN' THE
REST OF YOUR LIFE
YOU CAN ALWAYS TELL A YANK
HARMS
NEW YORK

AT MAIL CALL TODAY
By GENE AUTRY and FRED ROSE
Sgt. GENE AUTRY
WEST'RN
MUSIC PUBLISHING CO.

GOODBYE MAMA
(I'M OFF TO YOKOHAMA)
Words and Music by
J. Fred Coots
CHAPPELL
& CO · INC ·
RKO BUILDING
ROCKEFELLER
CENTER · N · Y · C
CHAPPELL
& CO · LTD · LONDON
MADE IN U. S. A.

Notes

Chapter 1

1. Hatch and Millward, *From Blues to Rock*, 1.

2. See "10 Best Sellers on Coin-Machines" and "15 Best Sheet Music Sellers," published weekly in *Variety*,1941–1945, and "Music Popularity Chart: Songs with Most Radio Plugs; National and Regional Best Selling Records; National and Regional Sheet Music Best Sellers; and Leading Music Machine Records," published weekly in *Billboard*, 1941–1945.

3. Mabry, *The Pop Process*, 41.

4. Browne, "Popular Culture," in *Popular Culture and Curricula*, eds. Browne and Ambrosetti, 31.

5. "Army Rules Out Double Hitches for Orks, Acts," *Billboard*, 22 Aug. 1942, 20. "'Show Must Go on,' Says La Guardia," *Billboard*, 27 Dec. 1941, 6. "Show Biz Takes Stock of Itself," and "Gov't Seizes H'Wood Arms," *Variety*,10 Dec. 1941, 3. In November 1942, the Office of War Information asked Selective Service deferments for Edgar Bergen, Red Skelton, Bob Hope, Nelson Eddy, Freeman Gosden (Amos of *Amos n' Andy*), Lanny Ross, Harold Peary (the Great Gildersleeve), and Kay Kyser. Only Bergen received a deferment; the rest were rejected by the military for medical reasons. "OWI Asked Deferring of 7 Radio Figures," *New York Times*, 11 Mar. 1943.

6. *Congressional Record*, 77th Cong., 2d sess., 1942, 88, pt. 1:1143; Rep. Clevenger, in *Congressional Record*, 88, pt. 1:1266.

7. *Congressional Record*, 77th Cong., 2d. sess., 1942, 88, pt. 1:1097.

8. Broyles, "Commercial Phonographs Build Morale," *Billboard*, 13 Dec. 1941, 64.

9. "Gov't Help for War Songs: To Encourage Fighting Tunes," *Variety*, 26 Aug. 1942, 3. "Too Few War Tunes," *Variety*, 25 Mar 1942, 3.

10. Sherman, "Music's Role in War Theme at Meeting of Teachers," *Musical America*, 10 Jan. 1942, 1.

11. "Not Singing About This War," *Variety*, 15 April 1942, 1. "Isham Jones on Why War Songs Flop," *Variety*, 10 June 1942, 43. "Public Seems Blah to 'Wrath' Songs, Pubs See OWI Hopes Scuttled by Facts," *Variety*, 14 Oct. 1942, 42.

12. "More Comedy, Less Drama," *Variety*, 20 May 1942, 2.

13. "Says We Need 5 Ct. Song," *New York Times*, 29 Jan. 1942.

14. "W & J Sloan," advertisement, *New York Times*, 7 Dec. 1941; "Davega Sale," advertisement, *New York Times*, 7 Dec. 1941; "For Christmas a Libertyphone," advertisement, *New York Times*, 7 Dec. 1941.

15. "Roosevelt Appeals to Hirohito," *New York Times*, 7 Dec. 1941.

16. DeLong, *The Mighty Music Box*, 240–41. *Radio Broadcast News*, 7 Dec. 1941. This publication, produced by Westinghouse Electric & Manufacturing Co. in East Pittsburgh, Pennsylvania, lists the daily/weekly program schedules for the major radio networks in Pittsburgh, New York, and the East; Chicago and the Midwest; and the South.

17. DeLong, 241.

18. "Music in Wartime," *New Republic*, 7 Feb, 1944, 175–78.

19. Blumer, "Morale: The State of the Problem," in *American Society in Wartime*, ed. Ogburn, 207.

20. Lazarsfeld and Stanton, eds., *Radio Research, 1942–1943*, 335.

21. OWI: RG 208; "Surveys of Public Attitudes," May 1943–June 1944, SG 118, WNRC.

22. Lazarsfeld and Stanton, 335.

23. Fussell, *Wartime*, 185.

24. OWI: RG 208; "Surveys of Public Attitudes," May 1944: SG 118, WNRC.

25. O'Neill, *A Democracy at War*, 326, 145.

26. OWI: RG 208; "Surveys of Public Attitudes," Aug. 1942–June 1943, SG 118, WNRC.

27. Broyles, "Commercial Phonographs Build Morale," *Billboard*, 13 Dec. 1941, 64.

CHAPTER 2

1. "Wax Execs Optimistic Despite War; No Shortage Scares Yet, and Study of War Songs is On," *Billboard*, 20 Dec. 1941, 9; "Tin Pan Alley Fires Song Salvo at Axis; Air News, Enlistments and Paper Shortages Might Hurt," *Billboard*, 20 Dec. 1941, 11.

2. "Japs to Jeeps, Doughboy's Rose to Der Fuehrer's Face—There's Nary an 'Over There' in the Lot," *Billboard*, 9 Jan. 1943, 9.

3. "Inevitably, the War Songs," *Variety*, 17 Dec. 1941, 2.

4. "Japs to Jeeps, Doughboy's Rose to Der Fuehrer's Face—There's Nary an 'Over There' in the Lot," *Billboard*, 9 Jan, 1943, 9.

5. "Wax Execs Optimistic," 9; "Tin Pan Alley Fires Song Salvo," 11.

6. "Inevitably, the War Songs," 2; "Disk Firms Make Haste Slowly on Recording New War Songs," *Billboard*, 3 Jan. 1942, 60. This listing of popular song titles and the sheet music or recordings can be located in the catalogs of the Music Division titled "United States Popular Music Collection, 1941–

1945," Fine Arts (Music) Reading Room, Music and Recorded Sound Division, Library of Congress, Washington, D.C. (hereafter cited as "U.S. Popular Music Collection, 1941–1945," Library of Congress.)

7. "Wartime Music," *Billboard*, 31 Jan. 1942, 68.

8. Ewen, *All the Years*, 427.

9. ABCD: American, British, Chinese, and Dutch forces. Name given to powers arrayed against Japan. *Newsweek*, 24 November 1941, P. 24–26.

10. "Inevitably, the War Songs," *Variety*, 17 Dec. 1941, 2; "Disk Firms Make Haste Slowly," *Billboard*, 3 Jan. 1942, 60.

11. The *Portland Oregonian* claimed to have first coined the battle cry "Remember Pearl Harbor" on the copy of its editorial page printed 9 December 1941, but not on the streets until after midnight, making it 10 Dec. 1941. The OPM's claim is substantiated by a *New York Times* article of Dec. 11, 1941. Cohen, *"V" for Victory*, 36.

12. *Your Hit Parade* (sometimes referred to as *Hit Parade* or *The Lucky Strike Hit Parade)*, a weekly radio program focusing on the most popular songs of the past week based on retail sales, was first broadcast on April 20, 1935. By 1940 both *Variety* and *Billboard* published weekly tallies of the most popular songs according to sales of records, sheet music, and totals from jukeboxes. They also listed songs that were played most frequently by the major radio networks.

13. "Raps 'Alamo' Lyric," *Variety*, 22 April 1942, 1.

14. "New U.S. War Songs," *LIFE*, 2 Nov. 1942, 42.

15. "'Praise the Lord's Great Press," *Variety*, 4 Nov. 1942, 41, 47.

16. Lingeman, *Don't You Know There's a War On?*, 212.

17. "'Praise the Lord's Great Press," 47.

18. "'Praise the Lord, Wow 450,000 Copies Despite Frowns from the Clergy," *Variety*, 18 Nov. 1942, 18.

19. "The Methodists Join the War," *Time*, 15 May 1944, 42. For further information concerning the pacifist stand of the Methodist Church and the eventual recanting of this position by its General Assembly in May 1944, see "The Church Is Not at War," *The Christian Century*, 25 Mar. 1942, 375–77; "Is the Church at War?" *The Christian Century*, 8 April 1942, 468–69; "Methodists Shift Position on War," *The Christian Century*, 17 May 1944, 624+; "The Methodist Recantation," *The Christian Century*, 21 June 1944, 742–44; "Correspondence," *The Christian Century*, 12 July 1944: 831–32.

20. "Church Paper Asks Radio Ban 'Praise the Lord,'" *Variety*, 2 Dec. 1942, 38.

21. "'Praise the Lord' Wow," 3, 18.

CHAPTER 3

1. "Tin Pan Alley Fires Song Salvos at Axis; Air News, Enlistments and Paper Shortages Might Hurt," *Billboard*, 20 Dec. 1941, 11.

2. "Disk Firms Make Haste Slowly," *Variety*, 3 Jan. 1942, 60.

3. "Old Timers Doom New War Songs and Suggest More Tschaikovsky," *Billboard*, 3 Jan. 1942, 11.

4. Harold Humphrey, "Wartime Music," *Billboard*, 31 Jan. 1942, 68.

5. "Music Popularity Chart," *Billboard*, 11 April, 1942, 21. The compilation of the best-sellers was based on reports from retail stores of their ten best-selling records and sheet music of the previous week. Retail stores in the following cities were included in the reports: New York City; Bridgeport, Conn.; Boston; Pittsburgh; Philadelphia; Salt Lake City; Portland, Ore.; Los Angeles; Cincinnati; Milwaukee; Detroit; Des Moines; Kansas City, Mo.; Springfield, Mo.; St. Louis; Birmingham; New Orleans; Washington, D.C.; Louisville, Ky.; Butte, Mont.; Richmond, Va.; St. Paul, Minn.; Atlanta; Phoenix; Seattle; and San Antonio. *Billboard Music Popularity Charts* began with the July 20, 1940, issue and continue to the present day.

6. Robert Mugge, dir., *Entertaining the Troops*.

7. "All Out for Uncle Sam," *Billboard*, 27 Dec. 1941, 128.

8. Irving Berlin, "Any Bonds Today?": Theme Song of the National Defense Savings Program, U.S. Defense Savings Bonds and Stamps, copyright by Henry Morgenthau Jr., Secretary of the Treasury, Washington, D.C., 1941.

9. "Berlin Slaps the Japs in His 'Any Bonds' Song," *Variety*, 17 Dec. 1941, 3.

10. *Billboard*, 31 Jan. 1942, 68.

11. Ibid.

12. Davis, *A History of Music In American Life, Volume III*, 337.

13. Pitts, *Kate Smith, A Bio-Bibliography*, 8.

14. Davis, 337.

15. Both Kate Smith and Irving Berlin donated, in perpetuity, all of their royalties from "God Bless America" to the Boy and Girl Scouts of America. Mrs. Ralph J. Bunch, Joe Dimaggio, and Theodore Roosevelt Jackson were appointed as trustees of the "God Bless America" Fund; Kate Smith was also responsible for selling over $600 million in war bonds—$112 million of this total in a twenty-four hour radio marathon on Feb. 1, 1944. DeLong, *The Mighty Music Box*, 255.

16. For an alternate view of Berlin's "God Bless America" see Pascal, "Walt Whitman and Woody Guthrie," 41–59.

17. "Pop Songs End War Before We've Begun," *Variety*, 8 July 1942, 1; Office of War Information: Record Group 208; Records of the Deputy Chief, Radio Division, New York, Dec. 1942–Dec. 1945: Subgroup 169, Washington National Records Center, Suitland, Maryland. (Hereafter referred to as OWI: RG 208; SG 169, WNRC).

18. Eddie Seiler, Sol Marcus, Bennie Benjemen, "When the Lights Go on Again (All Over the World)."

19. Martin Page, "*Kiss Me Goodnight, Sergeant Major*," 69–99; Brian Murdoch, *Fighting Songs and Warring Words*, 175–208.

20. Davis, *A History of Music in American Life*, 340.

21. Ewen, *All the Years*, 431.

22. Freedland, 127.

23. "Music Biz Still Hunting That Boff War Song," *Variety*, 6 Jan. 1943, 187.

24. "Jump Music and Solid Ballads Liked Best from Bands in Camps," *Variety* 6 Jan. 1943, vol. 149, no. 4: 188.

25. *Let's Talk Turkey to Japan*, NBC's Sixth War Loan Program, 23 November 1944, RG 208: OWI; SG 169, Records of the Deputy Chief of the Radio Bureau, New York, December 1942–December 1945, WNRC.

26. Ewen, *All the Years*, 430.

27. *Billboard Book of Number One Hits*, 120.

28. Freedland, 127.

29. Lissauer, *Encyclopedia of Popular Music*, 159.

30. "'Texas' Song a War Hazard," *Variety*, 22 July 1942, 1.

31. Ewen, *All the Years*, 431.

CHAPTER 4

1. Stokesbury, *A Short History of World War II*, 119.

2. Ewen, *All the Years*, 430.

3. Abel Green, "Irving Berlin Winds up 3–Year Hitch in 'Army,' Nets AER $10,000,000," *Variety*, 18 April 1945, 1

4. Rep. Emmanuel Celler, in *Congressional Record*, 77th Cong., 2nd sess., 7 July 1942, 88, pt. 1:6035–36.

5. Smith, *Lieutenant Colonel Emily U. Miller, a Biography*, 12.

6. SPAR, taken from the Coast Guard motto "Semper Paratus," was the name given to Women Reserves of the United States Coast Guard Reserve, created 22 Nov. 1942. *Education for Victory*, 15 January 1943, 27.

7. Irvin Graham and Robert Sour, "A Woman's Place," (New York: Chappell, 1943).

8. Dick Howard, Russ Morgan and Bob Ellsworth, "Somebody Else Is Taking My Place," (New York: Shapiro, Bernstein & Co., 1937). Although published in 1937, this song was revived and eventually became number one on *Your Hit Parade* in 1942.

9. Tyler, *Hit Parade, 1920–1955*, 115.

10. Shapiro, ed., *Popular Music*,137.

11. Malone, *Country Music, U.S.A.*, 196.

12. "'Pistol' in Black Market Demand," *Variety*, 15 Sept. 1943, 45.

13. "Music in the News," *Billboard*, 30 Oct. 1943, 62.

14. "Pistol Packin' Mama," *LIFE*, 13 Oct. 1942, 43.

15. *Charlotte (NC) Observer*, quoted in "Music in the News," *Billboard*, 13 Nov. 1943, 62.

16. Millard, *Country Music*, 56.

17. "Decca 'Rum & Coke' May Be Co.'s Biggest Seller Despite Net Ban," *Variety*, 14 Feb. 1945, 43.

18. Panati, *Panati's Parade of Fads, Follies, and Manias*, 228.

19. "Decca 'Rum & Coke' May Be Co.'s Biggest Seller Despite Net Ban," 43. "Rum and Coca-Cola" was the subject of a famous plagiarism case detailed in Louis Nizer's book *My Life in Court* (Doubleday & Company, Inc., 1961). The decision of the federal court was in favor of the plaintiff, music publisher Maurice Baron of Trinidad. For a financial settlement, Baron relinquished all future property rights and writer and publisher credits. Officially, the song is copyrighted by Morey Amsterdam, Jeri Sullivan, and Paul Baron for Leo Feist, Inc., music publishers, 1944.

20. Abel Green, "This Has Been the Year of Years for the Music Business," *Variety*, 9 Jan. 1946, 245.

21. "Victory Mail," or "V-Mail," was the name given soldiers' letters, which were photographed and reduced in size to expedite mail to and from service men. Taylor, comp., *The Language of World War II*, 207.

22. Jack Lawrence, "Linda," (New York: Warock Music Inc., 1946). This song did not become a best-seller until 1947.

23. OWI: RG 208; Records of the Deputy Chief, New York: SG 169, WNRC.

CHAPTER 5

1. "ASCAP Coin Up, Also Sheet Sales," *Variety*, 13 Dec. 1944, 1.

2. "Wax Execs Optimistic," 9; "No Further Shellac Cuts for Disc Cos.," *Variety*, 7 July, 1943, 44.

3. "Big Biz Despite War, ASCAP Ban," *Variety*, 25 Aug. 1943, 1.

4. Hamm, *Yesterdays*, 389.

5. Malone, *Country Music, U.S.A.*, 178–80.

6. "WLB Delving into AFM-Disc Battle," *Variety*, 28 July 1943, 37.

7. Sears, comp., *V-Discs*, vi-vii, 223–70; Wanda Marvin, "V-Disks Help Hasten the Day," *Billboard 1944 Music Year Book*, 30 Sept. 1944, 148–49, 204–16.

8. "Announce Record Fees: Decca-AFM Agreement to Boost Supply of Records," *Billboard*, 9 Oct. 1943, 62.

9. "Petrillo, AFM End Ban," *Variety*, 15 Nov. 1944, 1.

10. Malone, *Country Music, U.S.A.*, 181.

11. Shapiro, ed., *Popular Music*, 8.

12. Abel Green, "Popular Appeal Will Take Its Course Sans Any Synthetic Hypo," *Variety*, 5 Jan. 1944, 187.

13. "American Folk Music," *Billboard*, 7 Feb. 1942, 64.

14. Capt. Colin Kelley was a naval aviator who was awarded the Distinguished Service Cross posthumously for his bombing attack on a Japanese naval task force in the Philippines on 10 December 1941. His plane was hit and he died in the crash. There were conflicting stories concerning Kelley's actual deeds, but the national news media latched onto the story as a positive note in a very dark time for Americans. Perrett, *Days of Sadness, Years of Triumph*, 207; Fussell, *Wartime*, 35–36.

15. Green, "Popular Appeal," 187.

16. Woll, *The Hollywood Musical Goes to War*, 70.

17. Henry A. Wallace (1888–1965), newspaper editor, plant geneticist, founder of Pioneer Seed Co., secretary of agriculture (1933–1941), vice president (1941–1945), was among the most controversial politicians of his time. He was a champion of soil conservation, public assistance to poor farmers (including tenants and migrants), federal relief for urban poverty, dissolution of industrial monopolies, and civil rights for both black and white Americans. Blum, *V Was for Victory*, 284–85.

18. "Elaborate Push for Its Theme," *Variety*, 19 Nov. 1942, 37.

19. "Lunch Time Follies," *Billboard*, 23 Jan. 1943, 23.

20. Lewis Allen and Earl Robinson's song did not become popular until sung by Frank Sinatra in the film short *The House I Live In*, 1945.

21. Lingeman, *Don't You Know There's a War On?*, 222.

CHAPTER 6

1. Blum, *V Was for Victory*, 21–24.

2. Ibid., 22; MacLeish, quoted in Winkler, *The Politics of Propaganda*, 13.

3. Winkler, *The Politics of Propaganda*, 8–30; Blum, *V Was for Victory*, 23–25.

4. Ibid., 31–37; OWI: RG 208; Executive Order 9182: SG 169, WNRC.

5. Winkler, *The Politics of Propaganda*, 2.

6. Vaughn, *Holding Fast the Inner Lines*, 141.

7. Winkler, *The Politics of Propaganda*, 2–5, 24.

8. OWI: RG 208; WNRC

9. Winkler, *The Politics of Propaganda*, 5, 38–51.

10. Ibid., 52; Blum, *V Was for Victory*, 23.

11. Winkler, *The Politics of Propaganda*, 55–56.

12. Ibid., 57–58; OWI: RG 208; Bureau of Intelligence, Media Division, "Weekly Summaries and Analysis of Feature Motion Pictures," WNRC. These summaries were not issued regularly, despite their title.

13. Winkler, *The Politics of Propaganda*, 59–62.

14. OWI: RG 208; Domestic Radio Bureau, memo, "Why Government Radio Coordination": SG 169, WNRC.

15. Ibid.

16. Ibid.

17. Ibid; Summers, ed., *A Thirty Year History*, 99–113.

18. Weinberg, "What to Tell America," 73–89.

19. Ibid.

20. OWI: RG 208; Domestic Radio Bureau, "Guidelines for Radio in Wartime," SG 169, WNRC.

21. Ibid.

22. Ibid.

23. Ibid.

24. MacDonald, "Government Propaganda in Commercial Radio," 285–304.

25. In addition to OWI, several U.S. government agencies produced radio programs during WWII. The Department of War was responsible for *This Is the Army* and *The Army Hour*. Other government agencies and departments involved were the Office of Civilian Defense, Department of Labor, Department of Justice, Office of Emergency Management, and the Coordinator of Inter-American Affairs.

26. Ibid.

27. Ibid.

28. OWI: RG 209; Domestic Radio Bureau, "Why Government Radio Coordination?": SG 169, WNRC.

29. Ibid.

30. DeLong, *The Mighty Music Box*, 247.

31. OWI: RG 209; Domestic Radio Bureau, "Why Government Radio Coordination?": SG 169, WNRC.

32. Ibid.

33. Ibid.

34. Ibid.

35. OWI: RG 208; "When Radio Writes for War,": SG 169, WNRC; The National Association of Broadcasters calculated almost 36,000 hours of free programs aired during the period May-July 1942. This included 1,541,640 spot announcements, and 187,075 pre-recorded and live programs. The largest numbers of live programs were fifteen minute programs for the army, navy, Marine Corps, and civilian defense. Pre-recorded programs for the Treasury Department's war bonds and stamps and the army were tabulated at 510,090. "Radio to 'Sell' the War," *Variety*, 9 September 1942, 47.

Chapter 7

1. OWI: RG 208; "When Radio Writes for War,": SG 169, WNRC. Unless otherwise noted, my discussion of OWI in this chapter is based on this source.

2. "Congress Blast Against OWI Portends Assault on New Deal," *The Nation*, 22 February 1943, 25–26.

3. Winkler, *The Politics of Propaganda*, 70.

4. Baird, *Representative American Speeches, 1940–1941*, 185.

5. Winkler, *The Politics of Propaganda*, 5; OWI: RG 208; "The Four Freedoms," pamphlet, Records of the Deputy Chief, Domestic Radio Bureau: SG 169, WNRC; Burns, *The Lion and the Fox*, 459.

6. Quoted in Winkler, *Home Front U.S.A.*, 29.

Chapter 8

1. Winkler, *The Politics of Propaganda*, 60.

2. Ibid.

3. "Our President Speaks for Democracy," *The Etude*, 1 June 1942, 364; "President Praises Music," *New York Times*, 19 June 1941.

4. OWI: RG 208; Records of the Domestic Radio Bureau, memo 2696 from the Office of the Chief to all Domestic Radio Bureau offices: SG 169, WNRC.

5. Ibid.

6. Arnold, *Music and War*, 187.

7."Big Bill" Broonzy (William Lee Conley), an American blues singer who served in the army after WWI, had a powerful song delivery and driving rhythm but was not well known until the jazz revival of the late 1940s.

8. "Disney Song 'Der Feuhrer's Face' Razzes Nazis with a German Band," *Life*, 2 Nov. 1942, 44; Delehanty, "The Disney Studio at War," *Theatre Arts*, 31–39.

9. Wanda Marvin, "V-Disks Help Hasten the Day," *Billboard 1944 Music Year Book*, 30 Sept. 1944, 149.

10. Samuel T. Williamson, "A Singing Army? Not Yet, But—," *New York Times Magazine*, 15 November 1942.

11. Livingston, "'Still Boy-Meets-Girl Stuff,'" in Bindas, *America's Musical Pulse*, 34.

12. Vaughn, *Holding Fast the Inner Lines*, 187–195; Ewen, *Great Men of American Popular Song*, 260–61.

13. Ibid.

14. Wenzal and Binkowski, *I Hear America Singing*, 74.

15. Livingston, "'Still Boy-Meets-Girl Stuff,'" in Bindas, *America's Musical Pulse*, 34.

16. Ibid, 35.

17. Burns, *Roosevelt*, 380 *passim*; Leuchtenburg, *Franklin Roosevelt and the New Deal, 1932–1940*, 197 *passim*.

18. Denisoff, *Great Day Coming*, 100.

19. Sillen, "Battle in Search of a Hymn," *New Masses*, 19 May 1942, 22–23.

20. Denisoff, *Great Day Coming*, 95–97.

21. "Four Almanacs Washed Up as OWI Singers," *New York Times Herald*, 4 Jan. 1943.

22. Ibid.

23. "OWI Plows Under the Almanac Singers," *New York Times*, 5 Jan. 1943.

24. OWI: RG 208; Domestic Radio Bureau Records: SG 169, WNRC; "OWI Plows Under the Almanac Singers," *New York Times*, 5 Jan. 1943; Denisoff, *Great Day Coming*, 99–104; Bindas, ed., *America's Musical Pulse*, 35.

25. "Four Almanacs Washed Up as OWI Singers," *New York Times Herald*, 6 Jan. 1943.

26. Cook, *A Narrative History of Film*, 407–10.

27. OWI: RG 208; undated, unsigned memo from the office of the New York Deputy Chief, Domestic Radio Bureau: SG 169, WNRC.

28. Billy Harrington, interviewed by the author, Natchitoches, La., 30 May 1994.

29. Shaw, *Dictionary of American Pop/Rock*, 132.

30. Palmer, *All You Need Is Love*, 142–45.

31. Ibid.

32. Denisoff and Lewis, "The One Dimensional Approach to Popular Music," 912.

33. Ibid.

34. Margarethe R. Bartholomew, interviewed by the author, Natchitoches, La., 20 April 1994.

35. OWI: RG 208; Records of the Domestic Radio Bureau: SG 169, WNRC.

36. Ewen, *Great Men of American Popular Song*, 261–62.

37. "Songplugger" is a term derived from the era when music publishers introduced their songs through a systematic formula that was at the heart of Tin Pan Alley. Publishers became their own "pluggers." A "plugger"—originally a "boomer"—was a combined advanceman, advertising czar, con artist, and entertainer. Julie Witmark, E.B. Marks, Charles K. Harris, and Joseph Stern were four of the most famous songpluggers. In addition to their songwriting and publishing activities, they went from variety house to public theater to restaurant to burlesque show, bribing orchestras with drinks, greeting performers, giving out free songsheets, offering singers a percentage of profits on sheet-music sales, promising stars their pictures on sheet-music covers, and standing up and singing an extra chorus when their own song was on the bill. All this was to get their songs played more frequently, interpolated into shows, hummed by the public, and ultimately skyrocketed to hits through the sales of large quantities of sheet music. Pluggers often visited half-a-dozen establishments on a given evening, turning on their special brand of personal charm. Around the turn of the century, the songplugger blossomed into an incredibly important figure. Sales in excess of one million, a rarity before 1900, became frequent. Between 1900 and 1910, more than one hundred songs sold more than a million copies. Wenzal and Binkowski, 47–50.

38. OWI: RG 208; memo 2696, Domestic Radio Bureau, Office of the Deputy Chief: SG 169, WNRC.

CHAPTER 9

1. OWI: RG 208; Records of the Domestic Radio Bureau, National Wartime Music Committee Guidelines: SG 169, WNRC.

2. OWI: RG 208; National Wartime Music Committee; letter and memorandum from William B. Lewis to Merritt W. Barnum, 13 Jan. 1943; National Wartime Music Committee Guidelines: SG 169, WNRC.

3. "Songwriters Own Positive Approach to War Song Problem Shelves OWI Hypo; MWC Jumping All Hurdles," *Variety*, 26 May 1943, 1.

4. Ibid.

5. OWI: RG 208; Records of the Domestic Radio Bureau; American Theater Wing's Music War Committee: SG 169, WNRC.

6. OWI: RG 208; Domestic Radio Bureau: SG 169, WNRC; Shapiro, *Popular Music*, 32.

7. Fehr and Vogel, *Lullabies of Hollywood*, 180.

8. OWI: RG 208; American Theater Wing's War Music Committee: SG 169, WNRC.

9. *Entertaining the Troops: American Entertainers in World War II*, dir. Robert Mugge, RCA/Columbia Pictures Home Video, 1992, videocassette.

10. Carl Van Vechten, "An Ode to the Stage Door Canteen," *Theatre Arts* 27, no. 4 (April 1943): 229–31. Van Vechten states: "The place is absolutely democratic . . . English soldiers, sailors and RAF men dance beside, mingle and eat with Chinese airmen, Americans from every branch of the service, including Negroes and Indians, Canadians, Australians, South Africans, Dutch and French sailors [and] occasionally Russians."

11. "Doughboys Like It Hot: Jazz Records, Orchestrations in demand; Sad Stuff Fluffed," *Billboard*, 10 Oct. 1942, 21.

12. Scheele, *Songs of World Wars I & II*, 1. *Your Hit Parade* (also called *Hit Parade* and *The Lucky Strike Hit Parade*), a radio program, began on April 20, 1935, and presented the top-selling songs of the week. It was the forerunner of many music ratings and lists that have become an accepted part of the music industry (including *Billboard*, *Variety*, and ASCAP's "All-Time Hit Parade" listings). The program was a reflection of the growing power of radio in making or breaking song hits.

13. Mina Lederman, "Songs for Soldiers," *American Mercury*, Sept. 1943, 296.

14. Brown, "The American Girl and the Christmas Tree," *Journal of American Culture* 8, no. 2 (Summer 1985): 25. See also Fussell, *Wartime*, 129–43.

15. "G.I.'s Report on Their Sing-Songs," *Billboard*, 30 September 1944, 65; "Camp(us) Tune, Disk, Label Faves," *Billboard*, 23 July 1945, 15.

16. Ibid.

17. OWI: RG 208; SG 169, WNRC.

18. "Army *Hit Kit* Gets 1st Six," *Variety*, 17 Feb. 1943, 35.

19. Pitts, *Kate Smith, a Bio-Bibliography*, 10.

20. "Army's Pop Music Project Will Debut 1st Songs Feb. 25 on M.O.T. Program," *Variety* 10 Feb. 1943, 35. Leopold Stokowski, an American conductor of British birth, had unprecedented popularity, both for himself and the classical music he conducted; Fred Waring was a popular bandleader, composer, and publisher from Pennsylvania who had a national following.

21. Lederman, "Songs for Soldiers," 297.

22. Ibid., 297–98.

23. Ibid., 298.

24. Hamm, *Yesterdays*, 388.

25. Ibid.
26. Ibid., 389.
27. Thomson, *The Art of Judging Music*, 117.
28. Hamm, *Yesterdays*, 359.
29. Ibid., 361.
30. Ibid., 376.
31. Seldes, *The 7 Lively Arts*, 58.
32. Rodgers, *100 Best Songs of the 20's and 30's*, xiv.
33. Arnold, *Music and War*, 187.
34. Howe, *World of Our Fathers*, 165.
35. Hamm, *Yesterdays*, 378.
36. Ibid.
37. "What Makes the Hit Parade?" *Variety*, 6 Jan. 1943, 186; "Who Selects the Air Music?" *Billboard*, 17 Feb. 1945, 14, 16.
38. Lederman, "Songs for Soldiers," 300.
39. Scheele, *Songs of World Wars I & II*, 1.
40. Lederman, "Songs for American Soldiers," 299.
41. Ibid.
42. Ibid.
43. Ibid., 300.
44. "Doughboys Like It Hot," *Billboard*, 10 Oct. 1942, 21.
45. "Pubs Sour War Notes: Say Public, Writers, Maestri Set Up Obstacles to War Songs," *Billboard*, 22 Aug. 1942, 20; "War Songs Don't Sell," *Billboard*, 8 Aug. 1942, 22.

CHAPTER 10

1. "Amusement Industry and the War Effort," *Billboard*, 17 Jan. 1942, 4.
2. Ben Bodec, "Yank Music Pubs Recall England," *Variety*, 10 Dec. 1941, 1, 39.
3. "10 Best Sellers on Coin-Machines," *Variety*, 10 Dec. 1941, 38; "15 Best Sheet Music Sellers," *Variety*, 10 Dec. 1941, 39.
4. "Sift English War Songs for America Now," *Variety*, 17 Dec. 1941, 2.
5. Abel Green, "Selling Side of Song Plugging," *Variety*, 7 Jan. 1942, 156.
6. "'Advanced ' Dancemen Call War Songs Too Corny but the Public Buys Them," *Variety*, 4 Feb. 1942, 1.
7. Ibid., 13.
8. Ibid.
9. "U.S. Radio Coordinator Sets H'wood Straight on War-Aid Programs," *Variety*, 11 Mar. 1942, 4.
10. "Too Few War Tunes Good for Sales," *Variety*, 25 Mar. 1942, 3.
11. "Patriotic Slogans on Song Sheets Set Style Other Pubs May Follow," *Variety*, 1 April 1942, 1.

12. "Not Singing About This War," *Variety*, 15 April 1942, 1.
13. "Isham Jones on Why War Songs Flop," *Variety*, 10 June 1942, 43.
14. "Give 'Em the Old Ones," *Variety*, 10 June 1942, 43.
15. Ben Bodec, "Victories Help Song Sales," *Variety*, 10 June 1942, 1, 44.
16. OWI: RG 208; Surveys of Public Attitudes, SG 118, WNRC.
17. Ibid.
18. Ben Bodec, "Victories Help Song Sales," *Variety*, 10 June 1942, 44.
19. "Tactless War Songs," *Variety*, 15 June 1942, 3.
20. Ibid.
21. Abel Green, "First Steps Taken for Fighting Songs; Dreamy Stuff Doesn't Fit Long War," *Variety*, 22 June 1942, 1, 19.
22. Ibid., 1.
23. OWI: RG 208; Domestic Radio Bureau, New York Radio Division: SG 169, WNRC.
24. "OWI's Radio Head Tells Songwriters of War Idiom Need in Pop Numbers," *Variety*, 29 July 1942, 3.
25. Ibid.
26. "'War' Song, Really 'Boy-Girl' Songs!" *Variety*, 22 July 1942, 7.
27. "Tells Songwriters of War Need," *Variety*, 29 July 1942, 35.
28. Ibid.
29. Margaret S. Wells, "Music in the News," *Billboard*, 20 Nov. 1943, 67.
30. Ibid.
31. OWI: RG 208; Records of the Domestic Radio Bureau: SG 169; "No Hit War Song Yet," *Billboard*, 17 Oct. 1942, 62.
32. "Jack Robbins Challenges 'Boy-Girl' War Song Charges at SPA; Offers to Publish Any 10 Picked by OWI," *Variety*, 19 July 1942, 37.
33. "Pubs' Sour War Notes," *Billboard*, 22 Aug. 1942, 20.
34. Ibid.
35. "If the War Ended Today," *Time*, 20 July 1942, 74.
36. Ibid.
37. "To Encourage Fighting Tunes," *Variety*, 26 Aug. 1942, 3.
38. Ibid., 44.
39. "Pubs' Sour War Notes," *Billboard*, 22 Aug. 1942, 20, 59.
40. Ibid.
41. Ibid.
42. OWI: RG 208; Records of the Domestic Radio Bureau; Fred Waring papers: SG 169, WNRC.
43. OWI: RG 208; letter from Charles Hamlin to Barnum and Van Nostrand, 19 April 1943, Fred Waring Papers: SG 169, WNRC.
44. "Music Goes to War, *Variety 37th Anniversary Issue*, 6 January 1943, 189.
45. "'Praise the Lord's' Great Press," *Variety*, 4 Nov. 1942, 41, 47; Tyler, *Hit Parade*, 109.
46. John Powell Anderson, "Educators Mull Radio's Part in Peace," *Variety*, 11 Nov. 1942, 30.

47. "Raise the Cash to Buy the Ammunition," *Variety*, 25 Nov. 1942, 1.

48. Fussell, *Wartime*, 154–55.

49. OWI: RG 208; Records of the Domestic Radio Bureau; National Wartime Committee: SG 169, WNRC.

50. "Part of O.W.I.'s New War Song Tips Already Tried in Music Biz," *Variety*, 9 Dec. 1942, 40.

51. "Japs to Jeeps, Doughboy's Rose to Der Feuhrer's Face—There's Nary an 'Over There' in the Lot," *Billboard*, 9 Jan. 1942, 25.

52. OWI: RG 208; Records of the Domestic Radio Bureau; National Wartime Music Committee: SG 169, WNRC.

53. "10 Best Sellers in Coin-Machines," *Variety*, 2 Dec. 1942, 38.

54. Ibid.

55. "10 Best Sellers on Coin-Machines," *Variety*, 24 June 1942, 44; "10 Best Sellers on Coin-Machines," *Variety*, Aug. 12, 1942, 50.

56. Tyler, *Hit Parade*, 108.

57. Ibid., 108–10.

58. Abel Green, *Variety 37th Anniversary Issue*, 6 Jan. 1943, 187.

59. Ibid.

60. OWI: RG 208; Records of the Domestic Radio Bureau; National Wartime Music Committee: SG 169, WNRC.

61. "Wartime Music Committee Quits after Exposure of Failure to Get Co-op from Trade; New Group Due," *Variety*, 14 April 1943, 45.

Chapter 11

1. "Wartime Music Committee Quits after Exposure of Failure to Get Co-op from Trade; New Group Due," *Variety*, 14 April 1943, 54.

2. OWI: RG 208; Records of the Domestic Radio Bureau; Wartime Music Committee: SG 169, WNRC.

3. "Mobilizing Composers to Go All Out in Furthering War Effort via Music," *Variety*, 19 May 1943, 1, 32.

4. Ibid., 1.

5. Ibid., 32.

6. "Not What WAAC Wants," *Billboard*, 6 Feb. 1943, 21.

7. Treadwell, *The Women's Army Corps*, 184.

8. OWI: RG 208; "Surveys of Public Attitudes": 22 December 1943: SG 118, WNRC.

9. OWI: RG 208; memo from William Burk to Keagan Bayles, 17 Feb. 1943, Records of the Domestic Radio Bureau, Wartime Music Committee: SG 169, WNRC.

10. "Mobilizing Composers to Go All Out in Furthering War Effort via Music," *Variety*, 19 May 1943, 32.

11. Ibid.

12. "Songwriters' Own Positive Approach to War Song Problem Shelves OWI

Hypo; MWC Jumping All Hurdles," *Variety*, 26 May 1943, 3, 54. The following discussion of the Music War Committee's birth is based upon this source.

13. OWI: RG 208; letter, 23 Feb. 1944, from Wilder Breckenridge to John Van Nostrand, Records of the Domestic Radio Bureau; American Theater Wings' Music War Committee: SG 169, WNRC.

14. OWI: RG 208; Records of the Domestic Radio Bureau; American Theater Wings' Music War Committee: SG 169, WNRC.

15. "Songwriters' Own Positive Approach to War Song Problem Shelves OWI Hypo; MWC Jumping All Hurdles," *Variety*, 26 May 1943, 3.

16. "Soldier Songsmiths Seen Writing the Most Believable War Tunes," *Variety*, 9 June 1943, 1.

17. "Sifting Committee, Other Machinery Oiled to Speed Worthy War Songs," *Variety*, 16 June 1943, 41.

18. "'That Great War Song Will Write Itself sans Contests': Irving Berlin," *Variety*, 23 June 1943, 1, 31.

19. Abel Green, "Show Biz's Role in the War," *Variety*, 17 Dec. 1941, 1, 22.

20. "This War Doesn't Lend Itself to a Big Hit Song Thinks Harold Arlen," *Variety*, 23 June 1943, 54.

21. "10 Best Sellers on Coin-Machines," *Variety*, 14 October 1942, 40; 21 October 1942, 48; 28 October 1942, 40; 4 November 1942, 42; 11 November 1942, 38; 18 November 1942, 38; 25 November 1942, 42; 2 December 1942, 38; 9 December 1942, 38; 16 December 1942, 36; 23 December 1942, 40; "'Praise the Lord' Wow 450,000 Copies Despite Frowns from the Clergy,"18 November 1942, 3.

22. Abel Green, "Loesser on War Songs," *Variety*, 27 Oct. 1943, 37.

23. Roeder, *The Censored War*, 5–6.

24. "10 Best Sellers in Coin-Machines," *Variety*, 28 July, 1943, 36.

25. "Music War Group Picks 2 Tunes for Ballyhoo of Defense Bond Drive," *Variety*, 11 Aug. 1943, 39; Palmer, *All You Need Is Love*, 155.

26. "New Crop of War Songs Attuned to 3rd War Loan Drive," *Variety*, 25 Aug. 1943, 39.

27. "'Pistol' in Black Market Demand," *Variety*, 15 Sept. 1943, 45.

28. Tyler, *Hit Parade*, 113.

29. Margaret S. Wells, "Music in the News," *Billboard*, 29 Jan. 1944, 62.

30. OWI: RG 208; Domestic Radio Bureau; SG 169, "'Let's Talk Turkey to Japan: N.B.C.'s Sixth War Loan Program," 23 Nov. 1944: 1–55, WNRC.

31. Ibid, 2.

32. Participation in the effort to sell war bonds was not limited to musical variety shows; radio dramas like "Hasten the Day," written by Pauline Gilsdorf for CBS, included several shows comparing the relatively slight sacrifices of civilians with that of American soldiers, and in several scripts the remedy to assuage the guilt of both the characters and their audience was to purchase more war bonds. OWI: RG 208; "Hasten the Day," 119 scripts, August 1943–December 1944, SG 152, WNRC.

33. OWI: RG 208; Domestic Radio Bureau, Office of the Deputy Chief; SG 169, "Fact Sheet No. 324, Seventh Loan Drive," 14 May 1945, WNRC.

34. "U.S. Popular Music Collection, 1941–1945," Library of Congress; OWI: RG 208; Domestic Radio Bureau, Office of the Deputy Chief; SG 169, "Fact Sheet No. 324, Seventh Loan Drive," 14 May 1945, WNRC.

CHAPTER 12

1. John Desmond, "Tin Pan Alley Seeks the Song," *New York Times Magazine*, 6 June 1943, 14, 31; Chappell & Co., Inc., *80 Years of American Songs Hits, 1892–1972*, 5, 10.

2. "Decca 'Rum & Coke' Disc May Be Co's Biggest Seller Despite Net Ban, *Variety*, 14 February 1945, 43.

3. Olin Downes, "Music of the Times: The Need for Great War Songs," *New York Times*, 23 Aug. 1942.

4. "G.I.'s Tab Musical Favorites; Crosby, James, Shore Rated," *Billboard*, 16 Sept. 1944, 19.

5. "'Slush Tunes,' Nonetheless, Get Best Play in Camp Jukeboxes, Says Soldier," *Variety*, 2 Sept. 1942, 2, 50.

6. "Public Seems Blah to 'Wrath' Songs Pubs See OWI Hopes Scuttled by Facts," *Variety*, 14 October 1942, 42.

7. Tom Payne, "Give Us a Song We Can Fight To," in *Reveille*, 93–94.

8. "GI's Want Sentimental Numbers, Says Berlin; 'Marizy' Floors Him," *Variety*, 8 March 1944, 44.

9. Casdorph, *Let the Good Times Roll*, passim; O'Neill, *A Democracy at War*, 129–43.

10. Denisoff and Peterson, eds., *The Sounds of Social Change*, 20.

11. H.F. Mooney, "Popular Music Since the 1920's: The Significance of Shifting Taste," in Denisoff and Peterson, eds., *The Sounds of Social Change*, 189.

12. Stearns and Stearns, *Jazz Dance*, 323.

13. Stowe, *Swing Changes*, 40.

14. "This Is Not a Singing War," *New York Times Magazine*, 20 June 1943, 23.

15. "15 Best Song Sellers," *Variety*, 16 June 1943, 41.

16. Moeller, *Shooting War*, 204–6.

17. OWI: RG 208; "Surveys of Public Attitudes," 4 November 1943: SG 118, WNRC.

18. OWI: RG 208; "When Radio Writes for War," Domestic Radio Bureau: SG 169, WNRC.

19. John Lardner, "Lardner's Goes to War," *Newsweek*, 24 Aug. 1943, 24.

20. Gustav Klemm, "The Fighting Man and His Music," *The Etude* 61 (Nov. 1943): 711, 755.

21. Oscar Hammerstein II, "War Songs," *Variety Anniversary Thirty-eighth Anniversary Issue*, 5 Jan. 1944, 187.

22. Ibid.

23. Abel Green, "War Song of World War II Taking Care of Itself," *Variety Thirty-eighth Anniversary Issue*, 5 Jan. 1944, 187.

24. Quoted in "Music in the News," *Billboard*, 18 Sept. 1943, 64.

25. "G.I.'s Hit 'Hit Kit': Prefer Nickel and Dime Lyric Mags," *Billboard*, 29 July 1944, 21.

26. "Public Prefers Novelties to War Songs, Publishers Figure; Cite Escape Need," *Variety*, 2 Feb. 1944, 1, 46.

27. "Mairzy Day Too," *Newsweek*, 7 Feb. 1944, 97.

28. "Public Prefers Novelties to War Songs, Publishers Figure; Cite Escape Need," *Variety*, 2 Feb. 1944, 1, 46.

29. "10 Best Sellers on Coin-Machines," *Variety*, 21 June 1944, 46.

30. "Music Publishers Preparing V-E Day Songs for Fast Marketing," *Variety*, 11 Oct. 1944, 35.

31. In 1942 an anti-monopoly edict from the FCC ordered RCA to sell or disband one of its two networks. Robert Sarnoff kept the more profitable NBC Red network and reorganized the smaller NBC Blue network into a separate entity. The names Red and Blue derived from the red- and blue-colored pencils initially used by station engineers to map the station hookup of the NBS system. In 1943 Edward J. Noble bought the Blue chain and renamed it the American Broadcasting Company. DeLong, *The Mighty Music Box*, 249.

32. "Top Tunes of 1944," *Variety Thirty-ninth Anniversary Edition*, 3 Jan. 1945, 135.

33. Abel Green, "Music Industry Looks Ahead to Big 1945," *Variety Thirty-ninth Anniversary Edition*, 3 Jan. 1945, 135.

34. "Honor Roll of Hits," *Billboard*, 19 May 1945, 22. *Billboard* claimed its "Honor Roll of Hits" was determined by a "scientific, statistical tabulation" of a song's popularity based on various "*Billboard* Popularity Charts," "Songs with Most Radio Plugs," "Records Most Played on Disk Programs," "Play Status of Films with Leading Songs," "Best Selling Sheet Music," "Best Selling Retail Records," and "Most Played Juke Box Records."

35. "'Bell Bottom Trousers,' Old Sea Chantey, Rings the Bell as a Pop Hit," *Variety*, 6 June 1945, 1, 46.

36. "Leading Music Box Records of 1941," *Billboard*, 31 Jan. 1942, 66.

CHAPTER 13

1. O'Neill, *A Democracy at War*, 140–41.

2. Ibid., 254.

3. "Chicago Times for War Tune," *Billboard*, 6 June 1942, 60.

4. Ibid.

5. OWI: RG 208; Domestic Radio Bureau; SG 169, WNRC.

6. OWI: RG 208; "Surveys of American's Radio Listening Preferences;" SG 119, WNRC.

7. Bindas, ed., *America's Musical Pulse*, 37.

8. Mills Music Advertisement, *Billboard*, 31 Jan. 1942, 68-69.

9. "Socko Boom in Music Sales Sets In," *Variety*, 24 Dec. 1941, 1.

10. "War Jitters Down, Biz Up," *Variety*, 11 Feb. 1942, 5.

11. "Records Make Big Pay-Off," *Variety*, 8 April 1942, 41.

12. "Seek Washington Sympathy on Tires for Band, Important in Soldier Diversion; Meantime Biz Is Good," *Variety*, 8 April 1942, 41.

13. "Bumpy—But—Prosperous Biz," *Variety*, 24 June 1942, 41.

14. Ibid.

15. "Exit Red Ink for Bands," *Variety*, 8 Sept. 1943, 35.

16. "Ace Bands Peak Tallies," *Variety*, 7 April 1943, 1.

17. "75,000,000 Disc Sales in '43: Big Biz Despite War, AFM Ban," *Variety*, 25 Aug. 1943, 37.

18. Ben Bodec, "Music Biz Bouncing High: '43 Sales May Hit 40,000,000," *Variety*, 25 Aug. 1943, 1, 19.

19. "Novelty Songs, Per Usual, Lead Way in Critical '43: Music Biz Also Rode Wartime Prosperity Crest—800,000 to 1,000,000 Sheet-Seller," *Variety Thirty-eighth Anniversary Issue*, 5 Jan 1944, 187.

20. "OPA Eyes Price of Records," *Variety*, 20 June 1943, 37.

21. "No Further Shellac Cuts for Disc Cos.," *Variety*, 7 July 1943, 44; Elliott Grennard, "Music Goes to War," *Billboard 1943 Music Year Book*, 25 Sept. 1943, 20.

22. "Shellac Supply Hangs on '44 India Crop and Cargo Space," *Billboard*, 27 Nov. 1943, 98.

23. "Pre-War Shellac for Discs Apr. 1," *Variety*, 15 March 1944, 53.

24. "WPB Order Snags Pubs on Paper," *Variety*, 21 June 1944, 39.

25. "Sheet Music Biz at 15 Year Crest," *Variety*, 4 Oct. 1944, 1, 43.

26. "ASCAP Coin Up, Also Sheet Sales," *Variety*, 13 Dec. 1944, 1, 8.

27. Sales racks in music business refer to displays of sheet music in venues other than music stores: newsstands, department, grocery, and 5- and 10-cent stores.

28. "Stress Paper Dole Fallacy," *Variety*, 11 April 1945, 35.

29. "Even Stale Music Sells Like Nylons," *Variety*, 4 April 1945, 1, 20. *Billboard* reported that priorities for defense did not force advertisers from the radio. New manufacturing plants and army camps created markets where none had existed before. Old markets were booming. There were new markets in the South for foods, drugs, and toiletries. People who had been on welfare now worked in defense plants and on other war-related work. Ed Wood, general sales manager for the Mutual Broadcasting Company, said, "The purchasing power of the lower classes is so tremendously increased that it is now comparable to what it was in 1928—this despite the income tax." *Billboard*, 6 Dec. 1941, 6.

30. "Another Slump in Sheet Sales," *Variety*, 25 July 1945, 71.

31. "Musicians Have Lost $4,000,000 in Jobs, but Disc Cos. Hurt Little by AFM Ban," *Variety*, 4 August 1943, 47.

32. Ibid., 38.

33. "Dancemen Spin under Wartime Blows," *Variety*, 29 April 1942, 39.

34. "1945 Expected to See Start of Record Boom," *Variety Thirty-ninth Anniversary Issue*, 3 Jan. 1945, 135.

35. Abel Green, "This Has Been the Year of Years for the Music Business," *Variety Fortieth Anniversary Issue*, 9 Jan. 1946, 247.

CHAPTER 14

1. "Thank You for Your Letters," *Seventeen*, October 1945: 4.

2. "Thank You for Your Letters," *Seventeen*, May 1945: 124–27.

3. Lee J. Cronbach, "Research . . . Pupil-Morale After One Year of War," *School and Society*, 10 April 1943, 416–20.

4. Ibid., 418.

5. Jitterbugs take their name from a dance style in which partners two-step, balance, and twirl in set patterns. By the mid-1940s the term bobby-soxer became synonymous with teenagers, especially girls who donned the jitterbug "uniform" consisting of a pleated skirt, a baggy sweater, bobbysocks, and saddle shoes or penny loafers. "Victory Girls," or "V-Girls," was the label given to girls who picked up servicemen, usually at amusement centers. They were also called khaki wackies, patriotutes, and good-time Janes. *LIFE*, 20 Dec. 1943, 101–2.

6. Ella Merrit and Floy Hendricks, "Trend of Child Labor," in Richard Polenberg, ed., *America at War, 1941–1945*, 139.

7. O'Neill, *A Democracy at War*, 249.

8. Merrit and Hendricks, "Trend of Child Labor," 141.

9. James H.S. Bossard, "Family Backgrounds of Wartime Adolescents," *The Annals of the American Academy of Political and Social Science*, 246 (November 1944): 35–36.

10. "Honor Roll of Hits Tabbed," *Billboard*, 24 March 1945, 3, 12, 64.

11. "Home Jukes Set Motif for Postwar Play Rooms," *Billboard*, 25 Mar. 1944, 90.

12. R. Serge Denisoff, "What Is Popular Music: A Silly Question?," in *Solid Gold*, 19.

13. Ibid., 20.

CHAPTER 15

1. Fussell, *Wartime*, 188.

2. Brown, *The Year of the Century*, 26–41.

3. H.F. Mooney, "Popular Music Since the 1920's: The Significance of Shifting Taste," 68.

4. Denisoff, "What Is Popular Music?" 20.

5. Ibid., 18.

6. "Negro Jitterbugs Beyond Control," *Variety*, 29 July 1942, 41.

7. Lingeman, *Don't You Know There's a War On?*, 284–85.

8. George Simon, *The Big Bands*, 35.

9. Margaret S. Wells, "Music in the News," *Billboard*, 5 February 1944, 62.

10. "Waltz Big in Iowa Halls," *Variety*, 15 April 1942, 39.

11. Ibid.

12. Ibid.

13. The initial drafting of men under twenty started in January 1943 and continued at the rate of 100,000 per month. This number was included in the Office of War Information's statement that beginning in January 1943, 350,000 men per month would be called to service, so the U.S. fighting force would reach 9.7 million men by the end of 1943. Casdorph, *Let the Good Times Roll*, 86–87.

14. Ben Bodec, "Music Biz Bouncing High; Sheet Music Drawing Public's Surplus Coin," *Variety*, 25 Aug. 1943, 1, 19.

15. "Ideas on What People Like in Music—and Why They Like It—Keep Flowing, Like Good Music," *Billboard*, 3 Oct. 1942, 65.

16. Ibid. "Sweet-hot" refers to swing music that incorporates elements of the larger swing band sound with those of the traditional jazz ensemble. "Hot jazz" relies on freely improvised musical lines played by smaller groups—usually five to seven instruments. Shaw, *Dictionary of American Pop/Rock*, 179.

17. "Ideas on What People Like in Music—and Why They Like It—Keep Flowing, Like Good Music," *Billboard*, 3 Oct. 1942, 65

18. Margaret S. Wells, "Music in the News," *Billboard*, 29 Jan. 1944, 62.

19. "High Schoolers Say James Best," *Billboard*, 3 June 1944, 1, 12.

20. "Final Standing in *Billboard* Poll of Music Preferences of Hi School Kids," *Billboard*, 3 June 1944, 12, 65.

21. "Top Records High School Students Liked in 1943–'44 First Annual High School Music Poll," *Billboard*, 3 June 1944, 12.

22. "G.I.'s Tab Favorites; They're Still Kids at Heart," *Billboard*, 23 Sept. 1944, 20.

23. "G.I. Disk Label Ratings; Boys & Girls Tell Facts: Little Difference Between a Serviceman or High-schooler, According to Survey," *Billboard*, 23 Sept. 1944, 72.

24. Ibid.

25. "G.I.'s Report Their Sing-Songs," *Billboard*, 30 Sept. 1944, 11.

26. Ibid.

27. "2nd High-School Music Survey Tab," *Billboard*, 16 June 1945, 3.

28. "Bobby-Sox Tab Disk, Tune Faves," *Billboard*, 16 June 1945, 20.

29. "Record Labels No Mystery to Soxers," *Billboard*, 16 June 1945, 21.

30. "Bing Solid in Minnesota," *Billboard*, 16 June 1945, 21.

31. "Colleges Confirm Other BB Polls," *Billboard*, 21 July 1945, 3.

32. Ibid.

33. "They've Done It Again: G.I. and Soxers' Yens Repeat," *Billboard*, 21 July 1945, 15.

34. "Camp(us) Tune, Disk, Label Faves," *Billboard*, 28 July 1945, 15.

35. "They've Done It Again: G.I. and Soxers' Yens Repeat," *Billboard*, 21 July 1945, 15.

36. Don Matthews, "College Rhythm," *Variety*, 3 Dec. 1941, 50.

37. Donald R. Larrabee, "College Rhythm," *Variety*, 17 Dec. 1941, 50.

38. Harley Bowers, "College Rhythm," *Variety*,14 Jan. 1942, 38.

39. Jim Ward, "College Rhythm," *Variety*, 21 Jan. 1942, 52.

40. Bob J. Thomas, "College Rhythm," *Variety*, 31 Dec. 1942, 34.

41. O'Neill, *A Democracy at War*, 255.

42. Arnold, *Music and War*, 79.

43. Blum, *V Was for Victory*, 16.

44. OWI: RG 208; Survey of Public Attitudes, Dec. 1943: SG 118, WNRC.

45. OWI: RG 208; Survey of Public Attitudes, Mar. 15,1944: SG 118, WNRC.

46. Satterfield, *The Homefront*, 282.

47. Ibid.

48. "Meet Soozie Cue," *Billboard*, 3 Oct. 1942, 65.

49. O'Neill, *Democracy at War*, 142.

Bibliography

Government Records

National Archives and Record Administration, Washington, D.C.

"Powers of Persuasion: Poster Art from World War II," an Exhibition of Original World War II Poster Art at the National Archives, Washington, D.C., February 1994–February 1995.

Record Group 208: Records of the Office of War Information.

Subgroup 169: Records of the Domestic Radio Bureau, National Wartime Music Committee, and the Music War Council of the American Theater Wing.

Subgroup 118: "Survey of Public Attitudes."

Record Group 216: Records of the Office of Censorship.

Record Group 44: Records of the Public Relations Branch of the United States Army in World War II.

Music Division, Performing Arts (Music) Reading Room, Music and Recorded Sound Division, Library of Congress, Washington, D.C.

Leeds Original Manuscript Series Arrangements.

United States Popular Music Collection, 1900–1920; 1920–1940; 1941–1945.

Interviews

Margarethe R. Bartholomew, Natchitoches, La., 20 April 1994.

Billy Harrington, Natchitoches, La., 30 May 1994.

Music Lyrics

Adair, Tom, and Dick Hull. "Ev'rybody Ev'ry Payday." Washington, D.C.: Henry Morgenthau Jr., Secretary of the Treasury, 1942.

———. "It's the Little Things That Count!" Washington D.C.: War Savings Staff of the U.S. Treasury Department, 1942.
———. "Lend 'Til It Hurts the Axis." Washington, D.C.: Education Section, War Savings Staff, U.S. Treasury Department, 1942.
Adamson, Harold, and Jimmy McHugh. "Comin' In on a Wing and a Prayer." New York: Robbins Music Corp., 1943.
Alexander, Perry. "Pluggin' Jane." New York: Perry Alexander Music Publishing, 1945.
Allen, Lewis, and Earl Robinson. "The House I Live In (That's America to Me)." New York: Chappell & Co., 1942.
Almanac Singers. "The Ballad of October 16th." *Songs for John Doe*. New York: American Peace Mobilization, 1941.
———. "Dear Mister President," *Songs to Tear Hitler Down*. New York: New Theater League, 1942.
———. "Plow Under." *Songs for John Doe*. New York: American Peace Mobilization, 1941.
———. "Washington Breakdown." *Songs for John Doe*. New York: American Peace Mobilization, 1941.
Bergman, Dewey, Carley Mills, and Ann Roberts. "Some Peaceful Evening (In Some Peaceful Town)." New York: Campbell-Porgie, Inc., 1944.
Berk, Lew. "When I Get Back to My Home Town." New York: Lew Berk, 1944.
Berlin, Irving. "Any Bonds Today?": Theme Song of the National Defense Savings Program, U.S. Defense Savings Bonds and Stamps. Washington, D.C.: Henry Morgenthau Jr., Secretary of the Treasury, 1941.
———. "Arms for the Love of America." New York: Irving Berlin Music Corp, 1941.
———. "God Bless America." New York: Irving Berlin, Inc., Music Publishers, 1939.
———. "I'm Getting Tired So I Can Sleep." New York: Irving Berlin Music Corp, 1942.
———. "Just a Blue Serge Suit." New York: Irving Berlin Music Corp., 1945.
———. "Oh! How I Hate to Get Up in the Morning." New York: Waterson, Berlin, & Snyder Co., 1918.
———. "There Are No Wings on a Foxhole (For the Men of the Infantry)." New York: Irving Berlin Music Crop., 1944.
———. "White Christmas." New York: Irving Berlin Music Corporation, 1942.
Bryan, Alfred, and Al. Piantadosi. "I Didn't Raise My Boy to Be a Soldier." New York: Leo Feist, Inc., 1915.
Burton, Nat, and Walter Kent. "(There'll Be Bluebirds Over) The White Cliffs of Dover." New York: Shapiro, Bernstein & Company, 1941.
Cahn, Sammy, and Jule Styne. "I'll Walk Alone." New York: Morley Music Co., Inc., 1944.
———. "It's Been a Long, Long Time." New York: Morley Music Co., Inc., 1945.
———. "It Takes a Guy Like I." New York: Edwin H. Morris & Co., Inc., 1942.

———. "Vict'ry Polka." New York: Chappell & Co., Inc, 1943.
———. "You've Got to Study, Buddy." New York: Edwin H. Morris & Co., Inc., 1942.
Cohan, George M. "Over There." New York: Leo Feist, Inc., 1917.
Coots, J. Fred. "Goodbye, Mamma, I'm Off to Yokohama." New York: Chappell & Co., Inc., 1941.
Davis, Gussie L. "In the Baggage Coach Ahead." New York: Howley, Haviland & Co., 1896.
DeLange, Edgar, and Sam H. Stept. "This Is Worth Fighting For." New York: Harms, Inc., 1942.
De Vries, John, and Joe Bushkin. "(There'll Be a) Hot Time in the Town of Berlin (When the Yanks Go Marching In)." New York: Barton Music Corp., 1943.
Dexter, Al. "Pistol Packin' Mama." Santa Monica, Calif.: Vogue Music, Inc., 1943.
Drake, Milton, Al Hoffman, and Jerry Livingston. "Mairzy Doats." New York: Miller Music Corp., 1943.
Driggs, Collins. "Law-aw-aw-aw-aw-aw-ong Way Back Home." New York: Mills Music, Inc., 1944.
Egan, Raymond B., and Richard A. Whiting. "Till We Meet Again." New York: Remick Music Corp., 1918.
Evans, Redd. "He's 1–A in the Army and A-1 in My Heart." New York: Valiant Music Company, 1941.
Evans, Redd, and John Jacob Loeb. "Rosie the Riveter." New York: Paramount Music Corp., 1942.
Ford, Lena Guilbert, and Ivor Novello. "Keep the Home Fire Burning." London: Ascherberg, Hopwood, and Crew, Ltd., 1915.
Friend, Cliff, and Charlie Tobias. "We Did It Before and We Can Do It Again." New York: M. Witmark & Sons, 1941.
Gordon, Mack, and Harry Warrens. "I Had the Craziest Dream." New York: Bregman, Vocco & Conn, Inc., 1942.
Graham, Irvin, and Robert Sour. "A Woman's Place." New York: Chappell, 1943.
Harburg, E.Y. "Yip," and Burton Lane. "You Can Always Tell a Yank." New York: T.B. Harms Co., 1944.
Harris, Charles K. "After the Ball." New York: Charles K. Harris, 1892.
Hollingsworth, William H. "Wilson, Democracy, and the Red, White and Blue." Kansas City, Missouri: Howard Publishing Co., 1918.
Johnson, Howard, and Theodore Morse. "M-O-T-H-E-R, a Word That Means the World to Me." New York: Leo Feist, Inc., 1915.
Kahal, Irving, and Sammy Fain. "I'll Be Seeing You." New York: Williamson Music Co., 1938.
Lawrence, Jack. "Linda," New York: Warock Music, Inc., 1946.
Leslie, Edgar, and Joseph A. Burke. "We Must Be Vigilant." New York: Bregman, Vocco and Conn, Inc., 1942.
Lloyd, Robert. "Good Morning Mr. Zip, Zip, Zip." New York: Leo Feist, Inc., 1918.

Loesser, Frank. "Praise the Lord and Pass the Ammunition." New York: Famous Music Corp., 1942.

Loesser, Frank, and Arthur Schwartz. "They're Either Too Young or Too Old." M. Witmark & Sons, 1943.

Lombardo, Carmen, and John Jacob Loeb. "Ma, I Miss Your Apple Pie." New York: Fred Ahlert Music Corp., 1941.

Loveday, Carroll, and Jo Kern. "The Shrine of Saint Cecilia." Chicago: Braun Music Co., 1941.

Madden, Edward, and Theodore E. Morse. "Blue Bell." New York: F.B. Haviland Publishing Co., Inc., 1904.

Maschwitz, Eric and Michael Carr. "He Wears a Pair of Silver Wings." New York: Shapiro, Bernstein and Co., Inc., 1941.

McHugh, Jimmy, and Herb Magidson. "Say a Pray'r for the Boys Over There." New York: Southern Music Publishing Co., Inc., 1943.

Mercer, Johnny. "Dream." New York: Michael H. Goldsen, Inc., 1944.

———. "G.I. Jive." New York: Michael H. Goldsen, Inc., 1943.

Mercer, Johnny, and Harold Arlen. "I'm Doin' It for Defense." New York: Famous Music Corp., 1942.

———. "On the Swing Shift." New York: Famous Music Corp., 1942.

Moore, Phil. "Shoo-Shoo Baby." New York: Leeds Music Corp., 1943.

Mugge, Robert, dir. *Entertaining the Troops: American Entertainers in World War II.* RCA / Columbia Pictures Home Video, 1992.

Owen, Anita. "I Cannot Bear to Say Goodbye." New York: Waterson, Berlin & Snyder, 1918.

Parish, Mitchell, Bell Leib, and J. Pfeil. "The Blond Sailor." New York: Mills Music Co., 1937 & 1945.

Pease, Harry, Howard Johnson, and Harry Jentes. "I Don't Want to Get Well." New York: Leo Feist, Inc., 1917.

Porter, Cole. "Don't Fence Me In." New York: Harms, Inc., 1944.

Prichard, Henry. "Don't Let It Happen Again." New York: Broadcast Music, Inc., 1945.

Raye, Don, and Gene de Paul. "Milkman, Keep Those Bottles Quiet." New York: Leo Feist, Inc., 1944.

Reid, Don, and Irving Miller. "The Bells of Normandy (Are Ringing Again)." New York: Dorsey Brothers Music, Inc., 1944.

Reid, Don, and Sammy Kaye. "Remember Pearl Harbor." New York: Republic Music Corp., 1941.

Reisner, C. Francis, Benny Davis, and Billy Baskette. "Goodbye Broadway, Hello France." New York: Leo Feist, Inc., 1917

Roberts, Paul, and Shelby Darnell. "There's a Star Spangled Banner Waving Somewhere." New York: Bob Miller, Inc., Music Publishers, 1942.

Roeder, George H. *The Censored War: American Visual Experience During World War II.* New Haven: Yale University Press, 1993.

Russell, Bob, and Duke Ellington. "Don't Get Around Much Any More." New York: Robbins Music Corp., 1942.

Sanders, Joe. "Save the Grease: Dedicated to the American Housewife." New York: Words and Music, Inc., 1943.

Seiler, Eddie, Sol Marcus, and Bennie Benjemen. "When the Lights Go on Again (All Over the World)." New York: Campbell, Loft & Porgie, Inc., 1942.

Stanton, Frank N., and Ethelbert Nevin. "Mighty Lak' a Rose." Cincinnati: The John Church Company, 1901.

Taylor, Irving, and Vic Mizzy. "Three Little Sisters." New York: Santly-Joy-Select, Inc., 1942.

Tredwell, Mattie E. *The Woman's Army Corps.* Washington, D.C.: Office of the Chief of Military History, Dept. of the Army, 1953.

Tucker, Sophie. "The Bigger the Army and the Navy (Is the Better the Lovin' Will Be)." New York: Robbins Music Publishers, Inc., 1944.

Turk, Roy and Fred Ahlert. "I'll Get By (As Long as I Have You)." New York: Fred Ahlert Music Corp., 1928.

WAC Song Book. "In My Little GI Shoes." Fort Lee, Va.: Special Services, Women's Army Training Center, n.d.

Wallace, Oliver. "Der Feuhrer's Face." New York: Southern Music Publishing, Inc., 1942.

Waller, Thomas "Fats," and Ed Kirkeby. "Cash for Your Trash." New York: Robbins Music, Inc., 1942.

Waller, Thomas "Fats," and George Marion Jr. "When the Nylons Bloom Again." New York: Robbins Music, Inc., 1943.

Waring, Fred, and Jack Dolph. "Song of the M.P's." New York: Words & Music, Inc., 1943.

———. "(WAVES) In Navy Blue." New York: Words & Music, Inc., 1943.

Wentzel, Lynn and Carol J. Bitowski. *I Hear America Singing: A Nostalgic Tour of Popular Sheet Music.* New York: Crown Publishers, 1989.

Wheeler, Burt. "We'll Knock the Japs Right into the Laps of the Nazis!" New York: Mills Music, Inc., 1941.

Willson, Meredith. "America Calling." New York, Irving Berlin, Inc., 1942.

———. "FIRE UP! A Marching Song of the Chemical Warfare Service." New York: Words & Music, Inc., 1942.

———. "Yankee Doodle Girl." New York: Words & Music, Inc., 1943.

PERIODICALS

American Mercury, 1943

American Music, 1941–1945

The Billboard, 1941–1945

Charlotte (NC) Observer, 1943

Christian Century, 1942–1945

Cinema Journal, 1985–1990
Education for Victory, 1943
The Etude, 1941–1945
Hit Parader, 1941–1945.
Hollywood Quarterly
Journal of American History
Journal of Popular Culture
Journal of Popular Film
Life, 1941–1945
Music Educators' National Conference Journal, 1941–1945
Musical Courier
Musical America
Musician
New Masses, 1941–1945
New Republic, 1941–1945
Newsweek, 1941–1945
New York Times, 1941–1945
New York Times Herald, 1941–1945
New York Times Magazine, 1941–1945
Popular Music and Society
Prologue: The Journal of the National Archives
Seventeen, 1944–1945
Theatre Arts, 1941–1945
Time, 1941–1945
Variety, 1941–1945
Wall Street Journal, 1941–1945

Books, Articles, and Other Secondary Sources

Abrahamson, James L. *The American Home Front: Revolutionary War, Civil War, World War I, World War II.* Fort Lesley J. McNair, Washington, D.C.: National Defense University Press, G.P.O., 1983.

Adler, Kurt, ed. *Songs of Many Wars, from the 16th to the 20th Century*. New York: Howell, Soskin, 1943.

American Popular Music: Readings from the Popular Press, 2 Vols. Bowling Green, Ohio: Bowling Green State University Popular Press, 1989.

Anderson, Bruce W. "Popular American Music: Changes in the Consumption of Sound Recordings, 1940–1955." Thesis, University of Pennsylvania, 1974.

Anderson, John Powell. "Educators Mull Radio's Part in Peace." *Variety* 148, no. 10 (11 Nov. 1942): 30.

Anderson, Karen. *Wartime Women: Sex Roles, Family Relations, and the Status of Women during World War II*. Westport, Conn.: Greenwood Press, 1981.

Arnold, Ben. *Music and War: A Research and Informational Guide*. New York: Garland Publishing, Inc., 1993.

Ash, Lee. *Subject Collections: A Guide to Special Book Collections and Subject Emphases as Reported by University, College, Public, and Special Libraries and Museums in the United States and Canada*. 6th ed., 2 vols. New York: Bowker, 1985.

Baird, A. Craig. *Representative American Speeches, 1940–1941*. New York: H.W. Wilson, 1941.

Barnouw, Erik. *The Golden Web: A History of Broadcasting in the United States, 1933–1953*. New York: Oxford University Press, 1968.

Barzun, Jacques. *Music in American Life*. Bloomington, Ind.: Indiana University Press, 1965.

Basinger, Jeanine. *The World War II Combat Film: Anatomy of a Genre*. New York: Columbia University Press, 1986.

Bigsby, C.W.E., ed. *Approaches to Popular Culture*. Bowling Green, Ohio: Bowling Green University Popular Press, 1976.

Billboard, Music/Records/200, The. New York: *Billboard* Publications, 1976.

Billboard Book of Number One Hits, The. New York: *Billboard* Publications, 1985.

Billboard Book of Number One Hits, The. New York: *Billboard* Publications, 1988.

Bindas, Kenneth, ed. *America's Musical Pulse: Popular Music in Twentieth-Century Society*. Westport, Conn.: Greenwood Press, 1992.

Biocca, Frank. "Media and Perceptual Shifts: Early Radio and the Clash of Musical Cultures." *Journal of Popular Culture* 24, no. 2 (Fall 1990): 1–15.

Black, Gregory D. "*Keys of the Kingdom*: Entertainment or Propaganda?" *South Atlantic Quarterly* 75 (1976): 434–46.

Black, Gregory D., and Clayton R. Koppes. "OWI Goes to the Movies: The Bureau of Intelligence's Criticism of Hollywood." *Prologue* 6, no. 1 (Spring 1974): 48–64.

Blum, John Morton. *V Was for Victory*. New York: Harcourt, 1976.

Blumer, Herbert. "Morale: The State of the Problem." In *American Society in Wartime*, edited by William Fielding Ogburn, 207. Chicago: University of Chicago Press, 1943.

Bodec, Ben. "Music Biz Bouncing High: '43 Sales May Hit 40,000,000; Sheet Music drawing Public's Surplus Coin." *Variety* 151, no. 11 (25 Aug. 1943): 1, 19.

———. "Victories Help Song Sales: Midway Boosts Sheet Music Biz." *Variety* 147, no. 7 (10 June 1942): 1, 44.

———. "Yank Music Pubs Recall England." *Variety* 145, no. 1 (10 Dec. 1941): 1, 39.

Booth, Mark W. *The Experience of Songs*. New Haven, Conn.: Yale University Press, 1981.

———., comp. *American Popular Music: A Reference Guide*. Westport, Conn.: Greenwood Press, 1983.

Bordman, Gerald. *The American Musical Theatre: A Chronicle*. New York: Oxford University Press, 1978.

Bossard, James H.S. "Family Backgrounds of Wartime Adolescents." *The Annals of the American Academy of Political and Social Science* 246 (November 1944): 35–36.

Bowers, Harley. "College Rhythm." *Variety* 145, no. 6 (14 Jan. 1942): 38.

Bowman, Kent. *Voices of Combat: A Century of Liberty and War Songs, 1765–1965*. Contributions to the Study of Music and Dance, no. 10. Westport, Conn.: Greenwood Press, 1987.

Boyington, Gregory. *Baa, Baa Black Sheep*. Fresno, Calif.: Wilson Press, 1958.

Braggiotti, Mary. "'Stars and Spangles—A Soprano and a Song' (Lucy Monroe)." *New York Post*, 20 July 1943.

Bratlinger, Patrick. *Bread & Circuses: Theories of Mass Culture as Social Decay*. Ithaca: Cornell University Press, 1983.

Braun, D. Duane. *Toward a Theory of Popular Culture: The Sociology and History of American Music and Dance, 1920–1968*. Ann Arbor, Michigan: Ann Arbor Publications, 1969.

Brinkley, David. *Washington Goes to War*. New York: Knopf, 1988.

Broadcast Music, Incorporated. *Pop Hits: 1940–1966*. New York: BMI, 1967.

Bronson, Fred. *The Billboard Book of Number One Hits*. 2d ed. New York: Billboard Publications, 1988.

Brown, Dee. *The Year of the Century: 1876*. New York: Scribner's, 1966.

Browne, Ray. "Popular Culture: Notes Toward a Definition." In *Popular Culture and Curricula*, edited by Ray Browne and Ronald Ambrosetti, 27–48. Bowling Green, Ohio: Bowling Green State University Popular Press, 1970.

Brown, William R. "The American Girl and the Christmas Tree: World War II Soldier Poets Look at What the GIs Were Fighting For." *Journal of American Culture* 2 (1985): 25–30.

Broyles, J.E. "Commercial Phonographs Build Morale." *The Billboard* 53, no. 50 (13 December 1941): 64.

Burns, James MacGregor. *Roosevelt: The Lion and the Fox*. New York: Harcourt, 1956.

Burton, Jack. *The Blue Book of Broadway Musicals*. Watkins Glen, New York.: Century House, 1952.

———. *The Blue Book of Hollywood Musicals*. Watkins Glen, New York: Century House, 1953.

———. *The Blue Book of Tin Pan Alley: A Human Interest Encyclopedia of American Popular Music*. Rev. ed. Watkins Glen, New York: Century House, 1965.

———. *The Index of American Popular Music: Thousands of Titles Cross-Referenced to Our Basic Anthologies of Popular Song*. Watkins Glen, New York: Century House, 1957.

Buxton, Frank, and Bill Owen. *The Big Broadcast: 1920–1950*. New York: Viking, 1972.

Campbell, D'ann. *Women at War with America: Private Lives in a Patriotic Era*. Cambridge, Mass.: Harvard University Press, 1984.

Carothers, Diane Foxhill. *Radio Broadcasting from 1920–1990: An Annotated Bibliography*. New York: Garland Publishers, 1991.

Casdorph, Paul D. *Let the Good Times Roll: Life at Home in America During World War II*. New York: Paragon House, 1989.

Chappell & Co., Inc. *80 Years of American Song Hits, 1892–1972*. New York: Chappell & Co., Inc., 1973.

Chase, Gilbert. *America's Music: From the Pilgrims to the Present*. 3rd ed. New York: McGraw Hill,1987.

Cheseboro, James W., Davis A. Foulger, Jay E. Nachman, and Andrew Yanelli. "Popular Music as a Mode of Communication, 1955–1982." *Critical Studies in Mass Communication* 2 (1985): 115–35.

Chinn, Jeannie A. "There's a Star-Spangled Banner Waving Somewhere: Country and Western Songs of World War II." *John Edward Memorial Foundation Quarterly* 16 (1980): 74–80.

Chipman, John H. *Index to Top-Hit Tunes (1900–1950)*. Boston: Bruce Humphries, 1962.

Citron, Stephen. *Noel and Cole: The Sophisticates*. New York and Oxford: Oxford University Press, 1993.

Clarke, Donald. *The Penguin Encyclopedia of Popular Music*. London and New York: Viking, 1989.

Clarke, Garry E. *Essays on American Music*. Contributions in American History, no. 62. Westport, Conn.: Greenwood Press, 1977.

Cleveland, Les. "When They Send the Last Yank Home: Wartime Images of Popular Culture." *Journal of Popular Culture* 18, no. 3 (Winter 1984): 31–36.

Cohen, Stan. "*V for Victory: America's Home Front during World War II*. Missoula, Mont.: Pictorial Pictures Publishing Company, Inc., 1991.

Connor, D. Russell, and Warren W. Hicks. *BG on the Record: A Bio-discography of Benny Goodman*. New Rochelle, New York: Arlington House, 1969.

Congressional Record, 77th Cong., 2d Sess., 1942. Vol. 88, pt. 1.

Cook, David A. *A Narrative History of Film*. New York: Norton, 1981.

Cooper, B. Lee. *Images of American Society in Popular Music: A Guide to Reflective Teaching*. Chicago: Nelson-Hall, Inc., 1982.

———. *The Popular Music Handbook: A Resource Guide for Teachers, Librarians, and Media Specialists*. Littleton, Colo.: Libraries Unlimited, 1984.

———. *Popular Music Perspectives: Ideas, Themes, and Patterns in Contemporary Lyrics*. Bowling Green, Ohio: Bowling Green State University Popular Press, 1991.

Craig, Warren. *Sweet and Low Down: America's Popular Song Writers*. Metuchen, N.J.: Scarecrow Press, 1978.

Crichton, Kyle. "'The Star-Spangled Lady' (Lucy Monroe)." *Collier's*, 12 Nov. 1943.

Cronbach, Lee J. "Research . . . Pupil-Morale after One Year of War." *School and Society* 57, no. 1476 (10 April 1943): 416–20.

Cugat, Xavier. *Rumba in My Life*. New York: Didier, 1948.

Daniels, William R. *The American 45 and 78 RPM Record Dating Guide, 1940–1959*. New York: Greenwood Press, 1985.

Davis, Ronald L. *A History of Music in American Life, Volume III: The Modern Era, 1920–Present*. Malabar, Fla.: Robert L. Krieger Publishing Company, 1981.

De Charms, Desiree, and Paul F. Breed. *Songs in Collections: An Index*. Detroit: Information Service, 1966.

Delehanty, Thornton. "The Disney Studio at War." *Theatre Arts* 27, no. 1 (January 1943): 31–39.

DeLong, Thomas A. *The Mighty Music Box: The Golden Age of Music Radio*. New York: Hastings House Publishers, 1980.

Denisoff, R. Serge. *Great Day Coming: Folk Music and the American Left*. Urbana: University of Illinois Press, 1971.

———. "Massification and Popular Music." *Journal of Popular Culture* 9, no. 4 (Spring 1976): 886–94.

———. *Sing a Song of Social Significance*. Bowling Green, Ohio: Bowling Green State University Popular Press, 1972.

———. *Solid Gold: The Popular Record Industry*. New Brunswick, N.J.: Transaction Books, 1975.

———, comp. *Songs of Protest, War, and Peace: A Bibliography and Discography*. Santa Barbara, Calif.: American Bibliography Center-CLIO Press, 1973.

Denisoff, R. Serge, and Mark H. Lewis. "The One Dimensional Approach to Popular Music: A Research Note." *Journal of Popular Culture* 4, no. 4 (Spring 1971): 911–19.

Denisoff, R. Serge, and Richard A. Peterson, eds. *The Sounds of Social Change: Studies in Popular Culture*. Chicago: Rand McNally & Co., 1972.

Desmond, John. "Tin Pan Alley Seeks the Song." *The New York Times Magazine*, 6 June 1943, 14, 31.

Dick, Bernard F. *The Star-Spangled Screen: The American World War II Film*. Lexington, Ky.: The University Press of Kentucky, 1985.

Dolph, Edward Arthur, ed. *"Sound Off!": Soldier Songs from the Revolution to World War II*. New York and Toronto: Farrar & Rinehart, Inc., 1942.

Donovan, Timothy P. "Annie Get Your Gun: A Last Celebration of Nationalism." *Journal of Popular Culture* 12I, no. 3, (Winter 1978): 531–39.

———. "Oh, What a Beautiful Mornin': The Musical, *Oklahoma!* and the Popular Mind in 1943." *Journal of Popular Culture* 8, no. 3 (Winter 1974): 477–88.

Dower, John W. *War without Mercy: Race & Power in the Pacific War*. New York: Pantheon, 1986.

Downes, Olin. "Music of the Times: The Need for Great War Songs." *The New York Times*, 23 Aug. 1942, sec. 8, p. 5.

Duckles, Vincent, comp. *Music Reference and Research Materials: An Annotated Bibliography*. 3rd ed. New York: Free Press, 1974.

Dyer, Sherman. *Radio in Wartime*. New York: Greenberg Press, 1942.

Ellington, Edward Kennedy. *Music Is My Mistress*. New York: Doubleday, 1973.
Ellul, Jacques. *Propaganda*. New York: Random, 1973.
Engel, Lehman. *Their Words Are Music: The Great Theatre Lyricists and Their Lyrics*. New York: Crown Publishers, 1975.
Engel, Lyle K. *Popular Record Directory*. New York: Fawcett, 1958.
Entertaining the Troops: American Entertainers in World War II. Directed by Robert Mugge. RCA/Columbia Pictures Home Video, 1992. Videocassette.
Ewen, David. *All the Years of Popular Music*. Englewood Cliffs, N.J.: Prentice-Hall, Inc., 1977.
———. *American Popular Songs from the Revolutionary War to the Present*. New York: Random House, 1966.
———. *Great Men of American Popular Song*. Rev. and enl. ed. Englewood Cliffs, N.J.: Prentice-Hall, 1972.
———. *The Life and Death of Tin Pan Alley: The Golden Age of American Popular Music*. New York: Funk and Wagnalls Co., 1964.
———. *New Complete Book of the American Musical Theater*. New York: Holt, Rinehart and Winston, 1970.
Fehr, Richard, and Frederick G. Vogel. *Lullabies of Hollywood: Movie Music and the Movie Musical, 1915–1992*. Jefferson, N.C.: McFarland & Company, Inc., 1993.
Ferell, Robert H. *Woodrow Wilson & World War I, 1917–1921*. New York: Harper & Row, Publishers, 1985.
The Fifty Year Story of RCA Records. New York: Radio Corporation of America, 1953.
Freedland, Michael. *Irving Berlin*. New York: Stein & Day, 1974.
Frith, Simon, and Andrew Goodwin, eds. *On Record: Rock, Pop, and the Written Word*. New York: Pantheon Books, 1990.
Fry, Stephen M., comp. *The Story of the All Women's Orchestras in California, 1893–1955*. Northridge, Calif.: Department of Music, California State University, 1985.
Fuld, James J. *American Popular Music (Reference Book),1875–1950*. Philadelphia: Musical Americana, 1955.
———. *Book of World-Famous Music: Classical, Popular and Folk*. New York: Crown, 1971.
Fussell, Paul. *Wartime: Understanding and Behavior in the Second World War*. New York and Oxford: Oxford University Press, 1989.
Gammond, Peter. *The Oxford Companion to Popular Music*. Oxford: Oxford University Press, 1991.
Gammond, Peter, and Peter Clayton. *Dictionary of Popular Music*. New York: Philosophical Library, 1961.
Gans, H. *Popular Culture and High Culture*. New York: Basic Books, 1974.
Gelatt, Roland. *The Fabulous Phonograph, 1877–1977*. New York: Collier, 1977.
George, Nelson. *Top of the Charts: The Most Complete Listing Ever*. Piscataway, N.J.: New Century, 1983.

Gershwin, Ira. *Lyrics on Several Occasions*. New York: Viking Press, 1973.

Giddens, Gary. *Faces in the Crowd: Players and Writers*. New York and Oxford: Oxford University Press, 1992.

Gitler, Ira. *Swing to Bop: An Oral History of the Tradition in Jazz in the 1940s*. New York: Oxford University Press, 1985.

Gluck, Sherna Berger. *Rosie the Riveter Revisited: Women, the War and Social Change*. Boston: Twayne Publishers, 1987.

Goodman, Jack, ed. *While You Were Gone: A Report on Wartime Life in the United States*. New York: Simon & Schuster, 1946.

Gordon, Lois, and Alan Gordon. *American Chronicle: Six Decades of American Life, 1920–1980*. New York: Athenaeum Books, 1987.

Green, Abel. "First Steps Taken for Fighting Songs; Dreamy Stuff Doesn't Fit Long War." *Variety* 147, no. 7 (22 June 1942): 1, 19.

———. "Irving Berlin Winds up 3–Year Hitch in 'Army,' Nets AER $10,000,000." *Variety* 158, no. 6 (18 April 1945): 1.

———. "Loesser on War Songs." *Variety* 152, no. 7 (27 Oct. 1943): 37.

———. "Music Industry Looks Ahead to Big 1945." *Variety Thirty-ninth Anniversary Edition* (3 Jan. 1945): 135.

———. "Popular Appeal Will Take Its Course sans Any Synthetic Hypo." *Variety* 153, no. 4 (5 Jan. 1944): 187.

———. "Selling Side of Song Plugging." *Variety* 145, no. 5 (7 Jan. 1942): 156.

———. "Show Biz's Role in the War." *Variety* 145, no. 2 (17 Dec. 1941): 1, 22.

———. "This Has Been the Year of Years for the Music Business." *Variety Fortieth Anniversary Issue* 161, no. 5 (9 Jan. 1946): 245, 247.

———. *Variety 37th Anniversary Issue* 149, no. 4 (6 Jan. 1943): 187.

———. "War Song of World War II Taking Care of Itself." *Variety Thirty-eighth Anniversary Issue* 153, no. 4 (5 Jan. 1944): 187.

Green, Abel, and Joe Laurie Jr. *Show Biz from Vaude to Video*. New York: Henry Holt, 1951.

Green, Benny. *Let's Face the Music: The Golden Age of Popular Song*. London: Pavilion Books Limited, 1989.

Green, Stanley. *Encyclopedia of the Musical Theatre*. New York: Dodd, Mead, 1976.

Grennard, Elliott. "Music Goes to War." *The Billboard 1943 Music Year Book* 55, no. 38 (25 Sept. 1943): 20.

Hamilton, Dale. "Appearance Is Important." *The Parents' Magazine*, August 1942, 28–29, 76.

Hamm, Charles. *Yesterdays: Popular Song in America*. New York: Norton, 1979.

Hammerstein II, Oscar. "War Songs." *Variety Anniversary Thirty-eighth Anniversary Issue* 153, no. 4 (5 Jan. 1944): 187.

Hardy, Phil, and Dave Lanig. *The Faber Companion to 20th-Century Popular Music*. London and Boston: Faber and Faber, 1990.

Harkins, Philip. "Music Is Big Business." *Liberty*, 24 July 1943, 17–20.

Harris, Mark Jonathan, Franklin Mitchell, and Steven Schecter. *The Homefront: America During World War II*. New York: Putnam's, 1984.

Hartmann, Susan M. *The Home Front and Beyond: American Women in the Forties*. Boston: Twayne Publishers, 1982.

Hasbany, Richard. "Bromidic Parables: The American Musical Theatre During the Second World War." *Journal of Popular Culture* 6, no. 4, (Spring 1973): 642–65.

Hatch, David, and Stephen Millward. *From Blues to Rock: An Analytical History of Pop Music*. Manchester, UK: Manchester University Press, 1987.

Havlice, Patricia Pate. *Popular Song Index*. Metuchen, N.J.: Scarecrow Press, 1975.

Hayakawa, S.I. "Popular Songs vs. The Facts of Life." In *Mass Culture: The Popular Arts in America*, edited by B. Rosenberg and D. White, 393–403. New York: Free Press, 1957.

Hesbacher, Peter, and Les Waffen. "War Recordings: Incidence and Change, 1940–1980." *Popular Music and Society* 8, nos. 3/4 (1982): 77–101.

Higham, Charles, and Joel Greenburg. *Hollywood in the Forties*. New York: Paperback Library, 1970.

Hille, Waldemar, ed. *The People's Song Book*. New York: Boni and Gaer, 1948.

Hirsch, Paul. *The Structure of the Popular Music Industry*. Ann Arbor, Mich.: University of Michigan Press, 1969.

Hirsch, Paul, John Robinson, Elizabeth Keogh Taylor, and Stephen B. Whithey. "The Changing Popular Song: An Historical Overview." *Popular Music and Society* 1 (Winter 1972): 83–93.

Hirshhorn, Clive. *The Hollywood Musical*. New York: Crown, 1981.

Hitchcock, H. Wiley. *Music in the United States: A Historical Introduction*. 2nd ed. Englewood Cliffs, N.J.: Prentice-Hall, 1974.

Hitchcock, H. Wiley, and Stanley Sadie, eds. *The New Grove Dictionary of American Music*. 4 vols. London: Macmillan, 1984.

Hodgkinson, Anthony W. "'Forty-Second Street' New Deal: Some Thoughts about Early Film Musicals." *Journal of Popular Film* 4 (1975): 33–46.

Holsinger, M. Paul, and Mary Anne Schofield, eds., *Visions of War: World War II in Popular Literature and Culture*. Bowling Green, Ohio: Bowling Green State University Press, 1992.

Honey, Maureen. *Creating Rosie the Riveter: Class, Gender, and Propaganda during World War II*. Amherst: University of Massachusetts Press, 1984.

Hoover, Cynthia A. *Music Machines—American Style*. Washington, D.C.: Smithsonian Institution, 1971.

Hopkins, Anthony, ed. *Songs from the Front and Rear: Canadian Servicemen's Songs from the Second World War*. Edmonton: Hurtig, 1979.

Horton, Donald. "The Dialogue of Courtship in Popular Songs." *American Journal of Sociology* 62 (May 1957): 569–78.

Howard, Dick, Russ Morgan, and Bob Ellsworth."Somebody Else Is Taking My Place." New York: Shapiro, Bernstein & Co., 1937.

Howe, Irving. *World of Our Fathers: The Journey of the East European Jews to America and the Life They Found and Made*. New York: Simon and Schuster, 1989.

Huguunin, Marc. "ASCAP, BMI, and the Democratization of American Popular Music." *Popular Music and Society* 7 (1979): 8–17.

Humphrey, Harold. "Wartime Music." *The Billboard* 54, no. 5 (31 Jan. 1942): 68.

Hyland, William G. *The Song Is Ended: Songwriters and American Music, 1900–1950*. New York: Oxford University Press, 1995.

Inge, M. Thomas, ed.. *Concise Histories of American Popular Culture*. Westport, Conn.: Greenwood Press, 1982.

Iwaschkin, Roman, comp.. *Popular Music: A Reference Guide*. New York: Garland Publishing, Inc., 1986.

Jackson, Richard. *United States Music: Sources of Bibliographic and Collective Biography*. Brooklyn, N.Y.: Institute for Studies in American Music, 1973.

Jacobs, Lewis. "World War II and the American Film." *Cinema Journal* 7 (Winter 1967–68): 1–21.

Jasen, David A. *Tin Pan Alley: The Composers, the Songs, the Performers and Their Times: The Golden Age of American Popular Music from 1886 to 1956*. New York: Donald I. Fine, 1988.

Johnstone, John, and Elihu Katz. "Youth and Popular Music: A Study in the Sociology of Taste." *American Journal of Sociology* 62 (May 1957): 563–68.

Jones, Charles, and Eugene Jones. *The Face of War*. New York: Prentice-Hall, 1951.

Jones, Dorothy B. "The Hollywood War Film. 1942–1944." *Hollywood Quarterly* 1 (October 1945): 1–19.

Jones, James. *WWII*. New York: Ballantine, 1975.

Jones, Steve. "Ban(ned) in the U.S.A.: Popular Music and Censorship." *Journal of Communication Inquiry* 15, no. 1 (1991): 73–87.

Jowett, Garth. *Film: The Democratic Art*. Boston: Little, Brown, 1976.

Kimball, Robert, ed. *Music and Lyrics by Cole Porter: A Treasury of Cole Porter*. New York: Random House and Chappell & Co., 1972.

Kinkle, Roger D. *The Complete Encyclopedia of Popular Music and Jazz, 1900–1950*. 4 vols. New Rochelle, New York: Arlington House, 1974.

Kirby, Edward M., and Jack W. Harris. *Star-Spangled Radio*. Chicago: Ziff-Davis, 1948.

Klemm, Gustav. "The Fighting Man and His Music." *The Etude* 61 (Nov. 1943): 711, 755.

Koppes, Clayton, R,. and Gregory D. Black. *Hollywood Goes to War: How Politics, Profits, and Propaganda Shaped World War II Movies*. New York: The Free Press, 1987.

Krummel, D.W., Jean Geil, Doris J. Dyen, and Deane L. Root. *Resources of American Music History: A Dictionary of Source Materials from Colonial Times to World War II*. Urbana, Ill.: University of Illinois Press, 1981.

Landis, Carole. *Four Jills in a Jeep*. New York: Random House, 1944.

Landrum, Larry N. "World War II in the Movies: A Selected Bibliography of Sources." *Journal of Popular Film* 1 (Spring 1972): 147–53.

LaPrade. *Broadcasting Music*. New York and Toronto: Rinehart & Company, Inc., 1947.

Lardner, John. "Lardner's Goes to War." *Newsweek*, 24 Aug. 1943, 24.

Larrabee, Donald R. "College Rhythm." *Variety* 145, no. 2 (17 Dec. 1941): 50.

Lax, Roger, and Frederick Smith. *The Great Song Thesaurus*. 2nd ed. New York: Oxford University Press, 1989.

Lazarsfeld, Paul F., and Frank M. Stanton. *Radio Research, 1942–1943*. Reprint, New York: Arno Press, 1979.

Lederman, Mina. "Songs for Soldiers." *American Mercury*, Sept. 1943, 296–301.

Lees, Gene. "1918–1968: From 'Over There' to 'Kill for Peace.'" *High Fidelity* 18 (Nov. 1968): 56–60.

———. *Singers and the Song*. New York: Oxford University Press, 1987.

———. "War Songs: Bathos and Acquiescence." *High Fidelity*, 28 (Dec. 1978): 41–44.

———. "War Songs II: Music Goes AWOL." *High Fidelity* 29 (Jan. 1979): 20–22.

Leigh, Robert. *Index to Song Books: A Title Index to Over 11,000 Copies of Almost 6,800 Songs in 111 Song Books Published Between 1933 and 1962*. Stockton, Calif.: Robert Leigh, 1964.

Lennon, Mary Jane, and Syd Charendoff. "How to Spot a Jap." In *On the Homefront: A Scrapbook of Canadian World War II Memorabilia*. Erin, Ontario: The Boston Mills Press, 1981.

Leuchtenburg, William E. *Franklin Roosevelt and the New Deal, 1932–1940*. New York: Harper & Row, 1963.

Levine, Lawrence W. *The Unpredictable Past: Explorations in American Cultural History*. New York and Oxford: Oxford University Press, 1993.

Levy, Lester. *Give Me Yesterday: An American History in Song, 1890–1920*. Norman: University of Oklahoma Press, 1967.

———. *Grace Notes in American History: Popular Sheet Music from 1820–1900*. Norman: University of Oklahoma Press, 1967.

Lewine, Richard, and Alfred Simon. *Songs of the Theater: A Definitive Index to the Songs of the Musical Stage*. New York: H.W. Wilson, 1984.

Lewis, George H., ed. *Side-Saddle on the Golden Calf: Social Structure and Popular Music in America*. Pacific Palisades, Calif.: Goodyear Publishing Company, Inc., 1972.

———. "The Sociology of Popular Music: A Selected and Annotated Bibliography." *Popular Music and Society* 7 (1979): 57–68.

Lichty, Lawrence W., and Malachai C. Topping. *American Broadcasting: A Source Book on the History of Radio and Television*. New York: Hastings House, 1975.

Lieberman, Robbie. *"My Song Is My Weapon": People's Songs, American Communism, and the Politics of Culture, 1930–1950*. Urbana, IL: University of Illinois Press, 1989.

Lingeman, Richard R. *Don't You Know There's a War On?: The American Home Front, 1941–1945*. New York: Putnam's, 1970.

Lissauer, Robert. *Lissauer's Encyclopedia of Popular Music: 1888 to the Present*. New York: Paragon House, 1991.

Litoff, Judy, and David C. Smith. *Since You Went Away: World War II Letters from American Women on the Homefront*. New York and Oxford: Oxford University Press, 1991.

———. *"We're in This War, Too": World War II Letters from American Women in Uniform*. New York and Oxford: Oxford University Press, 1994.

Livingston, Jeffrey C. "'Still Boy-Meets-Girl Stuff': Popular Music and War." In *America's Musical Pulse: Popular Music in Twentieth-Century Society*, edited by Kenneth J. Bindas, 33–42. Westport, Conn.: Greenwood Press, 1992.

Lomax, Alan, comp., with Woody Guthrie and Pete Seeger. *Hard Hitting Songs for Hard-Hit People*. New York: Oak Publications, 1967.

Lombardo, Guy, and Jack Altshul. *Old Acquaintance*. New York: Doubleday, 1975.

Look Magazine. *Movie Lot to Beachhead*. New York: Doubleday, Doran, 1945.

Lull, James, ed. *Popular Music and Communication*. Newbury Park, Calif.: Sage Publications, 1987.

Mabry, Richard. *The Pop Process*. London: Hutchinson Educational Ltd., 1969.

MacDonald, Dwight. "A Theory of Mass Culture." In *Mass Culture: The Popular Arts in America*, edited by B. Rosenberg and D. White, 59–73. New York: Free Press, 1957.

MacDonald, J. Fred. "Government Propaganda in Commercial Radio—The Case of *Treasury Star Parade*, 1942–1943." *Journal of Popular Culture*, 12, no. 2 (Fall 1979): 285–304.

Maddox, Robert James. *The United States and World War II*. Boulder, Colo.: Westview Press, 1992.

Malone, Bill C. *Country Music, U.S.A.*. Rev. ed. Austin, Tex.: University of Texas Press, 1985.

———. *Southern Music, American Music*. Lexington, Ky.: University Press of Kentucky, 1979.

Marks, Edward B. *They All Had Glamour: From the Swedish Nightingale to the Naked Lady*. New York: Julian Messner, 1944.

Marvin, Wanda. "V-Disks Help Hasten the Day." *The Billboard 1944 Music Year Book* 56, no. 38 (30 Sept. 1944): 148–49, 204–16.

Mathias, Frank F. *GI Jive: An Army Bandsman in World War II*. Lexington, Ky.: The University Press of Kentucky, 1982.

Matthews, Don. "College Rhythm." *Variety* 144, no. 13 (3 Dec. 1941): 50.

Mattfield, Julius. *Variety Music Calvacade: Musical-Historical Review, 1620–1969*. 3rd ed. Englewood Cliffs, N.J.: Prentice-Hall, 1971.

Matthews, Peter, ed. *The Guinness Book of World Records*. New York: Bantam, 1993.

Mauldin, Bill. *Up Front*. New York: Henry Holt & Company, 1944.

McCarthy, Albert. *Big Band Jazz*. New York: Berkley, 1977.

McCarthy, John, Richard Peterson, and William Yancey. "Singing Along with the Silent Majority." In *Side Saddle on the Golden Calf: Social Structure and Popular Culture in America*, edited by George Lewis, 287–314. Pacific Palisades, Calif.: Goodyear, 1972.

McClure, Arthur F. "Hollywood at War: The American Motion Picture and World War II, 1939–1945." *Journal of Popular Film* 1 (Spring 1972): 123–35.

McCue, George, ed. *Music in American Society, 1776–1976: From Puritan Hymn to Synthesizer*. New Brunswick, N.J.: Transaction Books, 1977.

McMahon, Morgan E. *A Flick of the Switch: 1930–1950*. Palos Verdes Peninsula, Calif.: Vintage Radio, 1975.

Mead, Rita H. *Doctoral Dissertations in American Music: A Classified Bibliography*. Brooklyn, New York: Institute for Studies in American Music, 1974.

Meet the Artists: Biographical Sketches of Leading Performing Artists with Listings of Their Recordings of BMI-Licensed Songs. New York: Broadcast Music, Inc., 1952.

Mehr, Linda Harris. *Motion Pictures, Television and Radio: A Union Catalogue of Manuscript and Special Collections in the Western United States*. Boston: G.K. Hall, 1977.

Mellers, Wilfrid. *Angels of the Night: Popular Female Singers of Our Time*. New York: Basil Blackwell, 1986.

Merrit, Ella, and Floy Hendricks. "Trend of Child Labor." In *America at War: The Home Front, 1941–1945*, edited by Richard Polenberg, 140–52. Englewood Cliffs, N.J.: Prentice-Hall, Inc., 1968.

Merton, Robert K., Marjorie Fiske, and Alberta Curtis. *Mass Persuasion: The Social Psychology of the War Bond Drive*. New York, London: Harper & Brothers, 1946.

Meyer, Hazel. *The Gold in Tin Pan Alley*. Philadelphia and New York: J.B. Lippincott Co., 1958.

Middleton, Richard, and David Horn, eds. *Popular Music 1: Folk or Popular? Distinctions, Influences, Continuities*. Cambridge: Cambridge University Press, 1981.

———. *Popular Music 2: Theory and Method*. Cambridge: Cambridge University Press,1982

———. *Popular Music 3: Producers and Markets*. Cambridge: Cambridge University Press, 1983.

———. *Popular Music 4: Performers and Audiences*. Cambridge: Cambridge University Press, 1984.

———. *Popular Music 5: Continuity and Change*. Cambridge: Cambridge University Press, 1985.

Millard, Bob. *Country Music: 70 Years of America's Favorite Music*. New York: Harper Collins Publishers, 1993.

Miller, Francis Trevelyn. *A History of World War II*. New York: Winston, 1945.

Mirtle, Jack, comp. *Thank You Music Lovers: A Bio Discography of Spike Jones and His City Slickers, 1941–1965*. Westport, Conn.: Greenwood Press, 1986.

Moeller, Susan. *Shooting War: Photography and the American Experience of Combat*. New York: Basic Books, 1989.

Mohrmann, G.P., and F. Eugene Scott. "Popular Music and World War II: The Rhetoric of Continuation." *Quarterly Journal of Speech* 62 (Feb. 1976): 145–56.

Mooney, H.F. "Popular Music Since the 1920's: The Significance of Shifting Taste." *American Quarterly* 20, no. 1 (Spring 1968): 67–85.

———. "Popular Music Since the 1920's: The Significance of Shifting Taste." In *The Sounds of Social Change: Studies in Popular Culture*, edited by R. Serge Denisoff and Richard Peterson, 181–97. Chicago: Rand McNally & Co., 1972.

Moore, Jerrold Northrop. *A Matter of Records*. New York: Taplinger, 1976.

Morgan, Alfred Lindsey. "Radio Music Mitigates War's Alarms." *Etude* 60 (July 1942): 435, 488.

Morgereth, Timothy A. *Bing Crosby: A Discography, Radio Program List, and Filmography*. Jefferson, N.C.: McFarland & Company, Inc., Publishers, 1987.

Morrill, Dexter, comp. *Woody Herman: A Guide to the Big Band Recordings, 1936–1987*. Westport, Conn.: Greenwood Press, 1990.

Moving Picture Screen and Radio Propaganda. Subcommittee of the Committee on Interstate Commerce. Washington, D.C.: GPO, 1941.

Murdoch, Brian. *Fighting Songs and Warring Words: Popular Lyrics of Two World Wars*. London and New York: Routledge, 1990.

Murrells, Joseph. *Million Selling Records from the 1900s to the 1980s: An Illustrated Directory*. London: Batsford, 1984.

Niles, John Jacob. *Singing Soldiers*. New York: Scribner's, 1927.

Nye, Russel. *The Unembarrassed Muse: The Popular Arts in America*. New York: Dial, 1970.

O'Neill, William L. *A Democracy at War: America's Fight at Home and Abroad in World War II*. New York: The Free Press, 1993.

Oppenheimer, George. Liner notes to *The Vintage Irving Berlin*. New York: New World Records NW 238, 1977.

Page, Martin. *"Kiss Me Goodnight, Sergeant Major": The Songs and Ballads of World War II*. London: Granada Publishing, Limited, 1975.

Palmer, Tony. *All You Need Is Love: The Story of Popular Music*. New York: Grossman Publishers, 1976.

Panati, Charles. *Panati's Parade of Fads, Follies, and Manias: The Origins of Our Most Cherished Obsessions*. New York: HarperCollins Publishers, 1991

Pascal, Richard. "Walt Whitman and Woody Guthrie: American Prophet-Singers and Their People." *Journal of American Studies* 24, no. 1 (April 1990): 41–59.

Paymer, Marvin E. *Facts Behind the Songs: A Handbook of American Popular Music from the Nineties to the '90s*. New York: Garland Publishing, 1993.

Payne, Tom. "Give Us a Song We Can Fight To," *Reveille: War Poems by Members of Our Armed Forces*. Selected by Daniel Henderson, John Kieran, and Grantland Rice, 57–58. New York: A.S. Barnes and Company, 1943.

Perrett, Geoffrey. *Days of Sadness, Years of Triumph. The American People, 1939–1945*. New York: Coward, McCann, and Geoghegan, 1973.

Pessen, Edward. "Tin Pan Alley's Many Ways of Love, 1920–1945." *Popular Music in Society* 14, no. 4 (1990): 39–47.

Phillips, Cabell. *Decade of Triumph and Trouble: The 1940s*. New York: Macmillan, 1975.

Pitts, Michael R. *Kate Smith, A Bio-Bibliography*. Westport, Conn.: Greenwood Press, 1988.

Pleasants, Henry. *The Great American Popular Singers*. New York: Simon & Schuster, 1974.

Polenberg, Richard, ed. *America at War: The Home Front, 1941–1945*. Englewood Cliffs, N.J.: Prentice-Hall, Inc., 1968.

———. *War and Society: The United States, 1941–1945*. Philadelphia: Lippincott, 1972.

Pollock, Bruce. *Popular Music: An Annotated Index of American Popular Songs*. Detroit, Mich.: Gale Research Co., 1974.

Popular Music Periodicals Index. Metuchen, N.J.: Scarecrow Press, 1973.

Popular Music Perspectives 2: Papers from the Second International Conference on Popular Music Studies, Reggio Emilia, September 19–24, 1983. Ottawa: International Society for the Study of Popular Music, 1985.

Possett, Eric. *G.I. Songs Written, Composed and /or Collected by the Men in the Service*. New York: Sheridan House, 1944.

Pratt, Ray. *Rhythm and Resistance: Explorations in the Political Uses of Popular Music*. New York: Praeger, 1990.

Pyle, Ernie. *Here Is Your War*. New York: Henry Holt & Company, 1943.

Radio Broadcast News. East Pittsburgh, Penn.: Westinghouse Electric & Manufacturing Co., 7 Dec. 1941.

Raph, Theodore. *The Songs We Sang: A Treasury of American Popular Music*. New York: A.S. Barnes, 1964.

Reed, Peter Hugh. "Records to Meet War Usage." *Etude* 61 (March 1943): 251–52.

Reinartz, Kay. "The Paper Doll: Images of American Women in Popular Songs." In *Women: A Feminist Perspective*, edited by Jo Freeman, 292–308. Palo Alto, Calif.: Mayfield Publishing Company, 1975.

Roberts, John Storm. *The Latin Tinge: The Impact of Latin American Music on the United States*. New York: Oxford University Press, 1979.

Rodgers, Richard. Introduction to *100 Best Songs of the 20's and 30's*. New York: Harmony Books, 1973.

Rodgers, Richard, and Oscar Hammerstein II. *State Fair*. New York: Williamson Music Inc, 1944.

Rogers, Donald L. *Since You Went Away*. New Rochelle, New York: Arlington House, 1973.

Root, Robert L., Jr. *The Rhetorics of Popular Culture: Advertising, Advocacy, and Entertainment*. Westport, Conn.: Greenwood Press, 1987.

Rublowsky, John. *Popular Music*. New York: Basic Books, 1967.

Rust, Brian A.L. *The American Dance Band Discography, 1917–1942*. New Rochelle, New York: Arlington House, 1975.

Ryan, John. *The Production of Culture in the Music Industry: The ASCAP-BMI Controversy*. Lanham, Md.: University of America, Inc., 1985.

Sadie, Stanley, ed. "78 RPMs." *The New Grove Dictionary of Music and Musicians, Vol. 17*. London: Macmillan, 1980–1981.

Sadie, Stanley, et al., eds. *The New Grove Dictionary of Music and Musicians*. 6th ed. 20 vols. Washington, D.C.: *Groves Dictionary of Music*, 1980.

St. John, Robert. *Encyclopedia of Radio and Television Broadcasting*. Milwaukee: Cathedral Square Publishing, 1967.

Sanjek, Russell. *American Popular Music and Its Business—The First Four Hundred Years: Volume Three, 1900–1984*. New York: Oxford University Press, 1988.

Sann, Paul. *Fads, Follies and Delusions of the American People*. New York: Crown, 1967.

Satterfield, Archie. *The Homefront: An Oral History of the War Years in America, 1941–1945*. New York: Playboy Press, 1981.

Scheele, Carl H. *Songs of World Wars I & II*. Washington, D.C.: Recorded Anthology of American Music, Inc., 1977.

Schemel, Sidney, and M. William Krasilovsky. *This Business of Music*. New York: Billboard, 1985.

Scheurer, Timothy, ed. *American Popular Music: Readings from the Popular Press*. 2 vols., Bowling Green, Ohio: Bowling Green State University Popular Press, 1989.

———. *Born in the U.S.A.: The Myth of America in Popular Music from Colonial Times to the Present*. Jackson, Miss.: University of Mississippi Press, 1991.

Schilling, James Von. "Records and the Record Industry," In *Handbook of American Popular Culture—Volume Three*, edited by M. Thomas Inge, 385–411. Westport, Conn.: Greenwood Press, 1981.

Schuler, Gunther. *The Swing Era: The Development of Jazz, 1930–1945*. New York: Oxford University Press, 1985.

Sears, Richard S., comp. *V-Discs, First Supplement*. Discographies, no. 25. New York: Greenwood Press, 1980.

Seldes, Gilbert Vivian. *The 7 Lively Arts*. New York: Sagamore Press, 1957.

Shapiro, Nat, ed. *Popular Music: An Annotated Index of American Popular Song, Vol. 2, 1940–1949*. New York: Adrian Press, 1964.

Shapiro, Nat, and Bruce Pollock, comps. *Popular Music, 1920–1979: A Revised Compilation, 3 Vols*. Detroit, Mich.: Gale Research Company, 1986.

Shaw, Arnold. *Dictionary of American Pop/Rock*. New York: Schirmer Books, 1982.
Sherman, John K. "Music's Role in War Theme at Meeting of Teachers." *Musical America* 62 (10 Jan. 1942): 1.
Shindler, Colin. *Hollywood Goes to War: Film and American Society, 1939–1952*. London and Boston: Routledge & K. Paul, 1979.
Short, K.R.M. "The White Cliffs of Dover: Promoting the Anglo-American Alliance in World War II." *Historical Journal of Film, Radio, and Television* 2 (1982): 3–23.
Sillen, Samuel. "Battle in Search of a Hymn." *New Masses* (19 May 1942): 22–23.
Simon, George T. *The Big Bands*. Rev. ed. New York: MacMillan, 1975.
———. *Glenn Miller and His Orchestra*. New York: Macmillan, 1963.
———. *Simon Says: The Sights and Sounds of the Swing Era, 1935–1955*. New Rochelle, New York: Arlington House, 1971.
Simpson, Harold B. *Audie Murphy, American Soldier*. Hillsboro, Tex.: Hill Junior College Press, 1975.
Sklar, Robert. *Movie-Made America: A Cultural History of the Movies*. New York: Random House, 1975.
Smith, Cecil Michener. *Musical Comedy in America*. New York: Theatre Arts Books, 1950.
Smith, Kathleen E.R. *Lieutenant Colonel Emily U. Miller, a Biography*. Natchitoches, La.: Northwestern State University of Louisiana Press, 1984.
Spaeth, Sigmund. *The Facts of Life in Popular Song*. New York: McGraw-Hill, 1934.
———. A *History of Popular Music in America*. New York: Random House, 1948.
Spector, Ronald H. *Eagle against the Sun*. New York: The Free Press, 1985.
Stambler, Irwin. *Encyclopedia of Popular Music*. New York: St. Martin's Press, 1965.
Stanton, Frank N. "Impact on Radio Listening Less Severe Than Feared." *Variety* 155, no. 6 (19 July 1944): 34.
Stearns, Marshall, and Jean Stearns. *Jazz Dance: The Story of American Vernacular Dance*. New York: Macmillan, 1968.
Steele, C.H. Liner notes to *Praise the Lord and Pass the Ammunition*. New York: New World Records NW 222, 1977.
Steele, Richard. "Preparing the Public for War: Efforts to Establish a National Propaganda Agency, 1940–41." *American Historical Review* 75 (1970): 1640–53.
———. *Propaganda in an Open Society: The Roosevelt Administration and the Media, 1939–1941*. Westport, Conn.: Greenwood Press, 1985.
Stern, Dick, ed. *Those Wonderful Years: Unforgettable Songs from 1900–1920*. New York: The Big 3 Music Corporation, 1985.
Stokesbury, James L. *A Short History of World War II*. New York: William Morrow, 1980.

Stolz, Herbert R. "How Appearance Affects Personality." *The Parents' Magazine*, Jan. 1942, 20–21, 34, 84.

Stowe, David W. *Swing Changes: Big Band Jazz in New Deal America*. Cambridge, Mass.: Harvard University Press, 1994.

Suid, Lawrence H. *Guts and Glory: American War Movies*. Reading, Mass.: Addison-Wesley, 1978.

Summers, Harrison B., ed. *A Thirty Year History of Programs Carried on National Radio Networks in the United States 1926–1956*. 1958. Reprint, New York: Arno Press, 1971.

Suskin, Steven. *Berlin, Kern, Rodgers, Hart,and Hammerstein: A Complete Song Catalogue*. Jefferson, N.C.: McFarland & Company, Inc., Publishers, 1990.

Swartz, Jon David. *Handbook of Old-Time Radio: A Comprehensive Guide to Golden Age Radio Listening and Collecting*. Metuchen, N.J.: Scarecrow Press. 1993.

Taylor, A. Marjorie. *The Language of World War II: Abbreviations, Captions, Quotations, Slogans, Titles and Other Terms and Phrases*. New York: H.W. Wilson Co., 1948.

Taylor, Derek. *As Time Goes By*. San Francisco: Straight Arrow Books, 1973.

Taylor, John Russell, and Arthur Jackson. *Hollywood Musical*. New York: McGraw-Hill, 1971.

Terkel, Studs. *"The Good War": An Oral History of World War II*. New York: Pantheon, 1984.

Thomas, Mary Martha. *Riveting and Rationing in Dixie: Alabama Women and the Second World War*. Tuscaloosa, Ala.: University of Alabama Press, 1987.

Thomson, Virgil. *The Art of Judging Music*. New York: Knopf, 1948.

Thrasher, Frederic. *Okay for Sound: How the Screen Found Its Voice*. New York: Duell, Sloan and Pearce, 1948.

Tudor, Dean. *Popular Music: An Annotated Guide to Recordings*. Littleton, Colo.: Libraries Unlimited, 1983.

Tuttle, William M., Jr. *"Daddy's Gone to War": The Second World War in the Lives of America's Children*. New York and Oxford: Oxford University Press, 1993.

Tyler, Don. *Hit Parade: An Encyclopedia of the Top Songs of the Jazz, Depression, Swing, and Sing Eras*. New York: William Morrow, 1985.

———. *Hit Parade, 1920–1955*. New York: Quill, 1985.

United States Bureau of the Census. *Statistical Abstract of the United States: 1994*, 114th ed. Washington, D.C., 1994.

University of Washington Phonoarchive and Milo Ryan. *History in Sound: A Descriptive Listing of the KIRO-CBS Collection of Broadcasts of the World War II Years and After, in the Phonoarchive of the University of Washington, by Milo Ryan*. Seattle: University of Washington Press, 1963.

Van Vechten, Carl. "An Ode to the Stage Door Canteen." *Theatre Arts* 27, no. 4 (April 1943): 229–31.

Vaughn, Stephen. *Holding Fast the Inner Lines: Democracy, Nationalism, and the Committee on Public Information*. Chapel Hill, N.C.: The University of North Carolina Press, 1980.

"'The VOICE's Rival with the Bobbysoxers' (Lawrence Tibbett)." *New York Post*, 17 April 1945.
Walker, J. Samuel "The Decision to Use the Bomb: A Historiographical Update." *Diplomatic History* 14 (Winter, 1990): 97–114.
Ward, Jim. "College Rhythm." *Variety* 145, no. 7 (21 Jan. 1942): 52.
Waring, Fred. "The Music America Wants." *Etude* 63 (February 1945): 28, 43.
Weigley, Russell F. *Eisenhower's Lieutenants: The Campaigns of France and Germany, 1944–1945*. Bloomington: Indiana University Press, 1981.
Weinberg, Gerhard L. *A World at Arms: A Global History of World War II*. New York: Cambridge University Press, 1994.
Weinberg, Sidney. "What to Tell America. The Writers' Quarrel with the OWI." *Journal of American History* 55, no. 1 (June 1968): 73–89.
Wells, Margaret S. "Music in the News." *The Billboard* 55, no. 47 (20 Nov. 1943): 67.
———. "Music in the News." *The Billboard* 56, no. 5 (29 Jan. 1944): 62.
Whitburn, Joel. *Top Pop Records (1940–1955)*. Menomonee Falls, Wis.: Record Research, 1973.
Whitcomb, Ian. *After the Ball: Pop Music from Rag to Rock*. New York: Simon & Schuster, 1974.
Whitman, Wanda Wilson, ed. *Songs That Changed the World*. New York: Crown, 1969.
Wilder, Alec. *American Popular Song: The Great Innovators, 1900–1950*. New York: Oxford University Press, 1972.
Wilk, Max. *They're Playing Our Song*. New York: Athenaeum, 1973.
Williams, John R. "This Was 'Your Hit Parade.'" Rockland, Maine: Courier-Gazette, 1973.
Williams, John S. Liner notes for *The Great Band Era (1936–1945)*. RCA Custom Records, RD 3–25–1–10, made for *Readers Digest*, 1985.
Williamson, Samuel T. "A Singing Army? Not Yet, But—." *New York Times Magazine* 7 (15 Nov. 1942): 12–13.
Winkler, Allan M. *Home Front U.S.A.: America during World War II*. Arlington Heights, Ill.: Harlan Davidson, Inc., 1986.
———. *The Politics of Propaganda: The Office of War Information, 1942–1945*. New Haven: Yale University Press, 1978.
Witmark, Isidore, and Isaac Goldberg. *The Story of the House of Witmark: From Ragtime to Swingtime*. New York: L. Furman, 1939.
Woll, Allen L. *The Hollywood Musical Goes to War*. Chicago: Nelson-Hall, 1983.
———. *Songs from Hollywood Musical Comedies, 1927 to the Present: A Dictionary*. New York: Garland Publishing, Inc., 1976.
Wyden, Peter. *Day One: Before Hiroshima and After*. New York: Simon and Schuster, 1984.
Young, Margaret Labash, Harold Chester Young, and Anthony T. Kruzas. *Directory of Special Libraries and Information Centers*. Detroit: Gale Research, 1977.

Selected Discography

Abbreviations:

ARA	American Recording Association
Bb	Bluebird Records
Br	Brunswick Records
Cap	Capitol Records
Co	Columbia Records
De	Decca Records
Hit	Hit Records
Maj	Major Records
Mus	Music and Word Records
OK	Okeh Records
Vi	VVictor Records
Wor	World Records

1941

Allen, Red

OK 6281 *K.K. Boogie/Ol' Man River*
OK 6357 *A Sheridan "Square"/Indiana*

Andrews Sisters

De 3598 *Boogie Woogie Bugle Boy*
De 4097 *Shrine of Saint Cecilia/Jack of All Trades*

Armstrong, Louis

De 4140 *When It's Sleepy Time Down South/You Rascal You*

Barnet, Charlie

Bb 11153 *Merry-Go-Round*
Bb 11194 *Little Dip/Ponce de Leon*
Bb 11281 *Harlem Speaks/Swingin' on Nothin'*

Barron, Blue

Elite 5001 *Shepherd Serenade/Elmer's Tune*

Basie, Count

OK 6122 *Beau Brummel*
OK 6365 *H and J/Diggin' for Dex*
OK 6527 *Tom Thumb*

Berrigan, Bunny

Elite 5005 *'Tis Autumn Again/Two in Love*
Elite 5006 *I Got It Bad/The White Cliffs of Dover*

Bon Bon

De 3980 *I Don't Want to Set the World on Fire*

Boswell, Connie

De 3893 *Sand in My Shoes/Nighty-Night*

Bradley, Will

Co 36147 *Flamingo/Swingin' Down the Lane*
Co 36296 *City Called Heaven/I'm Tired of Waiting for You*

Brown, Les

OK 6367 *City Called Heaven/It's You Again*
OK 6377 *Joltin' Joe DiMaggio/The Nickel Serenade*
OK 6430 *'Tis Autumn/That Solid Old Man*
OK 6696 *Mexican Hat Dance*

Byrne, Bobby

De 3773 *Do I Worry?/Nighty-Night*
De 3774 *Two Hearts That Pass in the Night/These Things You Left Me*
De 3969 *I Went Out of My Way/It's You Again*

CALLOWAY, CAB

OK 6084 *Bye Bye Blues/Run Little Rabbit*
OK 6109 *Willow Weep for Me/Jonah Joins the Cab*
OK 6305 *Take the "A" Train/Chattanooga Choo Choo*

CARLISLE, UNA MAE

Bb 110033 *Walkin' By the River/I Met You Then*

CHESTER, BOB

Bb 11017 *I Could Write a Book/Beau Night in Hotchkiss Corners*
Bb 11227 *There Goes That Song Again/It's So Peaceful in the Country*

CLARK, BUDDY

OK 6392 *Moonlight Masquerade/Ma-Ma-Maria*
OK 6403 *Delilah/A Sinner Kissed an Angel*

CLINTON, LARRY

Bb 11166 *Loveliness and Love/You Started Something*

CROSBY, BING

De 3032 *'Til Reveille*
De 3636 *It's Always You/You Lucky People You*
De 4065 *Shepherd Serenade/The Anniversary Waltz*

CROSBY, BOB

De 4009 *Two in Love/A Sinner Kissed an Angel*
De 4027 *I'm Trusting in You/From One Love to Another*

DONAHUE, SAM

Bb 11131 *They Still Make Love in London/Au Ree*t

DORSEY, JIMMY

Br 03328F I *Remember You*
De 3629 *Amapola/Donna Marie*
De 3657 *Yours/When the Sun Comes Out*
De 3698 *Green Eyes/Maria Elena*
De 3775 *Blue Champagne/All Alone and Lonely*
De 3859 *Time Was/Isle of Pines*
De 3963 *Jim/A New Shade of Blue*
De 4102 *This Is No Laughing Matter/I Said No!*

DORSEY, TOMMY

Vi 27274 *Oh, Look at Me Now/You Might Have Belonged to Another*
Vi 27317 *Dolores/I Tried*
Vi 27338 *Do I Worry?/Little Man with a Candy Cigar*
Vi 27421 *Will You Still Be Mine?/Yes Indeed*
Vi 27508 *This Love of Mine/Neiani*
Vi 27690 *Violets for Your Furs/Somebody Loves Me*
Vi 27749 *How About You?/Winter Weather*

DUCHIN, EDDY

Bb 11200 *Sand in My Shoes/East Street*

ELLINGTON, DUKE

Vi 27326 *Flamingo/The Girl in My Dreams Tries to Look Like You*
Vi 27356 *Jumpin' Punkins/Blue Serge*
Vi 27380 *Take the "A" Train/Sidewalks of New York*
Vi 27502 *Bakiff/The Giddybug Gallop*
Vi 27740 *Chelsea Bridge/What Good Would I Do?*

GOODMAN, BENNY

Co 35962 *Perfidia/Let the Door Knob Hitcha*
Co 36039 *Breakfast Feud/I Found a New Baby*
Co 36050 *Amapola/Intermezzo*
Co 36421 *Pound Ridge/I Got It Bad*
Co 36429 *Buckle Down, Winsocki/Shady Lady Bird*
OK 6486 *Limehouse Blues/If I Had You*
OK 6544 *Clarinet a la King/How Long Has This Been Going On?*

HAMPTON, LIONEL

Vi 27409 *Give Me Some Skin/Three Quarter Boogie*
Vi 27529 *Chasin' with Chase/Now That You're Mine*

HERMAN, WOODY

De 3643 *Blue Flame/Fur Trappers' Ball*
De 3761 *South/Fan It*
De 3972 *Bishop's Blues/Woodsheddin' with Woody*
De 4113 *Someone's Rockin' My Dream Boat/Rose O'Day*

HINES, EARL

Bb 11126 *Jersey Bounce*
Bb 11237 *Up Jumped the Devil/South Side*

Bb 11374 *I Got It Bad/Straight to Love*
Bb 11432 *The Earl*
Bb 11465 *Swingin' on C*

JAMES, HARRY

Co 36069 *Dolores/Walkin' By the River*
Co 36246 *It's So Peaceful in the Country/Yes Indeed*
Co 36321 *He's 1–A in the Army and A-1 in My Heart* (Helen Forest, vocal)
Co 36322 *I Don't Want to Walk without You* (Helen Forest, vocal)
Co 36412 *You've Changed/Nobody Knows the Trouble I've Seen*

JARRETT, ART

Vi 27474 *Loveliness and Love/You Started Something*
Vi 27571 *Delilah/The Nickel Serenade*
Vi 27612 *The Bells of San Raquel/Ma-Ma-Marie*

JESTERS

De F8057 *Ma, I Miss Your Apple Pie*

JURGENS, DICK

OK 6289 *You and I/Starlight, Starbright*
OK 6401 *Moonlight Masquerade/Ma-Ma-Marie*

KASSEL, ART

Bb 11073 *Do I Worry?/Knocking at Your Door*

KAYE, SAMMY

Vi 27339 *My Ship/You Stepped Out of a Dream*
Vi 27391 *Daddy/Two Hearts That Pass in the Night*
Vi 27476 *Sand in My Shoes/Don't Cry, Cherie*
Vi 27498 *A Rose and a Prayer/Harbor of Dreams*

KENTON, STAN

De 4037 *This Love of Mine/The Nango*

KING, WAYNE

Vi 27373 *A Worried Man/Broken Melody*
Vi 27516 *Time and Time Again/Blue Danube Waltz*
Vi 27535 *Time Was/The Corporal Takes Command*

Krupa, Gene

OK 6130 *Let's Get Away from It All/Just a Little Bit South of North Carolina*
OK 6266 *The Cowboy Serenade/'Til Reveille*
OK 6278 *After You've Gone/Kick It*
OK 6352 *Tunin' Up/Rockin' Chair*
OK 6447 *Two in Love/This Time the Dreamin' Is on Me*

Kyser, Kay

Co 36244 *The Cowboy Serenade/You and I*
Co 36354 *He Wears a Pair of Silver Wings* (Henry Babbitt, vocal)
Co 36445 *The White Cliffs of Dover* (Harry Babbitt, vocal)/*The Nadocky*

Lombardo, Guy

De 3675 *You Stepped Out of a Dream/The Band Played On*

Lucas, Lucas

Elite 5009 *How About Me?/The Shrine of Saint Cecilia*

Lunceford, Jimmie

De 3807 *Battle Axe/Chocolate*
De 4032 *Hi Spook/Yard Dog Mazurka*
De 4083 *Gone/Impromptu*

Martin, Freddy

Bb 11167 *Flamingo/'Til Reveille*
Bb 11211 *Piano Concerto in B Flat (Tonight We Love)/Why Don't We Do This More Often?*
Bb 11256 *Blue Champagne/Be Honest with Me*
Bb 11393 *'Tis Autumn/Until the Stars Fall Down*
Vi 14587 *The Hut Sut Song (A Swedish Serenade)*

Merrill, Joan

Bb 11125 *I Went Out of My Way/Summertime*

Merry Macs

De 4023 *Rose O'Day/By-U By-O*

Miller, Glenn

Bb 10982 *Anvil Chorus (1 & 2)*
Bb 11042 *You Stepped Out of a Dream/Ring, Telephone, Ring*

Bb 11063 *I Dreamt I Dwelt in Harlem*
Bb 11219 *Adios/Under Blue Canadian Skies*
Bb 11230 *I Know Why/Chattanooga Choo Choo*
Bb 11234 *Perfidia*
Bb 11235 *The Cowboy Serenade/Below the Equator*
Bb 11248 *You and I* (Ray Eberle, vocal)
Bb 11369 *This Is No Laughing Matter/Humpty Dumpty Heart*
Bb 11382 *A String of Pearls*
Bb 11386 *Elmer's Tune*
Bb 11388 *Jersey Bounce*
Bb 11397 *The White Cliffs of Dover/We're the Couple in the Castle*

MILLS BROTHERS

De 1542 *I Don't Want to Set the World on Fire*

MONROE, VAUGHN

Bb 10976 *The Last Time I Saw Paris/High on a Windy Hill*
Bb 11273 *Two in Love/Cherry Blossoms on Capitol Hill*

NOBLE, RAY

Co 36271 *Harbor of Dreams/If It's You*

PASTOR, TONY

Bb 11008 *Adios/Paradiddle Joe*
Bb 11067 *Number Ten Lullaby Lane/For Whom the Bell Tolls*

POWEL, TEDDY

Bb 11089 *Two Hearts That Pass in the Night/The Wise Old Owl*
Bb 11092 *Talking to the Wind*
Bb 11152 *I Went Out of My Way*

RAY, ALVINO

Bb 11108 *Amapola*
Bb 11216 *Harbor of Dreams*
Bb 11272 *Don't Take Your Love from Me/Jealous*
Bb 11275 *Deep in the Heart of Texas*

RAYMOND SCOTT ORCHESTRA

Co 36103 *Just A Little Bit South of North Carolina/In the Hush of the Night*

ROBERTSON, DICK

De 3791 *Be Honest with Me/Goodbye Dear, I'll Be Back in a Year*
De 3981 *I Don't Want to Set the World on Fire/I'm Alone Because I Love You*

SHAW, ARTIE

Vi 27069 *Blues in the Night*
Vi 27536 *It Had to Be You/If I Had You*
Vi 27664 *Rockin' Chair/If I Love Again*
Vi 27885 *Frenesi*
Vi 27895 *St. James Infirmary (1 & 2)*
Vi 27945 *Moonglow/My Blue Heaven*

SHORE, DINAH

Bb 11204 *Jim/I'm Through with Love*

SPIVAK, CHARLIE

OK 6257 *Time Was/I'll Never Let a Day Pass By*
OK 6280 *The Angels Came Through/A Rose and a Prayer*

STONE, LEW

De F7987 *When They Sound the Last All Clear*
De F8057 *(There'll Be Bluebirds Over) The White Cliffs of Dover*

TEAGARDEN, JACK

De 3844 *St. James Infirmary/Black and Blue*

THORNHILL, CLAUDE

Co 36341 *The Bells of San Raquel/I Found You in the Rain*
Co 36391 *Orange Blossom Lane/Moonlight Masquerade*

TODD, DICK

Bb 11195 *Wasn't It You?/Just a Little Street Where Old Friends Meet*
Bb 11387 *'Tis Autumn/Tropical Magic*

TUCKER, TOMMY

OK 6320 *I Don't Want to Set the World on Fire/This Love of Mine*

WOOD, BARRY

Vi 27369 *The Things I Love/Talking to the Wind*

1942

Andrews Sisters

De 18312 *Don't Sit Under the Apple Tree/At Sonya's Cafe*
De 18398 *Pennsylvania Polka/That's the Moon, My Son*
De 18470 *Mr. Five by Five/The Strip Polka*

Barnet, Charlie

De 18541 *That Old Black Magic/I Don't Want Anybody at All*

Berrigan, Bunny

Elite 5020 *Me and My Melinda/Somebody Else Is Taking My Place*
Elite 5048 *Skylark/My Little Cousin*

Boswell, Connie

Br 0333 *One Dozen Roses*

Bradley, Will

Co 36470 *Who Can I Turn To?/Sleepy Time Gal*

Breese, Lou

De 4107 *Humpty Dumpty Heart/How Long Did I Dream?*

Brit, Elton

Bb 9000 *There's a Star Spangled Banner Waving Somewhere/When the Roses Bloom Again*

Brown, Les

Co 36602 *Sweet Eloise/Here You Are*
OK 6557 *Fooled/Ya Lu-Blu*
OK 6696 *When the Lights Go on Again*

Calloway, Cab

OK 6720 *Let's Go Joe/A Smo-o-oth One*

Chester, Bob

Bb 11562 *He's My Guy/By the Light of the Silvr'y Moon*

Crosby, Bing

Br 03456 *I'm Thinking Tonight of My Blueyes*

De 4193 *Skylark/Blue Shadows and White Gardenias*
De 4249 *Lamplighter's Serenade/Mandy Is Two*
De 18424 *Happy Holidays/Be Careful It's My Heart*
De 18429 *White Christmas/Let's Start the New Year Right*
De 18513 *Moonlight Becomes You/Constantly*

CROSBY, BOB

De 4316 *Poor You/Last Call for Love*
De 4368 *Over There/Smile, Smile, Smile*
De 4390 *Sugar Foot Stomp/King Porter Stomp*
De 4415 *Black Zephyr/Blue Surreal*

CUGAT, XAVIER

Co 36559 *Sleepy Lagoon/Nightingale*

DAVIS, SCAT

Hit 7012 *White Christmas/Hip Hip Hooray*

DONAHUE, AL

OK 6617 *Candles in the Wind/My Heart's on Fire*

DORSEY, JIMMY

De 4103 *(There'll Be Bluebirds Over) The White Cliffs of Dover*
De 4122 *Not Mine/Arthur Murray Taught Me Dancing in a Hurry*
De 4123 *Tangerine* (Helen O'Connell and Bob Eberly, vocals)*/Ev'rything I Love*
De 4132 *I Remember You/If You Build a Better Mousetrap*
De 4197 *I'm Glad There Is You/Tomorrow's Sunrise*
De 18376 *Take Me/This Is Worth Fighting For*

DORSEY, TOMMY

Vi 27701 *Who Can I Turn To?/I Think of You*
Vi 27849 *Poor You/Last Call for Love*
Vi 27876 *Moonlight on the Ganges*
Vi 27887 *Well, Git It!*
Vi 27903 *Just as Though You Were Here/Street of Dreams*
Vi 27923 *Take Me/Be Careful, It's My Heart*
Vi 27947 *In the Blue of the Evening/A Boy on Khaki, a Girl in Lace*

ELLINGTON, DUKE

Vi 27856 *C-Jam Blues/Moon Mist*
Vi 27880 *Perdido/Raincheck*

Fields, Shep

Bb 11325 *Who Can I Turn To?/Autumn Nocturne*
Bb 11537 *Wonder When My Baby's Coming Home/This Is Worth Fighting For*
Bb 11583 *When the Lights Go on Again/Better Not Roll Those Eyes*

Garland, Judy

De 18323 *Poor You/Last Call for Love*
De 18549 *That Old Black Magic/Poor Little Rich Girl*

Goodman, Benny

Co 36580 *Not Mine/If You Build a Better Mousetrap*
Co 36613 *Take Me/Idaho*
Co 36622 *Serenade in Blue/I've Got a Gal in Kalamazoo*
Co 36652 *Why Don't You Do Right?*
OK 6482 *Jersey Bounce/String of Pearls*
OK 6497 *Somebody Else Is Taking My Place/That Did It Marie*
OK 6580 *The Lamp of Memory/When the Roses Bloom Again*
OK 6644 *We'll Meet Again*

Gray, Glen

De 4166 *I'll Never Forget/Darling, How You Lied*
De 4298 *Here You Are/Oh. the Pity of It All*
De 18479 *Don't Get Around Much Anymore/Don't Do It Darling*

Hampton, Lionel

De 18394 *Flying Home/In the Bag*

Heidt, Horace

Co 36645 *Pennsylvania Polka/When You Lips Met Mine*
Co 36667 *Where the Mountains Meet the Sky/This Is the Army, Mister Jones*

Herman, Woody

De 4188 *Fooled/You Can't Hold a Memory in Your Arms*
De 4353 *Elise/Yardbird Shuffle*
De 18469 *Please Be There/There Will Never Be Another You*
De 18526 *Four or Five Times/Hot Chestnuts*
De 18544 *Down Under/Ten Day Furlough*

Hines, Earl

Bb 11512 *Skylark/She'll Always Remember*

HUTTON, INA RAE

OK 6335 *At Last/What's the Good of Moonlight?*

INK SPOTS

De 18503 *Don't Get Around Much Anymore*

JAMES, HARRY

Co 36478 *I Don't Want to Walk without You*
Co 36518 *I Remember You/Last Night I Said a Prayer*
Co 36533 *Skylark*
Co 36549 *Sleepy Lagoon*
Co 36566 *One Dozen Roses/You're Too Good for Good-for-Nothing Me*
Co 36614 *He's My Guy/You're in Love with Someone Else*
Co 36644 *Manhattan Serenade/Daybreak*
Co 36659 *I Had the Craziest Dream* (Helen Forest, vocal)/*A Poem Set to Music*

JARRETT, ART

Vi 27693 *How Long Did I Dream?/Humpty Dumpty Heart*
Vi 27851 *You Can't Hold a Memory in Your Arms/Don't Sit Under the Apple Tree*

JENKINS, GORDON

Cap 106 *He Wears a Pair of Silver Wings/I'm Always Chasing Rainbows*
Cap 124 *White Christmas/Heaven for Two*

JONES, SPIKE

Vi 27843 *Der Fuehrer's Face*

JORDA, LOUIS

De 8593 *I'm Gonna Move to the Outskirts of Town/Knock Me a Kiss*

JURGENS, DICK

OK 6535 *I'll Never Forget/How About You?*

KAYE, SAMMY

Vi 27832 *I Left My Heart at the Stage Door Canteen/South Wind*
Vi 27870 *Here You Are/Johnny Doughboy Found a Rose in Ireland*
Vi 27944 *Where the Mountains Meet the Sky/I Came Here to Talk for Joe*
Vi 27949 *There Will Never Be Another You/Let's Bring New Glory to Old Glory*

KRUPA, GENE

OK 6607 *Skylark*
OK 6619 *Me and My Melinda*

KYSER, KAY

Co 36433 *Humpty Dumpty Heart/Romeo Smith and Juliet Jones*
Co 36521 *Johnny Doughboy Found a Rose in Ireland*
Co 36526 *Who Wouldn't Love You?/How Do I Know It's Real?*
Co 36567 *Don't Sit Under the Apple Tree/There Won't Be a Shortage of Love*
Co 36604 *He Wears a Pair of Silver Wings/Jingle Jangle Jingle*
Co 36635 *The Strip Polka/Ev'ry Night About This Time*
Co 36640 *I Came Here to Talk for Joe/Praise the Lord and Pass the Ammunition*

LOMBARDO, GUY

De 4199 *How Do I Know It's Real?/There Won't Be a Shortage of Love*

LOPEZ, VINCENT

Elite 5014 *When the Roses Bloom Again/Somebody Nobody Loves*

LUNCEFORD, JIMMIE

De 4125 *Blues in the Night (1 & 2)*
De 18534 *You're Always in My Dreams/Easy Street*

LYMAN, ABE

Bb 11542 *Amen/He Wears a Pair of Silver Wings*

MARTIN, FREDDY

Bb 11426 *I Remember You/Fun to Be Free*
Bb 11495 *Last Call for Love/You Can't Hold a Memory in Your Arms*
Bb 11509 *Here You Are/Oh, the Pity of It All*

MARX, CHICO

Hit 7004 *Here You Are/Sweet Eloise*

MCINTYR, HAL

Vi 27777 *Fooled/I'll Never Forget*
Vi 27803 *Tangerine/When the Roses Bloom Again*
Vi 27859 *The Story of a Starry Night/We'll Meet Again*

MCKINLEY, RAY

Hit 7006 *This Is Worth Fighting For*

MERCER, JOHNNY

Cap 103 *The Strip Polka/The Air-Minded Executive*

MERRILL, JOAN

Bb 11551 *Take Me/Wonder When My Baby's Coming Home?*
Bb 11574 *There Will Never Be Another You/You Can't Say No to a Soldier*

MILLER, GLENN

Bb 11401 *Moonlight Cocktail/Happy in Love*
Bb 11438 *When the Roses Bloom Again/Always in My Heart*
Bb 11445 *A String of Pearls*
Bb 11462 *Skylark/The Story of a Starry Night*
Vi 1059 *Juke Box Saturday Night*
Vi 27935 *Serenade in Blue/That's Sabotage*
Vi 27943 At *Last/I've Got a Gal in Kalamazoo*
Vi 27879 *Sweet Eloise/Sleep Song*

MILLINDER, LUCKY

De 18497 *When the Lights Go on Again/That's All*

MILLS BROTHERS

Br 03436 *I Met Her on Monday*

MONROE, VAUGHN

Bb 11433 *Tangerine/Tica-Ti Tica-Ta*
Bb 11483 *Me and My Melinda*
Vi 27821 *This Is Worth fighting For/The Corporal Told the Private*
Vi 27910 *All I Need Is You*
Vi 27925 *My Devotion/When I Grow Up*
Vi 27945 *When the Lights Go on Again (All Over the World)/Hip, Hip, Hooray*

MORGAN, RUSS

De 4300 *Sweet Eloise/All Those Wonderful Years*
De 18374 *Just as Though You Were Here/Windmill Under the stars*

PASTOR, TONY

Bb 11435 *Lamp of Memory/Absent-Minded Moon*

Rhodes, Betty Jane

Br 03315 *I Don't Want to Walk without You*

Ross, Lanny

Vi 27799 *Lamp of Memory/Blue Shadows and White Gardenias*

Sherwood, Bobby

Cap 123 *Moonlight Becomes You/Harlem Butterfly*

Shore, Dinah

Vi 27963 *A Boy in Khaki a Girl in Lace*

Slack, Freddy

Cap 102 *Cow Cow Boogie/Here You Are*
Cap 115 *Mr. Five by Five*
Cap 126 *That Old Black Magic/Hit the Road to Dreamland*

Smith, Kate

Co 36609 *Wonder When My Baby's Coming Home/Old Sad Eyes*
Co 36618 *He Wears a Pair of Silver Wings/Be Careful, It's My Heart*

Spivak, Charlie

Co 36620 *My Devotion/I Left My Heart at the Stage Door Canteen*
Co 36642 *At Last/People Like You and Me*
Co 36649 *White Christmas/Yesterday's Gardenias*
OK 6646 *I'll Remember April/What Does a Soldier Dream Of?*

Stabile, Dick

De 4351 *Be Careful, It's My Heart/You're Easy to Dance With*
De 4352 *At Last/He's My Guy*

Todd, Dick

Bb 11577 *When the Lights Go on Again/I'm Old Fashioned*

Tucker, Orin

Co 36565 *Tangerine/Always in My Heart*

Tucker, Tommy

OK 6702 *Just as Though You Were Here/There Will Never Be Another You*

WHEELER, DOC

Bb 11529 *Me and My Melinda*

1943 (THE YEAR OF THE AMERICAN FEDERATION OF MUSICIANS RECORDING BAN)

ANDREWS SISTERS

De 18752 *Shoo Shoo, Baby/Down in the Valley*

CARTER, BENNY

Cap 144 *Poinciana/Hurry Hurry*

CROSBY, BING

De 18564 *People Will Say We're in Love/Oh, What a Beautiful Mornin'*
De 18586 *Poinciana/San Fernando Valley*
De 18651 *If You Please/Sunday. Monday or Always*

CUGAT, XAVIER

Co 36651 *Brazil/Chiu Chiu*

DORSEY, JIMMY

De 18532 *Let's Get Lost/"Murder" He Says*
De 18571 *Star Eyes/They're Either Too Young or Too Old*
De 18574 *Besamé Mucho/My Ideal*
De 18582 *When They Ask about You/My First Love*
De 18593 *Holiday for Strings/Ohio*

DORSEY, TOMMY

Vi 26054 *Boogie Woogie/Weary Blues*

DURHAM, SONNY

Hit 7073 *I'll Be Around/When They Ask about You*
Hit 7074 *Holiday for Strings/Don't Worry, Mom*

DURBIN, DEANNA

De 18575 *Say a Prayer for the Boys Over There/God Bless America*

ELLINGTON, DUKE

Vi 20–1556 *Main Stem/Johnny Come Lately*
Vi 26610 *Don't Get Around Much Anymore/Never No Lament*

Garland, Judy

De 18584 *No Love, No Nothin'/A Journey to a Star*

Goodman, Benny

Co 35869 *Cabin in the Sky/Taking a Chance on Love*
Co 36680 *Mission to Moscow*
Co 36684 *Solo Flight/The World Is Waiting for the Sunrise*

Gray, Glen

De 18567 *My Shining Hour/My Heart Tells Me*

Hall, Adelaide

De F8292 *As Time Goes By*

Hallett, Mal

Hit 7013 *Let's Get Lost/There Will Never Be Another You*

Hanna, Phil

De 4432 *My Heart Tells Me/Besamé Mucho*

Haymes, Dick

De 18556 *You'll Never Know/Wait for Me, Mary*
De 18557 *In My Arms/It Can't Be Wrong*
De 18558 *I Heard You Cried Last Night/I Never Mention Your Name*

Herman, Woody

De 18578 *By the River of the Roses/Do Nothin' Till You Hear from Me*

James, Harry

Co 36668 *I've Heard That Song Before/Moonlight Becomes You*
Co 36672 *Velvet Moon*
Co 36677 *I Heard You Cried Last Night*

Jordan, Louis

De 8654 *Ration Blues*

Kaye, Sammy

Vi 20–1527 *Taking a Chance on Love/Cabin in the Sky*

Kyser, Kay

Co 36657 *Can't Get Out of This Mood/Moonlight Mood*
Co 36673 *Let's Get Lost/The Fuddy Duddy Watchmaker*

Lombardo, Guy

De 18573 *Speak Low/Take It Easy*

Long, Johnny

De 4427 *No Love, No Nothin'/You Better Give Me Lots of Lovin'*

Mercer, Johnny

Cap 141 *G.I. Jive*

Miller, Glenn

Vi 20–1523 *A Pink Cocktail for a Blue Lady/That Old Black Magic*

Millinder, Lucky

De 18569 *Sweet Slumber/Don't Cry Baby*

Mills Brothers

De 18318 *Paper Doll/I'll Be Around*

Monroe, Vaughn

Vi 20–1524 *Happy-Go-Lucky/Let's Get Lost*

Morse, Ella Mae

Cap 143 *No Love, No Nothin'*

Renard, Jacques

Br 6205 *As Time Goes By/I'm Sorry Dear*

Shore, Dinah

Vi 1519 *You'd Be So Nice to Come Home To*

Sinatra, Frank

Co 36678 *You'll Never Know/Close to You*
Co 36679 *If You Please/ Sunday, Monday or Always*
Co 36682 *People Will Say We're in Love/Oh, What a Beautiful Mornin'*

SLACK, FREDDIE

Cap 146 *Silver Wings in the Moonlight*

SONG SPINNERS, THE

De 18445 *Johnny Zero*
De 18553 *Comin' In on a Wing and a Prayer*

VALLEY, RUDY

Vi 20–1526 *As Time Goes By*

WALD. JERRY

De 4431 *Shoo, Shoo, Baby*
De 4433 *Poinciana/Mississippi Dreamboat*
De 4443 *Silver Wings in the Moonlight/And So Little Time*

1944

ANDREWS SISTERS

De 18606 *Tico-Tico/Straighten Up and Fly Right*
De 18754 *(There'll Be a) Hot Time in the Town of Berlin* (with Bing Crosby)

BARNET, CHARLIE

De 18620 *Come Out, Come Out, Wherever You Are/What a Difference a Day Made*
De 18685 *There's No You/Any Old Time*

BASIE, COUNT

Co 36766 *I Didn't Know About You*

BROWN, LES

Co 36701 *My Dream Are Getting Better All the Time* (Doris Day, vocal)
Co 36763 *Sleigh Ride in July/Robin Hood*
Co 36769 *Sentimental Journey* (Doris Day, vocal)/*Twilight Time*

BUTTERFIELD, BILLY

Cap 182 *Moonlight in Vermont/There Goes That Song Again*

CALLOWAY, CAB

Co 36611 *I'll Be Around/Virginia, Georgia and Caroline*
Co 36786 *Let's Take the Long Way Home/Foo a Little Ballyhoo*

Carle, Frankie

Co 36760 *A Little on the Lonely Side* (Paul Allen, vocal)/*I Had a Talk with the Lord*
Co 36764 *Evelina/Right as the Rain*
Co 36777 *Saturday Night*

Cavallaro, Carmen

De 18631 *In the Middle of the Nowhere/Wouldn't It Be Nice?*

Crosby, Bing

De 18580 *It Could Happen to You/The Day After Forever*
De 18597 *Going My Way/Swinging on a Star*
De 18608 *Amor/Long Ago and Far Away*
De 18640 *Sleigh Ride in July/Like Someone in Love*
De 18649 *Strange Music/More and More*
De 18665 *I'll Be Home for Christmas*

———, and the Andrews Sisters

De 18754 *(There'll Be a) Hot Time in the Town of Berlin*
De 23350 *Is You Is or Is You Ain't My Baby?*

Cugat, Xavier

Co 36780 *Tico-Tico/Linda Mujer*

Dorsey, Jimmy

De 18637 *I Dream of You/Magic Is the Moonlight*
De 18647 *More and More/Don't You Know I Care?*

Dorsey, Tommy

Vi 20–1608 *I Dream of You*
Vi 20–1614 *More and More/You're Driving Me Crazy*
Vi 20–1622 *Sleigh Ride in July/Like Someone in Love*
Vi 20–1607 *Opus One*
Vi 1574 *I'll Be Seeing You* (Frank Sinatra, vocal)

Ellington, Duke

Vi 20–1618 *Don't You Know I Care?/I'm Beginning to See the Light*

Ennis, Skinny

ARA 110 *Sleigh Ride in July/Jumpin' Jimminy*

Fitzgerald, Ella

De 18605 *Time Alone Will Tell/Once Too Often*

Forest, Helen

De 18600 *Time Waits for No One/In a Moment of Madness*

———, and Dick Haymes

De 18661 *Long Ago (And Far Away)*

Carroll Gibbons and the Savoy Hotel Orpheans

Co FB3049 *I'll Be Seeing You*

Benny Goodman Quintet

Co 46767 *Ev'ry Time We Say Goodbye/Only Another Boy and Girl*

Gray, Glen

De 18596 *Suddenly It's Spring/Sure Thing*

Haymes, Dick

De 18604 *How Blue the Night/How Many Times Do I Have to Tell You?*

Heidt, Horace

Co 36761 *I Promise You/Don't Fence Me In*
Co 36776 *More and More/Lucky to Be Me*

Herman, Woody

Br 03517 *I'll Get By (As Long As I Have You)*
De 18577 *The Music Stopped/I Couldn't Sleep a Wink Last Night*
De 18603 *Irresistible You/Milkman, Keep Those Bottles Quiet*
De 18619 *Let Me Love You Tonight/Who Dat Up There?*
De 18641 *I Didn't Know About You/Saturday Night*

Hill, Tiny

De 4447 *How Many Hearts Have You Broken?/Rose of Santa Rosa*

Hutton, June, with Paul Weston Orchestra

Cap 177 *Sleigh Ride in July/Don't You Know I Care?*

INK SPOTS

De 18579 *I'll Get By as Long as I Have You*
De 18583 *A Lovely Way to Spend an Evening/Don't Believe Everything You Dream*

JAMES, HARRY

Co 36758 *The Love I Long For/I'm Beginning to See the Light*

JORDAN, LOUIS

De 8659 *G.I. Jive/Is You Is or Is You Ain't My Baby?*

KENTON, STAN

Cap 166 *And Her Tears Flowed Like Wine/How Many Hearts Have You Broken?*
Cap 187 *Ev'ry Time We Say Goodbye/Are You Livin,' Old Man?*

KING, WAYNE

Vi 20–1587 *Amor*

KING COLE TRIO, THE

Cap 167 *Straighten Up and Fly Right*

KRUPA, GENE

Co 36768 *I Walked In/I'll Remember Suzanne*

KYSER, KAY

Co 36757 *There Goes That Song Again/Gonna See My Baby*
Co 36771 *Like Someone in Love/Ac-cent-tchu-ate the Positive*

LEADER, LEADER

Regal Zonophone MT3735 *Goodnight Wherever You Are*

LOMBARDO, GUY

De 18634 *The Trolley Song/Always*

LONG, JOHNNY

De 4439 *Time Waits for No One/Featherhead*

LUNCEFORD, JIMMY

De 18618 *Jeep Rhythm/I Dream a Lot About You*

Martin, Freddy

Vi 20–1615 *Strange Music/Magic Is the Moonlight*

Martin, Mary

De 23456 *I'll Walk Alone*

Mercer, Johnny

Cap 180 *Ac-cent-tchu-ate the Positive*

Merry Macs

De 18684 *Sentimental Journey/Choo Choo Polka*

Mills Brothers

De 18599 *Till Then*

Monroe, Vaughn

Vi 20–1619 *The Love I Long For/This Heart of Mine*

Morse, Ella Mae

Cap 137 *Milkman, Keep Those Bottles Quiet*

Pied Pipers

Cap 123 *The Trolley Song*
Cap 146 *Marizy Doats*

Prima, Louis

Hit 7083 *Robin Hood/I'll Walk Alone*
Hit 7096 *Kentucky/A Fellow on a Furlough*

Rains, Gray

Hit 7087 *Time Alone Will Tell/Once Too Often*

Rogers, Roy

RCA Victor 2808 *San Fernando Valley*

Sinatra, Frank

Co 36687 *I Couldn't Sleep a Wink Last Night/A Lovely Way to Spend an Evening*
Co 36762 *I Dream of You/Saturday Night*

Co 36768 *Saturday Night (Is the Loneliest Night of the Week)*
Co 36797 *There's No You/Dream*

SMITH, KATE

Co 36759 *There Goes That Song Again/Don't Fence Me In*

SPIVA, CHARLIE

Vi 20–1636 *Ev'ry Time We Say Goodbye/Only Another Boy and Girl*

STAFFORD, JO

Cap 153 *Long Ago (And Far Away)*
Cap 158 *It Could Happen to You*
Cap 171 *I Didn't Know About You/Tumbling Tumble Weeds*

STRONG, BOB

Hit 7097 *Come Out, Come Out, Wherever You Are/And Then You Kissed Me*

THREE SUNS

Hit 7114 *The Love I Long For/Don't Fence Me In*
Hit 7122 *Sleigh Ride in July/Oh, Maria!*
Hit 7985 *Long Ago and Far Away/And So Little Time*

TILTON, MARTHA

Cap 157 *I'll Walk Alone*

WELK, LAWRENCE

De 4444 *Amor/I've Learned a Lesson I'll Never Forget*

1945

ANDREWS SISTERS

De 18636 *Rum and Coca Cola/One Meat Ball*

ARMSTRONG, LOUIS

De 18652 *I Wonder*

ARMEN, KAY, WITH GUY LOMBARDO ORCHESTRA

De 18672 *All at Once/Back Home for Keeps*

BAIRD, EUGENIE, WITH MEL TORME'S MELTONES

De 18707 *I Fall in Love Too Easily/Am I Blue?*

BRITO, PHIL

Mus 15047 *Don't Let Me Dream/A Cottage For Sale*

BROWN, LES

Co 36769 *Sentimental Journey*
Co 36779 *My Dreams Are Getting Better All the Time*
Co 36875 *Aren't You Glad You're You?/The Last Time I Saw You*
Co 36896 *We'll Be Together Again/A Red Kiss on a Blue Letter*

CARPENTER, THELMA, WITH THE HERMAN CHITTISON TRIO

Mus 320 *All of My Life/I Should Care*

CAVALLARO, CARMEN

De 18671 *The More I See You/In Acapulco*

COMO, PERRY

Vi 20–1676 *If I Loved You/I'm Gonna Love That Gal*
Vi 20–1709 *Till the End of Time/That Feeling in the Moonlight*

CROSBY, BING

Br 03618 *It's Been a Long, Long Time* (with Les Paul and His Trio)
De 18658 *A Friend of Yours/All of My Life*
De 18675 *Out of This World/June Comes Around Every Year*
De 18686 *If I Loved You/Close as Pages in a Book*
De 18690 *I'd Rather Be Me/On the Atchison.Topeka & Santa Fe*
De 18720 *Aren't You Glad You're You?/In the Land of Beginning Again*

DIETRICH, MARLENE

De 23456 *Lili Marlene* (German version)

DEMARCO SISTERS

Maj 7157 *It's Been a Long, Long Time*

DORSEY, JIMMY

De 18656 *I Should Care/Twilight Time*
De 18670 *Dream/There. I've Said It Again*

Dorsey, Tommy

Vi 20–1669 *Out of This World/June Comes Around Every Year*
Vi 20–1710 *Nevada/That's It*

Garland, Judy

De 18660 *This Heart of Mine/Love*

Goodman, Benny

Co 36813 *Symphony/My Guy's Come Back*
Co 36908 *Give Me the Simple Life/I Wish I Could Tell You*

Gray, Glen

De 18639 *This Heart of Mine/Robin Hood*
De 18665 *I Walked In/I Don't Care Who Knows It*

Haymes, Dick

De 18662 *I Wish I Knew/The More I See You*
De 18706 *That's for Me/It Might as Well Be Spring*
De 18740 *It's a Grand Night for Singing/All I Owe I Owe I-oway*
De 18747 *Slowly/I Wish I Could Tell You*

Heidt, Horace

Co 36798 *Anywhere/My Baby Said Yes*

Herman, Woody

Co 36785 *Laura/I Wonder*
Co 36789 *Caldonia/Happiness Is a Thing Called Joe*

Holiday, Billie

De 23391 *Lover Man (Oh, Where Can You Be?)*

Ives, Burl

De 23378 *(The Ballad of) Rodger Young*

James, Harry

Co 36478 *I Don't Want to Walk without You*
Co 36778 *I Don't Care Who Knows It/I Guess I'll Hang My Tears Out to Dry*
Co 36794 *I Wish I Knew/The More I See You*
Co 36833 *I'll Buy That Dream/Memphis in June*

Co 36838 *It's Been a Long, Long Time* (Kitty Kallen, vocal)/*Autumn Serenade*
Co 36867 *I Can't Begin to Tell You/ Waitin' for the Train to Come In*

KAYE, SAMMY

Vi 20–1642 *All of My Life/Just a Prayer Away*
Vi 20–1662 *The More I See You/I Miss Your Kiss*
Vi 20–1684 *Gotta Be This or That/Good,Good, Good*
Vi 20–1738 *It Might As Well Be Spring/Give Me the Simple Life*

KENTON, STAN

Cap 202 *Tampico*
Cap 219 *Don't Let Me Dream/It's Been a Long, Long Time*

KRUPA, GENE

Co 36784 *I Should Care/Cry and You Cry Alone*

KYSER, KAY

Co 36801 *Can't You Read Between the Lines?/Bell Bottom Trousers*
Co 36844 *That's for Me/Choo Choo Polka*

LANGFORD, FRANCES

ARA 121 *Close As Pages in a Book/Ev'ry Time We Say Goodbye*

LEE, PEGGY

Cap 218 *Waitin' for the Train to Come In*

LOMBARDO, GUY

De 18642 *My Heart Sings/A Little on the Lonely Side*
De 18737 *Symphony/Seems Like Old Times*

MARTIN, FREDDY

Vi 20–1655 *Laura/A Song to Remember*
Vi 20–1747 *Symphony/In the Middle of May*

MCINTYRE, HAL

Bb 30–0831 *I'm Making Believe/I'm in a Jam with a Baby*

MERRY MACS

De 18630 *Ten Days with Baby/Thank Dixie for Me*

MERCER, JOHNNY, AND THE PIED PIPERS

Cap 195 *On the Atchison, Topeka and Santa Fe*

MONROE, VAUGHN

Vi 20–1619 *This Heart of Mine/The Love I Long For*
Vi 20–1637 *There, I've Said It Again/Rum and Coca Cola*

NOBLE, RAY

Co 36834 *The Wish That I Wish Tonight/So-o-o-o-o in Love*
Co 36893 *It Might as Well Be Spring/Full Moon and Empty Arms*

PIED PIPERS

Cap 185 *Dream*
Cap 207 *We'll Be Together Again*

RAVAZZA, CARL

WOR 1010 *This Heart of Mine/Waiting*

REISMAN, LEO

De 18693 *If I Loved You/What's the Use of Wond'rin?*

SHAW, ARTIE

Vi 20–1716 *That's for Me/Yolanda*

SINATRA, FRANK

Co 36814 *Out Your Dreams Away/If You Are but a Dream*
Co 36825 *If I Loved You/You'll Never Walk Alone*
Co 36839 *I Fall in Love Too Easily/The Charm of You*

SPIVAK, CHARLIE

Vi 20–1663 *There Must Be a Way/You Belong to My Heart*
Vi 20–1675 *Can't You Read Between the Lines?/Santa Luci*a
Vi 20–1721 *It's Been a Long, Long Time/If I Had a Dozen Hearts*

TILTON, MARTHA

Cap 184 *A Stranger in Town/I Should Care*

TORME, MEL

De 18653 *A Stranger in Town/You've Laughed at Me for the Last Time*

WALD, JERRY

Maj 7137 *A Friend of Yours*

WHITING, MARGARET

Cap 214 *It Might As Well Be Spring/How Deep Is the Ocean?*

WILSON, TEDDY

Mus 317 *This Heart of Mine/Ev'ry Time We Say Goodby*

INDEX